STUDIES IN WELSH HISTORY

Editors

RALPH A. GRIFFITHS   CHRIS WILLIAMS
ERYN M. WHITE

31

EXODUS FROM CARDIGANSHIRE

CW00763109

EXODUS FROM CARDIGANSHIRE

RURAL-URBAN MIGRATION IN VICTORIAN BRITAIN

by

KATHRYN J. COOPER

*Published on behalf of the
University of Wales*

**CARDIFF
UNIVERSITY OF WALES PRESS
2011**

www.uwp.co.uk

British Library Cataloguing-in-Publication Data
A catalogue record for this book is available from the British Library.

ISBN 978-0-7083-2399-1
e-ISBN 978-0-7083-2410-3

Printed by CPI Antony Rowe, Chippenham, Wiltshire

SERIES EDITORS' FOREWORD

Since the foundation of the series in 1977, the study of Wales's history has attracted growing attention among historians internationally and continues to enjoy a vigorous popularity. Not only are approaches, both traditional and new, to the study of history in general being successfully applied in a Welsh context, but Wales's historical experience is increasingly appreciated by writers on British, European and world history. These advances have been especially marked in the university institutions in Wales itself.

In order to make more widely available the conclusions of original research, much of it of limited accessibility in postgraduate dissertations and theses, in 1977 the History and Law Committee of the Board of Celtic Studies inaugurated this series of monographs, *Studies in Welsh History*. It was anticipated that many of the volumes would originate in research conducted in the University of Wales or under the auspices of the Board of Celtic Studies, and so it proved. Although the Board of Celtic Studies no longer exists, the University of Wales continues to sponsor the series. It seeks to publish significant contributions made by researchers in Wales and elsewhere. Its primary aim is to serve historical scholarship and to encourage the study of Welsh history.

To my parents, Edwin and Elaine Rothwell

CONTENTS

FIGURES

TABLES

TABLES

ACKNOWLEDGEMENTS

This book would not have seen the light of day without the help, support and encouragement of many people, and in particular Rob Cooper, Richard Thompson, Nicola Thompson, Professor Keith Snell, Professor Ralph Griffiths, Aelwyn Rees, Sylvia Garner and Christine Clarke.

I am most grateful to the Friends of the Centre for English Local History, Leicester, for their generous financial assistance towards the funding of my research.

Finally, I should like to say a special thank you to the interviewees whose family histories have helped to give this book a human dimension.

Image credits:
Mrs H. J. Lloyd: Lloyd's Dairy (figure 6.2).
Ceredigion County Library: The brig *Credo* (figure 8.4).
Dewi Thomas Jones: *Er Cof* ring (figure 8.5).
All other photographs by the author.

ABBREVIATIONS

CN	*Cambrian News*
Cards.	Cardiganshire
Carms.	Carmarthenshire
Cumb.	Cumberland
Lancs.	Lancashire
Mer.	Merioneth
Mon.	Monmouthshire
Montgom.	Montgomeryshire
NLW	National Library of Wales
Pembs.	Pembrokeshire
Warks.	Warwickshire
Yorks.	Yorkshire

INTRODUCTION

> One of the best indicators of the pattern of experience of a place is its population levels.[1]

The nineteenth century witnessed a shift in economic emphasis in Britain from agriculture to commerce and industry. No longer subject to the Malthusian checks of an agriculturally based economy, the population rise that had begun in the mid-eighteenth century continued at an 'unparalleled rate of natural increase' throughout the nineteenth.[2] Despite considerable emigration, the population of England and Wales doubled between 1801 and 1851 and then again by 1911.[3] Even so, it was not until mid-century that the urban population of England and Wales finally began to exceed that of the rural areas.[4] This urban growth, however, was due to more than just natural increase: it was continually being augmented by 'the constant flow of the country population into the town'.[5] The transition from a rural to an urban society was thus accompanied by accelerating population growth, new forms of economic organization and by lasting changes in the distribution of the people of Britain.[6] Population studies have demonstrated that short-distance moves within rural areas had long been the norm and that towns of the pre-industrial era had depended on a continuous flow from the country merely to maintain their numbers.[7] These long-

---

[1] K. Tiller, *English Local History: An Introduction* (2nd edn, Stroud, 2002), p. 173.

[2] J. Saville, *Rural Depopulation in England and Wales, 1851–1951* (London, 1957), p. 2.

[3] R. Woods, *The Population of Britain in the Nineteenth Century* (Basingstoke, 1992), p. 22.

[4] W. A. Armstrong, 'The flight from the land', in G. E. Mingay (ed.), *The Victorian Countryside* (London, 1981), p. 118.

[5] *Census of Great Britain, 1851. Population Tables. 1.*, vol. 1, p. lxxxii.

[6] Woods, *Population of Britain*, p. 25; R. Lawton, 'Population changes in England and Wales in the later nineteenth century: an analysis of trends by registration districts', *Transactions of the Institute of British Geographers*, 44 (1968), 55.

[7] Armstrong, 'Flight from the land', p. 118.

established migration patterns were now being disrupted by the escalating trend of the movement away from rural areas.

In 1911 there were just six counties in England and Wales whose populations were smaller than in 1841, and one of these was Cardiganshire.[8] The population of Cardiganshire mirrored the national increase until 1871 but thereafter declined dramatically, suggesting that considerable out-migration was taking place, and the agricultural nature of the county suggests that the majority of that movement was away from the land.[9] This raises important questions: what factors operating within Victorian Cardiganshire influenced the decision to move and the choice of destination; and to what extent was migration influenced by socio-economic features unique to that county? It has long been recognized that some factors responsible for the nineteenth-century rural exodus were general to all the rural areas of England and Wales.[10] The decision to move, however, is essentially a personal one, and scarcity of information from the migrants them-selves means that our interpretation of nineteenth-century migration is somewhat conjectural. By considering sending areas in detail, we can confirm the socio-economic factors that were operating generally and reveal those specific to a particular region. This book, then, will examine key aspects of the causes and effects of Cardiganshire's rural exodus that took place during the 'long' nineteenth century.

A major achievement of historical demography has been to establish the importance of population levels and trends in the understanding of communities at both local and national level.[11] The richness of English demographic data, as compared with that of Wales and Scotland, has meant that population studies have tended to concentrate on England.[12] Wales has been rather neglected in the

[8] The others were Montgomery, Radnor, Cornwall, Huntingdon and Rutland. B. R. Mitchell, *Abstract of British Historical Statistics* (Cambridge, 1962), pp. 20, 22. Cardiganshire is now Ceredigion. County names and registration districts as they appear in the Victorian census will be used throughout this book.

[9] The population decline continued until the 1950s. Mitchell, *Statistics*, pp. 20, 22.

[10] See, for example, Saville, *Rural Depopulation*, p. 201.

[11] D. Hey, *The Oxford Companion to Local and Family History* (3rd edn, Oxford, 2002), p. 372.

[12] For example, E. A. Wrigley and R. S. Schofield, *The Population History of England, 1541–1871: A Reconstruction* (Cambridge, 1981).

literature.[13] Conclusions derived from English studies, however, do not necessarily apply to Welsh communities where traditional values and cultural perspectives often differed from those operating in England.

Work on nineteenth-century geographical mobility reflects a variety of perspectives, in particular those of statisticians, geographers and social and economic historians.[14] Now, an increasingly wide range of sources on migration patterns and processes is being used to reinforce or challenge traditional assumptions.[15] Perhaps the richest source for migration studies, however, is the Victorian census and in particular the enumerators' manuscript returns or schedules, although historians have not always been aware of the full potential of the information contained in these data.[16]

The 1841 census marked the transition to modern census-taking and the nineteenth-century censuses from 1851 onwards followed a common administrative pattern.[17] It was from this date that birthplace data were included.[18] Among many other lines of research these can be used for analysing migratory trends and identifying population movements within England and Wales.[19] The published census reports are readily accessible and fairly easy to use. A significant

---

[13] Hey, *Oxford Companion*, p. 371. Exceptions to this have included B. Thomas, *Migration and Urban Development* (London, 1972); R. Lawton, 'Regional population trends in England and Wales, 1750–1971', in J. Hobcraft and P. Rees (eds), *Regional Demographic Development* (London, 1977); D. Baines, *Migration in a Mature Economy: Emigration and Internal Migration in England and Wales, 1861–1900* (Cambridge, 1985); C. G. Pooley and J. C. Doherty, 'The longitudinal study of migration: Welsh migration to English towns in the nineteenth century', in C. G. Pooley and I. D. Whyte (eds), *Migrants, Emigrants and Immigrants* (London, 1991); C. Pooley and J. Turnbull, *Migration and Mobility in Britain since the Eighteenth Century* (London, 1998).

[14] Pooley and Turnbull, *Migration and Mobility*, p. 11.

[15] These have included Poor Law, apprenticeship and trade union records, diaries, letters and oral testimonies. C. G. Pooley and J. Turnbull, 'Migration and urbanization in north-west England: a reassessment of the role of towns in the migration process', in D. J. Siddle (ed.), *Migration, Mobility and Modernization* (Liverpool, 2000), p. 187.

[16] E. Higgs, *Making Sense of the Census: The Manuscript Returns for England and Wales, 1801–1901* (2nd edn, London, 1991), p. ix.

[17] Ibid., pp. 7, 10.

[18] *Census of Great Britain, 1851. Population Tables. 1*, vol. 1, p. lxxxiii. There was an unsatisfactory attempt to include some birthplace data in 1841.

[19] Pooley and Turnbull, *Migration and Mobility*, p. 23.

disadvantage with the data is that they give only the position on a given day in every ten years, and cannot tell us, for
instance, the number of moves an individual may have made,
any intervening stages there may have been in the migration
process, or the extent to which permanent and temporary
moves were mingled.[20] The enumerators' returns can throw
more light on these themes through an analysis of the birthplace data of children, and high rates of family mobility that
are not apparent from the decennial census reports can
often be revealed in this way.

The enumerators' returns are less accessible than the
abstracts, and are subject to a 100-year embargo. All the
Victorian manuscript returns are now available for public
consultation, and recent technological advances have allowed
them to become a major source for social and economic
historians, genealogists, biographers, local historians and
demographers of nineteenth-century society. Developments
in electronic data processing coincided with a shift away from
the study of eminent individuals and towards an attempt
to capture the life experiences of ordinary people; and the
range of topics on which the enumeration books have been
used is now vast. As a result, new areas of knowledge have
been opened up, and older theories confirmed or modified,
particularly concerning family life and mobility.[21]

Administrative changes to county and parish boundaries
in the Victorian censuses have meant that areas of reference
have not always remained constant. This can make statistical comparisons between geographical units in different
censuses difficult or unsafe. In the case of Cardiganshire,
the registration county differed significantly from the
'ancient' (or geographical) county, although this latter is
virtually contiguous with the later administrative county.[22]

---

[20] Armstrong, 'Flight from the land', p. 118; Pooley and Turnbull, *Migration and Mobility*, p. 3; Pooley and Turnbull, 'Migration and urbanization', p. 187.

[21] See, for example, M. Anderson, 'Recent work on the analysis of nineteenth-century census returns', *Family History*, 11 (1980), 152–3; Pooley and Turnbull, 'Migration and urbanization', pp. 186–214.

[22] Registration counties originated with the civil registration of births, marriages and deaths and were formed by grouping together registration districts. The registration county of Cardigan included parts of Pembrokeshire and Carmarthenshire and covered, in 1891, 595,285 acres with a population of 86,383 as against 443,071 acres with a population of 63,467 in the administrative county. In Wales the

Demographic studies using data for the registration county of Cardigan, the unit used in the Registrar General's Annual Reports until 1911, can obviously lead to anomalies.[23] This book will use only data for either the ancient or the administrative county, unless otherwise stated, as these relate directly to the geographical unit of nineteenth-century Cardiganshire.

Further limitations in using census data for comparative purposes lie in both the instructions given to census takers and the answers received. Questions sometimes varied from census to census, and inaccuracies, both intentional and unintentional, could occur in the answers. In this context, areas of concern include errors in individuals' ages, confusion over occupational terminology and the under-recording of women's occupations and child labour.[24] Also problematical is the birthplace data, the accuracy of which is difficult to assess as there are few other sources against which to check it. From 1851, the county of birth, followed by the town or parish, was required for each individual except for those born outside England and Wales where only the country of birth was required, but the quality of responses in the enumerators' books varied greatly. The problems with the birthplace data were already recognized by the beginning of the twentieth century.[25] These problems of inaccuracy sprang from a variety of causes. Variations in spelling of place-names were quite common throughout the period, but Welsh place-names were particularly problematical for the enumerators, especially those outside Wales. Furthermore, the geographical awareness of household heads and enumerators was often rather hazy so that towns/parishes could be placed in the wrong counties.[26] Studies have revealed significant rates of discrepancies in the birthplace data of individuals in study populations in successive censuses.[27] It was also not

administrative counties, formed as a result of Local Government Acts of 1888 and 1894, largely coincided with the ancient/geographical counties. J. Williams, *Digest of Welsh Historical Statistics*, 2 vols (Cardiff, 1985), vol. 1, pp. 2, 43.

[23] Ibid., vol. 1, p. 75.

[24] For more on these problems, see Higgs, *Making Sense*, pp. 67–74.

[25] Ibid., p. 72.

[26] However, this could sometimes have been a result of boundary changes.

[27] See, for example, M. Anderson, *Family Structure in Nineteenth-Century Lancashire* (London, 1971), p. 75.

unknown for a person to claim the earliest place at which they remember living as their place of birth, which may or may not have been the case.[28]

Bearing in mind the care needed in interpreting the information, data from the Victorian census are central to the research for this book. The trend of rural out-migration in nineteenth-century England and Wales is examined, and the experience of Cardiganshire is set within this context. Information has been sought from data in the published census reports and also by sampling unpublished manuscript returns. Analysis of this data focuses on key aspects of the Cardiganshire migration and poses important questions. Which sectors of the community were leaving Cardiganshire, and were males more migratory than females? Did the migrants move to other rural regions or to urban/industrial areas? Were moves mostly short- or long-distance, and which were the most significant destinations? What types of employment were attracting the migrants, and can any conclusions be drawn about their age structure and socio-economic status? How far were individuals able to maintain contact with 'home' and what effect did this have on the migration process? Population studies relating to Wales have tended to concentrate on the urban, industrial south.[29] While the significance of that region for Cardiganshire's migrants is addressed, this book also focuses on those migrants who left Wales. It assesses the extent to which these individuals became integrated in the host society and how far they were able to preserve their cultural identity in their new environment.

In order to understand the impetus behind Cardiganshire's rural exodus it is first essential to consider the

[28] For more on this, see Higgs, *Making Sense*, pp. 71–4.

[29] For example, B. Thomas, 'The migration of labour into the Glamorganshire coalfield (1861–1911)', *Economica*, 10 (1930); D. Friedlander and J. Roshier, 'A study of internal migration in England and Wales: part 1', *Population Studies*, 19 (1966), 239–79; P. N. Jones, 'Some aspects of immigration into the Glamorgan coalfield between 1881 and 1911', *Transactions of the Honourable Society of Cymmrodorion* (1969), 82–98; A. M. Williams, 'Migration and residential patterns in mid-nineteenth-century Cardiff', *Cambria*, 6, part 2 (1980), 1–27; H. Carter and S. Wheatley, *Merthyr Tydfil in 1851* (Cardiff, 1982); P. N. Jones, *Mines, Migrants and Residence in the South Wales Steamcoal Valleys: the Ogmore and Garw Valleys in 1881* (Hull, 1987).

county's socio-economic development and its distinctive *pays*. This background offers a framework for understanding factors that would influence the decision to move. How was rural society organized and what was the state of the local economy? What economic and social factors may have induced some people to leave while others chose to stay? Did the timing of the outward movement and the choice of destination vary from region to region within the county, and what features of rural life and social organization informed the migration process? In order to gain as accurate a picture of this background as possible, considerable use has been made of nineteenth-century materials in the form of government reports, newspapers, journal articles and books. It must be remembered, however, that the opinions of historians and commentators may be biased for a variety of reasons and that the evidence of witnesses before government enquiries was often subjective and even contradictory, so that it is sometimes difficult to reach a balanced view. However, these nineteenth-century sources do have the advantage of highlighting the concerns of the day and illustrating contemporary opinions, and care has been taken to seek corroborative evidence where such exists.

Ultimately, though, migration is the outcome of a multitude of decisions taken by individuals who do not necessarily respond to similar situations in the same manner. A major problem in researching nineteenth-century migration is the scarcity of first-hand personal histories so that our interpretation of such factors as motivation has to be deduced from context and background. Oral history, family stories and traditions can help, and should not necessarily be dismissed as 'mere hearsay'. Oral history has added a new dimension to the study of the recent past, but should be treated just as rigorously as evidence from other sources.[30] In order to test various migration theories and also to add a personal dimension to this book, descendents of Cardiganshire's nineteenth-century migrants were sought through Family History Research Centres and Societies and by word of mouth. Interviewees' anonymity has been respected where requested.

---

[30] Hey, *Oxford Companion*, p. 332.

No study of out-migration in the nineteenth century would be complete without some mention of emigration which, for Britain, reached its peak during the later decades of the century. The emigration from Europe of between 44 and 52 million people in the period 1816 to 1915 has inevitably attracted a large and varied literature, although recent research has tended to centre on the local background and structure of migrant groups.[31] This book concludes with a brief overview of nineteenth-century emigration from Britain, and then focuses on emigration from Cardiganshire, drawing heavily on contemporary newspaper reports, harbour records and private letters.

---

[31] For a select bibliography see Baines, *Migration*, pp. 338–49; ibid., p. 2. For one such study, see A.K. Knowles, *Calvinists Incorporated* (London, 1997).

I

NINETEENTH-CENTURY CARDIGANSHIRE:
ITS ECONOMY AND SOCIETY

Cardiganshire lies on the western seaboard of Britain. Geographically it is in the highland zone, the land rising steeply from the narrow coastal plain to the Cambrian mountains (see figure 1.1). The absence of limestone in the county significantly reduces the range of native flora, and the soil is mainly poor and acidic. Heather moorland and blanket bog carpet much of the peaty uplands, and stands of hanging sessile oak woodland clothe many of the steep valley sides. The characteristics of the upland climate have been described as cool temperate with a foreshortened growing season, low temperatures and a high annual rainfall (200 to 220 wet days per year).[1] The mixed farming pattern of early modern Cardiganshire has gradually been superseded so that it is now essentially a pastoral county; the uplands of the north and east are characterized by sheep and cattle rearing, the rich alluvial soils of the Teifi and Aeron valleys until recently by dairying.[2]

Bounded by the substantial natural barriers of the Cambrian mountains to the east, the rivers Dyfi to the north and Teifi to the south and the Irish Sea to the west, Cardiganshire was for centuries a rather remote county. The main means of contact with the outside world was through coastal trade; travel along the pre-turnpike roads and mountain tracks was difficult and often hazardous and there were no satisfactory cross-country links until the later eighteenth century.[3] Moreover, there were few roads in the county

[1] A. J. Newson, *Some Aspects of the Rainfall of Plynlimon, Mid-Wales* (Wallingford, 1976), p.1.

[2] R. J. Moore-Colyer, 'Agriculture and land occupation in eighteenth- and nineteenth-century Cardiganshire', in G. H. Jenkins and I. G. Jones (eds), *Cardiganshire County History*, vol. 3, *Cardiganshire in Modern Times* (Cardiff, 1998), p. 36.

[3] A. J. Parkinson, 'Wheat, peat and lead: settlement patterns in west Wales, 1500–1800', *Ceredigion*, 10 (1985), 127; M. I. Williams, 'Commercial relations', in Jenkins and Jones (eds), *Cardiganshire County History*, vol. 3, p. 198.

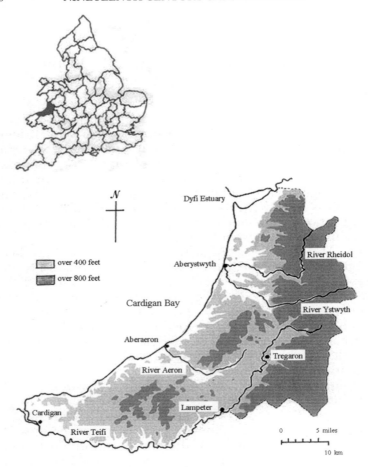

Figure 1.1 Cardiganshire in the nineteenth century
Based on: J. L. Davies and D. P. Kirby (eds), *Cardiganshire County History*, vol. 1 (Cardiff, 1994), pp. 8, 13.

suitable for more sophisticated wheeled traffic until well into the nineteenth century.[4]

Gradually, contact between Cardiganshire and the rest of Britain grew as coastal trade flourished, improvements

---

[4] A. K. Knowles, 'The structure of rural society in north Cardiganshire, 1800–1850', in Jenkins and Jones (eds), *Cardiganshire County History*, vol. 3, p. 77.

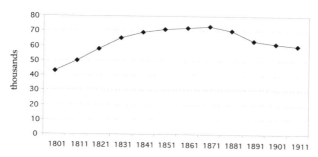

Figure 1.2 Population of Cardiganshire in the 'long' nineteenth century
Source: Population censuses, 1801–1911.

were made to the mountain roads and regular coach services to other parts of England and Wales were established. Nevertheless, even at the beginning of the nineteenth century a contemporary historian wrote that he knew of 'no district so confined within itself', and he noted that a letter took 'two complete days in going from Havod to Cardigan a distance of only forty miles within the county'.[5]

The population of nineteenth-century Cardiganshire had mirrored the national increase until 1871 after which it declined dramatically, and these trends are illustrated in figure 1.2. Given the rate of natural increase in Britain

[5] B. H. Malkin, *The Scenery, Antiquities, and Biography of South Wales*, 2 vols (London, 1807), vol. 2, p. 25.

at this time, it is clear that from the 1870s the county was experiencing a significant loss by migration. Why did the experience of Cardiganshire differ so markedly from the norm? Can the state of the county's economy and the way in which society was organized provide any answers?

URBAN AND COASTAL ECONOMY

For both strategic and economic reasons, Cardiganshire's two main towns had been established on Cardigan Bay at the mouths of its main rivers: Cardigan, in the extreme south of the county, situated at the head of the Teifi estuary, and Aberystwyth in the north at the confluence of the rivers Rheidol and Ystwyth. In addition, there was a network of creeks and landing places dotted around the coastline of Cardigan Bay that gave rise to the development of a scatter of small coastal settlements.

The only centres of any urban standing in Cardiganshire at the turn of the nineteenth century besides Cardigan and Aberystwyth were Lampeter and Tregaron.[6] Lampeter's commerce was described as being 'chiefly of a confined and domestic nature' while Tregaron 'consists chiefly of one street . . . a place of very little trade'.[7] However, the thriving fishing industry and maritime trade and the growth of shipbuilding, which were crucial to the economy of late eighteenth- and early nineteenth-century coastal Cardiganshire, resulted not only in the expansion of the ports of Aberystwyth and Cardigan but also in the establishment of two new harbours with their associated urban communities: one at Aberaeron and one at New Quay.[8]

From the Middle Ages until the end of the nineteenth century sea fishing made a substantial contribution to the economy of the coastal towns and villages that ringed

[6] S. Lewis, *A Topographical Dictionary of Wales*, 2 vols (2nd edn, London, 1850), vol. 1, p. 167.

[7] *Pigot & Co.'s National Commercial Directory* ([1835] Norwich, 1996 facsimile edn.), pp. 480 and 512.

[8] C. R. Lewis and S. E. Wheatley, 'The towns of Cardiganshire, 1800–1995', in Jenkins and Jones (eds), *Cardiganshire County History*, vol. 3, p. 220. Throughout the book, 'Aberaeron' will refer to the town and 'Aberayron' to the Victorian registration district.

Cardigan Bay. Within Cardiganshire, nineteenth-century New Quay was noted for 'Fish of a very superior quality . . . soles, oysters and turbot being taken in great numbers'.[9] Herring, however, was the principal catch on this coast but it was also a seasonal one, with the result that fishing was often part of a dual economy for those living in the coastal parishes:

> the herring generally make their first appearance . . . between the middle and the end of September, which is considered the best period of the season, as they will then bear carriage to distant markets, and the harvest being commonly over, the fishermen can be better spared from agricultural labours.[10]

The county's numerous sailing vessels were also well established in maritime commerce, and by the early nineteenth century were trading with Europe and even as far away as North America.

Cardiganshire's coastal economy gave rise to a variety of occupations besides providing employment for fishermen and mariners. The settlements that dotted the county's coastline produced a range of specialized craftsmen to support those whose livelihood was based on the sea and its harvest. Moreover, Cardiganshire's ports, as well as serving as retail and service centres for their rural hinterlands, developed flourishing shipbuilding centres with all their ancillary industries including foundries, rope works, smithies and sail lofts. These industries, in addition to servicing the shipyards, also supplied their local rural communities with such items as farm machinery and implements, rickcloths and even, occasionally, water wheels.[11] Between 1800 and 1880 over 700 ships were built in the county's main boatyards, the majority being small smacks and schooners intended for the coastal trade. These vessels were rarely owned by one person; according to custom each ship was divided into sixty-four shares and these were mostly held by local farmers, merchants and seamen.[12] Thus for much of the century the

[9] J. G. Jenkins, 'Rural industries in Cardiganshire', in Jenkins and Jones (eds), *Cardiganshire County History*, vol. 3, p. 155.

[10] Lewis, *Topographical Dictionary of Wales*, p. 245.

[11] Lewis and Wheatley, 'Towns of Cardiganshire', p. 217.

[12] D. Jenkins, 'Shipping and shipbuilding', in Jenkins and Jones (eds), *Cardiganshire County History*, vol. 3, p. 185.

shipbuilding industry, along with coastal trading, was a major facet of the county's economy. It expanded the occupational structure of the towns, requiring a significant input of skilled as well as unskilled labour, while the shareholders benefitted from the profits of the trade of their vessels in proportion to their shareholding.

By 1811 Aberystwyth was already overtaking Cardigan in terms of population, trading links and commercial diversity. One significant factor had been the economic boost due to the transference of the Customs House from Aberdyfi in 1763.[13] A trade directory of the 1830s conveys the optimism felt for the continued economic development of the town:

> Aberystwyth is a sea-port town . . . A line of road is to be formed . . . by which a more direct conveyance from London will be obtained . . . The trade and commerce of Aberystwyth is extensive . . . [and it] bids fair to arrive at the consequence of a great commercial port . . . [Trading links are] kept up with Ireland, London, Liverpool, Bristol, and the towns on the coast of Wales.[14]

Nevertheless, despite the thriving coastal trade the county's populace was still largely self-sufficient at this time.

Aberystwyth, as well as being a busy seaport in the early nineteenth century, had been gaining in popularity since the late eighteenth century as a watering-place for affluent visitors, particularly the gentry of mid Wales and the borderlands, and the annual influx of these visitors boosted the town's economy, status and range of services.[15] By 1835 there were three hotels and eighty-five lodging houses to accommodate those visitors who did not have their own town houses there.[16]

Aberystwyth never developed into the 'great commercial port' anticipated by Pigot in the 1830s.[17] As the size of ships increased with the transition from sail to steam, activity at the numerous small ports along Britain's coastline declined, and the arrival of the railway network in Cardiganshire

---

[13] Williams, 'Commercial relations', p. 203; Parkinson, 'Wheat, peat and lead', 127.

[14] *Pigot, 1835*, p. 449.

[15] Lewis and Wheatley, 'Towns of Cardiganshire', p. 218.

[16] *Pigot, 1835*, pp. 451–2.

[17] Ibid., p. 449.

from the 1860s merely hastened the demise of both the coastal trade and shipbuilding in the county. The major ports of England and Wales were now becoming a magnet for displaced seamen and the majority of Welsh mariners headed for Liverpool or Cardiff.[18] Improved land transport links within Cardiganshire, however, led to a new phase of urban economic development, encouraging the expansion of Aberystwyth, Aberaeron and New Quay as seaside resorts for a mainly middle- and working-class clientele, as spare time and spare cash increased. In addition, the founding of colleges at Lampeter and Aberystwyth would have significant long-term implications for the economy, employment structure and demographic mix of these towns.[19]

Figure 1.3 charts Cardiganshire's urban growth in the nineteenth century. Aberystwyth became established as the dominant urban centre, not just in the county but also in mid Wales. Its population growth rate, however, suggests that natural increase was continually being augmented by considerable in-migration, and the fact that by the end of the century Aberystwyth was classified as an English-speaking zone within the Welsh-speaking area that covered most of west Wales is suggestive of considerable inward movement from outside the region.[20]

The increase in Cardiganshire's urban population during the nineteenth century is in marked contrast to the overall county trend of population decline from 1871. Diversification of the economy of the towns, especially that of Aberystwyth into tourism and education, secured a stable though narrow economic base that nonetheless was accompanied by the growth of the professional classes, retail outlets and the service sector. However, the absence in the county of any major manufacturing or industrial concerns meant that

---

[18] J. G. Jenkins, *Welsh Ships and Sailing Men* (Llanrwst, 2006), pp. 12–13.

[19] St David's theological college was established at Lampeter in 1827. The first University College of Wales was founded at Aberystwyth in 1872.

[20] D. Jones, *Statistical Evidence relating to the Welsh Language, 1801–1911* (Cardiff, 1998), p. 330. Also contributing to this anglicization would have been education, which was conducted through the medium of English rather than Welsh at this time.

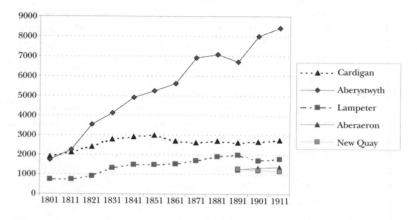

Figure 1.3 Population of Cardiganshire towns, 1801–1911
Source: Population censuses, 1801–1911.
Note: Statistics for urban Aberaeron and New Quay are only available from 1891.

it was unlikely that Cardiganshire's towns would be able to absorb much surplus rural population.

THE RURAL BACKGROUND

Cardiganshire has always been primarily an agricultural county. At the start of the nineteenth century 90 per cent of the people lived in rural areas (see figure 1.4), and the rural population continued to increase until the 1860s. Numbers then began to fall, the greatest percentage decrease occurring between 1881 and 1891. By contrast, as we have seen, there was a steady gain in the urban component throughout the century, although it remained a very minor part of the county's population.

RURAL TRADES AND OCCUPATIONS

Agriculture was the main occupation in Cardiganshire throughout the century, providing for about half of male employment in the county, but the occupation of farmer was by no means a completely male preserve. The census reveals that the percentage of female farmers in the county

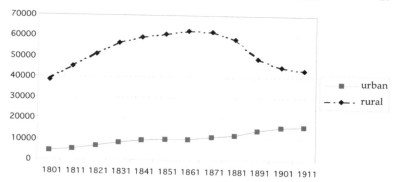

Figure 1.4 Cardiganshire's rural and urban population trends, 1801–1911
Source: Population censuses 1801–1911.
Note: The urban population is calculated using Aberystwyth, Cardigan and Lampeter figures only for 1801–81. Statistics for urban New Quay and Aberaeron are available for 1891 onwards and this slightly exaggerates the upward urban swing between 1881 and 1911.

rose during the second half of the nineteenth century – from 14 per cent in 1851 to just over 19 per cent in 1911.[21] Assisting on the farms were agricultural labourers and farm servants. The labourers were married farm hands who lived in rented cottages, often with their own small plot of land; while unmarried male and female farm servants lived and boarded on the farm.[22] Farming households also included the wives, children and sundry other relatives who helped on or around the farm. In addition, those engaged in rural trades and industries often occupied plots of land sufficient 'to keep from half-a-dozen to a score of sheep'.[23]

The rural community in nineteenth-century Cardiganshire was an economic as well as a social entity. Much of the food could usually be produced locally; neighbouring craftsmen produced tools and farming equipment, domestic articles,

[21] One possible contributory factor to this increase was the migration of males to work in the coalfields of Glamorgan, leaving the farms in the charge of their womenfolk. See, for example, *Report on the Decline in the Agricultural Population of Great Britain, 1881–1906* (London, 1906), pp. 94–5. See also chapter V.
[22] *Royal Commission on Agriculture. Reports of the Assistant Commissioners. Mr Doyle's Reports* ([1882] 2nd edn, Shannon, 1969), p. 66.
[23] Ibid., p. 10.

clothing and boots and shoes, and those households that were not within easy reach of their local market or service centre could be visited by itinerant traders and craftsmen.[24]

The most common non-agricultural male occupation in the county at this time, after lead mining, was that of general labourer. In nineteenth-century Cardiganshire the major task of these labourers was the construction and upkeep of roads.[25] As for the county's female occupations, domestic service, both rural and urban, was the major form of employment. Females, however, were also responsible for a wide range of domestic activities that contributed to the self-sufficiency and economy of many rural households. These included butter- and cheese-making, brewing, knitting and quilting, but these occupations rarely found their way into the Victorian census occupational data.

RURAL INDUSTRIES

Although a rural county with a modest population, nineteenth-century Cardiganshire nevertheless comprised several distinct regions. The coastal plain, the central uplands, the lead-mining districts of the north and the fertile river valleys in the south each had a different economic base that was reflected in the nature of its rural industries, and the full range of trades, crafts and industries was surprisingly diverse. In a society whose communities were not only scattered but also largely self-sufficient, some trades, such as that of the blacksmith, miller, shoemaker and carpenter, were ubiquitous. Others developed to meet local needs, such as the hatters of Tre'rddol and the weavers of Talybont who provided clothing for the lead miners. Others arose due to the presence locally of specific raw materials, such as the alder groves throughout the county that attracted the itinerant cloggers who were regular visitors to the county. Although clogs were widely used on farms, they were also worn in factories and mines, and the bulk of the soles made

---

[24] J. G. Jenkins, 'Rural industry in Cardiganshire', *Ceredigion*, 6 (1968–71), 90–1.
[25] S. Thomas, 'The enumerators' returns as a source for a period picture of the parish of Llansantffraid, 1841–1851', *Ceredigion*, 4 (1963), 414.

in Cardiganshire were destined for the clogging factories in the north of England.[26]

Topographical and geographical features also provided opportunities for small-scale rural industries. On the Teifi, coracle fishing, particularly for salmon, had been thriving since at least the Middle Ages and at the turn of the nineteenth century it was noted that there was 'scarcely a cottage in the neighbourhood of the Tivy . . . without its coracle hanging by the door'.[27] The plentiful water supply supported wood turning and leather production, and the many fast-flowing streams provided waterpower for the county's modest textile industry.[28]

Wool had long been an important commodity in rural Cardiganshire, and in medieval times raw wool from the vast flocks owned by the Cistercians at Strata Florida Abbey was regularly taken by packhorse to south Wales and Bristol. Spinning and weaving in the county, however, remained a cottage industry, supplying a strictly local need, and was usually combined with farming.[29] Fulling mills had gradually been built along the county's many swiftly flowing streams and, in the early nineteenth century, in the light of water-powered industrial developments elsewhere in Britain, it was considered that these streams might 'afford every advantage for the establishment of mills and factories' in the region.[30] This did happen, but only to a limited extent. Some small-scale mills were built, mostly to supply local needs; and mill villages were established in the Teifi Valley in the south of the county. These latter formed part of the industrial complex of neighbouring Carmarthenshire that attained considerable prosperity between 1860 and 1920; as far as Cardiganshire was concerned it was a very short-lived prosperity.[31] Moreover, the textile industry in the rest of the county was too remote from urban-industrial markets to justify the large-scale investment needed for mechanized textile production, and it remained

[26] Jenkins, 'Rural industry', 95.
[27] Malkin, *Scenery, Antiquities, and Biography*, p. 206.
[28] Jenkins, 'Rural industries', p. 157.
[29] Ibid., p. 107; E. West, *Woollen Mills of Wales* (n.p., 1974), p. 7; Parkinson, 'Wheat, peat and lead', 206.
[30] *Pigot, 1835*, p. 450.
[31] Jenkins, 'Rural industry', 113–14.

a 'vaguely organized, widely scattered domestic industry'.[32] Nevertheless, cloth production made a significant contribution to the county's rural economy by providing both full- and part-time work. It continued to supply the needs of local markets throughout most of the century, and the presence of a thriving lead-mining industry in the north of the county generated small weaving villages such as Talybont to supply clothing for the miners. Towards the end of the nineteenth century, however, the woollen industry was in decline in many parts of the county as improvements to overland transportation brought cheap mass-produced clothing within the physical and financial reach of most rural communities.[33]

One rural industry that developed along the full length of the county's coastline was that of lime burning. Although the lime was mainly used for improving the poor soils, it was also used for lime mortar and for whitewashing cottages, and thus it was a commodity required throughout the county. As the limestone was brought in by sea to the many small landing places along the coast where it then had to be burnt before it could be used for the various processes, the coastline became dotted with lime kilns, and the remains of some of them are still to be found.[34]

Extractive industries included a modest slate-quarrying concern in the south of the county, near Cardigan, and peat cutting from the extensive upland bogs and low-lying marshy areas such as Cors Caron and Cors Fochno. In the north, however, the underlying geology gave rise to the county's most important rural industry, second only in terms of employment to agriculture itself: that of lead mining. The role of the lead-mining industry in Cardiganshire's socio-economic history and its ultimate significance for rural out-migration was such that it will be explored more fully in chapter II.

---

[32] Knowles, 'Structure of rural society', p. 83; J. G. Jenkins, *The Welsh Woollen Industry* (Cardiff, 1969), p. 114.

[33] Knowles, 'Structure of rural society', p. 83.

[34] For more on this, see R. J. Moore-Colyer, 'Coastal limekilns in south-west Wales', *Folklife*, 28 (1989–90), 19–30.

Rural economy

Livestock droving was a long-standing and valuable part of Cardiganshire's rural economy and the chief agricultural export; historical records show that the trade in livestock between England and Wales had been important for centuries.[35] In the early eighteenth century Defoe recorded that highland Cardiganshire was so full of cattle that it seemed to be 'the nursery, the breeding place for the whole kingdom of England south of the Trent'. He further commented that this was not due to the fertility of the region, for although rearing cattle requires a rich soil and good pastures 'the breeding of them does not'.[36] In time, some of the more enterprising Welsh cattle farmers crossed the border and settled down among the greener pastures of the Midland counties, notably Leicestershire, Northamptonshire and Warwickshire; obtaining their cattle from Wales, they now became their own graziers and supplied the meat markets directly.[37]

Sheep gradually came to replace cattle as the mainstay of the county's upland economy, and these sometimes joined the cattle that were driven down the long-established trackways to be fattened on the superior grazing lands of the Midlands, East Anglia and Kent ready for the markets of England.[38] Traces of the network of drovers' routes from north, mid and south Cardiganshire to the counties of Shropshire, Herefordshire and onwards can still found today.[39] As the nineteenth century progressed, however, and the railway network spread throughout England and Wales, the droving of livestock was gradually replaced by trucking, so that the drovers eventually became redundant.[40]

---

[35] Knowles, 'Structure of rural society', p. 77; Moore-Colyer, 'Agriculture and land occupation', p. 36; J. L. Davies, 'The livestock trade in west Wales in the nineteenth century', *Aberystwyth Studies*, 13 (1934), 85; C. Skeel, 'The cattle trade between Wales and England from the fifteenth to the nineteenth centuries', *Transactions of the Royal Historical Society*, 4th series, 9 (1926), 137.

[36] Williams, 'Commercial relations', p. 202.

[37] P. G. Hughes, *Wales and the Drovers* ([1943] Carmarthen, new edn, 1988), p. 21.

[38] Moore-Colyer, 'Agriculture and land occupation', pp. 44, 49.

[39] See, for example, R. J. Moore-Colyer, *Welsh Cattle Drovers* (Ashbourne, 2002), pp. 125–49.

[40] Davies, 'Livestock trade', 95; R. J. Colyer, *The Welsh Cattle Drovers* (Cardiff, 1976), p. 86.

Although the actual numbers involved in droving were fairly small, their trade made a significant contribution to the economy of Cardiganshire. Not only were they involved with the county's main agricultural export, but the drovers of west Wales also exercised a wider influence on the business life of the community by being a key element in the development of the Welsh banking system. Drovers returning home with quantities of gold coin gained from their sales at the cattle markets of London faced constant dangers on the road and needed a way to safeguard their money. They began to establish their own banks associated with London agents, a notable one being the Black Ox Bank, so called because the banknotes featured a black ox.[41] This bank was established by the drover David Jones at Llandovery on the Carmarthenshire/Cardiganshire border in 1799.[42] Moreover, the regular and growing trade, especially with London's Smithfield market, provided a convenient and relatively secure way for the drovers to carry out financial transactions and commissions in the city on behalf of others by means of bills of exchange that were now readily accepted in London.[43]

The fortunes of agriculture waxed and waned during the nineteenth century, but even in the good times 'want was never far from the door' in rural Cardiganshire.[44] One significant means of supplementing a subsistence income and ensuring that the family had the means to pay the rent was widespread throughout Europe by the beginning of the nineteenth century: seasonal or temporary migration.[45] Two such well-established traditions in Cardiganshire were the summer movements of female labour – *merched y gerddi* – to work in the market gardens of London and the hop fields of Kent, and

[41] I. W. Jones, *Money Galore: The Story of the Welsh Pound* (Ashbourne, 2004), p. 77.

[42] R. C. Jones, *Arian: The Story of Money and Banking in Wales* (Swansea, 1978), p. 103. In the early nineteenth century many towns in England and Wales had their own banks which had been founded by local merchants and businessmen and which issued their own banknotes.

[43] S. Toulson and F. Godwin, *The Drovers' Roads of Wales* (London, 1977), p. 16; Jones, *Money Galore*, p. 77.

[44] W. J. Lewis, 'The condition of labour in mid-Cardiganshire in the early nineteenth century', *Ceredigion*, 4 (1963), 333.

[45] Knowles, 'Structure of rural society', p. 89.

the migration of male labour to help with the harvests in the English border counties and the Vale of Glamorgan.[46] These movements were naturally tied to the working cycle of the predominantly pastoral home farms; they were also linked to the life cycle of the migrants, who tended to be either young unmarried adults or in a situation in which they could leave their farms and households in the charge of wives and older children.[47]

Another method of boosting a marginal agricultural livelihood was by diversifying into non-farming occupations and here, as in most spheres of the rural family economy, Cardiganshire women were very active. One of the most widespread of these occupations, that required no capital outlay and very little skill, was the knitting of stockings. After gathering the coarse wool that had been shed by the mountain sheep in the uplands in early summer, the women would take it home to be washed, carded, spun and dyed. The stockings were knitted in any spare moments – while feeding the baby, in the evenings or even, according to tradition, on the seasonal migrations to south-eastern England.[48] The stocking trade in some parts of England and Wales developed into organized industries as the demand for cheap durable clothing for the rapidly developing urban and industrial areas grew, but in Cardiganshire it remained a modest cottage industry that nevertheless made a vital contribution to the income of many rural families. The home-knitted stockings were bought by itinerant stocking sellers, who had a ready market for them in the lead-mining districts in the north of the county, while some were traded on and eventually reached the English Midlands and industrial south Wales.[49]

---

[46] Ibid., p. 89; Lewis, 'Condition of labour', 333; B. Hill, 'Rural-urban migration of women and their employment in towns', *Rural History*, 5 (1994), 192.

[47] Knowles, 'Structure of rural society', p. 89.

[48] Ibid., pp. 82–3; Lewis, 'Condition of labour', 331.

[49] Lewis, 'Condition of labour', 331; Knowles, 'Structure of rural society', p. 82.

ENCLOSURES AND LAND HUNGER

From the early sixteenth century, the population of England and Wales had been growing steadily despite some short-term fluctuations. As farming was the main means of earning a living, pressure began to grow to enclose and improve the wastes in order to create more farm units, and Cardiganshire's remaining open lowlands were gradually enclosed, either by mutual agreement between landholders or by private Act of Parliament. Meanwhile, the uplands were attracting squatter holdings, and the expansion of sheep farming from the late seventeenth century and the decline of transhumance meant that landowners were beginning to enclose their *hafodydd* or summer grazing lands in the uplands to form sheep walks.[50]

The later eighteenth century had witnessed an escalation in changes to the upland landscape. A large proportion of upland Cardiganshire was Crown land although the boundaries were not clear.[51] Encroachment on this land occurred widely in the eighteenth and nineteenth centuries as the county's landowners wished to extend the limits of their estates, despite the fact that this often resulted in expensive litigation with the Crown.[52] Moreover, the Napoleonic wars created in Britain a demand for home-produced food that encouraged capital investment countrywide in improvement of the wastes to bring more land into cultivation. In Cardiganshire, enclosure of wastes and commons gained momentum from the same incentive, but continued well into the nineteenth century due to the demands of a continually rising population. This latter put pressure on the often

[50] Knowles, 'Structure of rural society', p. 80; E. Wiliam, *The Historical Farm Buildings of Wales* (Edinburgh, 1986), p. 9.

[51] The *Report on Land Revenues of the Crown* of 1787 reported that 'The waste lands in the Principality, in which the Crown has an interest, are known to be very extensive, though the extent has not been ascertained'. D. Ll. Thomas, *Bibliographical, Statistical and other Miscellaneous Memoranda, being Appendices to the Report of the Royal Commission on Land in Wales and Monmouthshire* (London, 1896), p. 11.

[52] R. J. Moore-Colyer, 'The landed gentry of Cardiganshire', in Jenkins and Jones (eds), *Cardiganshire County History*, vol. 3, pp. 55–6. According to Thomas in the *Appendices to the Royal Commission on Land*, by the end of the nineteenth century the highest proportion of unenclosed waste land in Wales still belonging to the Crown lay in Cardiganshire, that is almost 26,500 acres out of a total of just over 84,000 (p. 12). This accounts for the extensive tracts of softwood plantations that characterized the county's uplands in the twentieth century.

barely subsistence incomes of existing holdings, generating a need to create new farm units, and thereby exacerbating the 'land hunger' that was to be such a feature of the county throughout the century.[53]

While enclosures were welcomed by many small occupiers who were glad of the opportunity to increase the size of their holdings or create new ones, commoners deeply resented any attempt to deprive them of their traditional rights. For the rural poor, the commons had for generations offered the only alternative to destitution, and they also attracted squatter settlements. These, although illegal and resented by the commoners, were often tacitly condoned by the more influential members of the local community as tending to reduce the burden on the poor rates for which they were responsible.[54] Indeed, the Welsh Land Commission concluded that the cottages in many areas of rural Wales 'appear to have almost entirely originated in squatters' settlements', the result being 'the existence of perhaps a greater number of cottages unfit for the habitation of human beings than is to be found within an equal area in any part of Great Britain'.[55] Efforts to promote enclosures created an undercurrent of bitterness and discontent countrywide that erupted into violence in many areas, including parts of Cardiganshire. However, the effects of enclosures on the rural poor in this predominantly pastoral farming system were far less pronounced than in areas of England where arable land was being converted to pasture and causing large reductions in employment opportunities and the failure of cottage economies and industries as cottagers were denied free grazing on the commons and access to raw materials.

By the mid-nineteenth century, Britain's rural exodus was well under way, although, as noted above, the main movement out of Cardiganshire came in later decades. Even by the end of the century, despite the steady flow of migrants leaving rural Wales for the urban and industrial areas of Britain and the consequent dramatic fall in the populations

[53] Moore-Colyer, 'Agriculture and land occupation', p. 20.
[54] Ibid., p. 21.
[55] D. Ll. Thomas, *The Welsh Land Commission: A Digest of its Report* (London, 1896), p. 322.

of Welsh rural counties, the Welsh Land Commission reported that unoccupied farms were 'unknown in Wales'. Indeed, the commissioners noted:

> a land hunger of the most insatiable type exists throughout Wales, and that excessive competition and that a reckless bidding for farms are its inevitable results were but too clearly demonstrated to us.[56]

The problem of land hunger persisted in Cardiganshire throughout the nineteenth century, fuelled not only by the natural increase of the population but also by multiple occupation of holdings and the trend to permanent farm amalgamations on many of the larger estates.[57] However, there was also a further dimension to this competition for farms: it represented 'the great craving for land which we found to be a most marked characteristic of the Welsh in common with other branches of the Celtic races'.[58] In this context, the report of the Welsh Land Commission drew particular attention to the occupiers of

> scores of mountain farms of all sizes . . . with their mud hovels and the defective buildings, where even in the good times, they were able to exist with infinite difficulty, eking out a miserable and laborious life.[59]

It went on to pose the question:

> Why are there in Wales so many holdings with inhabited homesteads, at extreme altitudes, where, owing to the variations of the climate and the sterility of the land, the remoteness of the situation, the badness of the roads and the consequent inferiority of the buildings, their occupiers have but little share in the comforts and amenities which science and civilization have placed at the service of the humblest and most laborious toiler in almost every other sphere of life?[60]

The report concluded that:

> surely there is nothing but the consuming passion, the leech-craving for land, that can account for such a state of things. These men and their families would not persist in prolonging this miserable existence unless they were wholly possessed with the feeling that they must at all costs have a little holding . . . and that without it, life for them would not be worth living.[61]

---

[56] Ibid., pp. 137, 138.
[57] Moore-Colyer, 'Agriculture and land occupation', pp. 26–7.
[58] Thomas, *Digest*, p. 137.
[59] Ibid., p. 139.
[60] Ibid.
[61] Ibid.

FARMHOUSES, FARM BUILDINGS AND RURAL COTTAGES

Before the coming of the railways, materials for the construction of rural dwellings and farm buildings would generally have been sourced locally, preferably no further away than a day's journey by cart, so that different localities came to be characterized by the use of particular materials. For instance, in the western counties of Cardiganshire, Carmarthenshire and Pembrokeshire, that were particularly deficient in good building materials, earth-walled (or clay) buildings were widespread.[62]

By the early nineteenth century some Welsh landowners were spending heavily on their estates and rebuilding their farmhouses.[63] On most of Cardiganshire's landed estates the rebuilding and maintenance efforts were impeded by financial constraints, while the county's small landowners and owner-occupiers could afford only minimal improvements at best. Inevitably, the poor condition of Cardiganshire's rural dwellings and the archaic and unsuitable nature of farm buildings received much criticism in government enquiries that reported that, generally, livestock sheds were cramped, dark and ill ventilated, barns were inadequate and farmhouses and cottages often little better than cattle byres, with low, damp, smoke-filled rooms and poorly thatched roofs.[64]

Major changes in the rural settlement pattern took place throughout Wales during the eighteenth and nineteenth centuries. In Cardiganshire, small cottages proliferated. Those along the roadsides would generally have belonged to landless labourers and cottagers, and those in the expanding villages belonged to the growing numbers of artisans serving the local community. In mid and north Cardiganshire small hamlets of terraced dwellings grew with the increased exploitation of the lead mines, while the county's commons and

[62] These were made from a composition of clay, gravel and straw; sometimes also called cob or clom. Wiliam, *Historical Farm Buildings*, p. 52; P. Smith, 'The domestic architecture of the county. I. The rural domestic architecture', in Jenkins and Jones (eds), *Cardiganshire County History*, vol. 3, p. 252.

[63] Wiliam, *Historical Farm Buildings*, p. 45. See, for example, NLW, RA 33 Gogerddan Estate Rental, 1797–98, disbursements.

[64] R. J. Colyer, 'The gentry and the county in nineteenth-century Cardiganshire', *Welsh History Review*, 10 (1980–1), 526–8.

uplands attracted squatter cottages.[65] The squatter cottage in Wales, or *ty un-nos* (one-night house), was an interesting phenomenon:

> there survives in Wales a traditional notion, erroneous in point of law, but practically universal, that by building on a common a *ty un-nos* . . . freehold rights could be acquired . . . They were erected . . . in a single night, and an essential point was that smoke should be seen issuing from the chimney by dawn.[66]

The squatter's *ty un-nos*, usually of turf with a rough thatch, was later replaced by a more permanent structure, itself often little more than a 'mere hovel', whereupon the original reverted to use as a byre.[67] The ultimate fate of Cardiganshire's eighteenth- and nineteenth-century squatter settlements has varied. Some developed into sizeable communities that survived the county's rural exodus and are now becoming desirable places in which to live, while all that remains of others are the eroded dry-stone or earthwork structures that litter the uplands. The deserted rural settlement sites of upland Cardiganshire, however, are more than failed squatter settlements. They are the former dwellings of farmers, agricultural labourers, shepherds, peat cutters and lead miners (see figure 1.5), and provide evidence that there are few corners of even the county's uplands that have not been settled at some time.[68]

EDUCATION

As might be expected in a rather poor, isolated region, Cardiganshire was not well provided with schools in the early nineteenth century, and, with some notable exceptions such as Aberystwyth, which was 'an oasis in the wilderness', the available schooling was generally of a poor quality. Very few teachers had received adequate training, and the great majority of day schools in Wales were 'held under temporary

---

[65] Parkinson, 'Wheat, peat and lead', 122; Thomas, *Miscellaneous Memoranda*, p. 63, citing Andrew Doyle's report to the *Richmond Commission*.
[66] Thomas, *Digest*, pp. 320–1.
[67] Thomas, *Miscellaneous Memoranda*, p. 63; Wiliam, *Historical Farm Buildings*, p. 52.
[68] For more on the historic landscape, see *http://www.dyfedarchaeology.org.uk/*

Figure 1.5 Derelict dwelling, north Cardiganshire uplands (SN 730 850)
Photo: K. Cooper

occupation in rooms of private houses which degenerate in Cardiganshire . . . into mere outhouses'.[69]

Although some educational advances had been made in the preceding decades, on the eve of the 1870 Elementary

---

[69] W. G. Evans, 'Education in Cardiganshire, 1700–1974', in Jenkins and Jones (eds), *Cardiganshire County History*, vol. 3, p. 551.

Education Act the state of elementary education in Cardiganshire could 'only be said to be in a moderate condition ... especially in country places' and was considered inferior to that in the surrounding counties of Montgomery, Carmarthen and Pembroke.[70] Although the aim of the legislation was to establish a national system of elementary education to serve the needs of Britain as a whole, it was also another piece of legislation aimed at limiting the worst excesses of child labour, particularly in mines and factories. Elementary school attendance became compulsory from 1880, initially up to the age of 10 although this had been raised to 12 years by 1899, except for those employed in agriculture.[71] Absenteeism in the early decades, especially until payment of fees was abolished in 1891, was a serious problem, reflecting the social pressures of parental attitudes and poverty, although boards of guardians were now compulsorily involved in ensuring that the poorer children had money and appropriate clothing to attend school.[72] Children's labour was an essential element in the economy of working-class families, and this in turn affected school attendance as is often graphically illustrated in school log books. The following entries from the log book of Trisant school, in rural Cardiganshire, in 1898 are typical examples:

> 22 April School was re-opened on Monday, attendance was very small throughout the week. Many of the children are kept at home planting potatoes.

> 13 September The attendance has not yet got up to what it ought to have been. This is due to many of the children being kept at home [to help with] the corn harvest.[73]

In addition, many children had to work after school and on Saturdays to help boost the family income.

Nineteenth-century Cardiganshire was a stronghold of the Welsh language; even in the closing decades of the century

[70] Ibid., p. 553.

[71] A. L. Trott, 'The implementation of the 1870 Elementary Education Act in Cardiganshire during the period 1870–1880', *Ceredigion*, 3 (1956–9), 207; D. Hey, *The Oxford Companion to Local and Family History* (3rd edn, Oxford, 2002), p. 148.

[72] H. Palmer, 'Documentary evidence on the lives of the poor in the later nineteenth century in Cardiganshire', *Ceredigion*, 13 (1998), 20.

[73] Ceredigion Archives, Ed. Bk. 88.

when some areas such as Aberystwyth were becoming more anglicized, over 90 per cent of the population spoke Welsh, while over half were monoglot Welsh.[74] This linguistic bias was not reflected in the schools and colleges, however, where the language of instruction was predominantly English. Following a new code of regulations in 1890, Welsh became more widely used in the curriculum but the majority of schools remained anglicized. English was regarded as the language of social advancement, and a lack of it was regarded by school inspectors, head teachers and many parents as an educational handicap.[75] In the main, it was left to the Nonconformist Sunday schools that predominated in Cardiganshire to teach Welsh children and adults to read and write in their native language, using the scriptures as an aid.[76] Indeed, the chapel and Sunday school were central to the community, providing for the social and cultural life of its members as well as for its spiritual needs. Chapel membership also had a significant role to play in the migration process, as we shall see later in this book.

By the end of the nineteenth century, educational opportunities had undeniably improved dramatically in Britain; a basic, free elementary education was finally available to all. Education was now increasingly perceived as the means of improving one's station in life, although for many families in Cardiganshire the potential for achieving this was limited. Families on low incomes could not afford the fees of the intermediate schools that were the avenues to the professions and white-collar occupations. Nevertheless, even some basic schooling had the potential for raising the individual's personal expectations and for creating an awareness of the wider opportunities that were increasingly becoming available in late Victorian Britain.

---

[74] J. W. Aitchison and H. Carter, 'The Welsh language in Cardiganshire, 1891–1991', in Jenkins and Jones (eds), *Cardiganshire County History*, vol. 3, p. 573.

[75] Evans, 'Education in Cardiganshire', p. 556; *Cambrian News*, 30 May 1913, obituaries.

[76] Evans, 'Education in Cardiganshire', p. 550; K. D. M. Snell and P. S. Ell, *Rival Jerusalems* (Cambridge, 2000), p. 205.

SOCIAL STRUCTURE OF NINETEENTH-CENTURY CARDIGANSHIRE

The flourishing commercial activity that centred on Cardiganshire's ports in the late eighteenth and early nineteenth centuries generated social as well as economic changes. The increasing variety of goods imported into the county reflected the 'emergence of new social classes [that] created new patterns of material requirements', and this in turn promoted the expansion in the number and variety of retailers in the towns.[77] Urban expansion was accompanied by changes to the internal structure of the towns as the mixed land-use arrangement of the compact pre-industrial town was gradually superseded by the trend towards suburbanization to accommodate the growing middle and professional classes, a process that had already been under way for some time in England.[78] Cardiganshire's shopkeepers formed a 'new bourgeoisie' who came to play a dominant role in local financial, political and religious affairs.[79] Some of those involved in commerce and the professions became among the richest members of local society, building houses that reflected their new wealth and status and rivalled those of the local landed gentry.

In the countryside, small farms predominated although the tenant farms were generally larger than the minority of freeholds.[80] Welsh agriculture in general was characterized by a lack of capital and there was often not a great deal of difference between the mode of life and standard of living of the tenant farmer, the small owner-occupier and the agricultural labourer:

> The Welsh farmer presents a stronger contrast than even the Welsh labourer to the same class in England ... [He] is but little removed either in his mode of life ... his dwelling or his habits from the day labourers.[81]

[77] Williams, 'Commercial relations', p. 206.
[78] Lewis and Wheatley, 'Towns of Cardiganshire', p. 225.
[79] Williams, 'Commercial relations', p. 206.
[80] Knowles, 'Structure of rural society', p. 81.
[81] Mr Doyle's Reports, p. 8.

In general, Welsh farmers worked alongside their labourers, they took their meals together in the farmhouse kitchens and they worshipped together in the Nonconformist chapels.[82]

The countryside of nineteenth-century Cardiganshire, and indeed of the whole of Wales, was 'overwhelmingly dominated' by a landowning class, many of whom claimed a lineage of some antiquity.[83] This concentration of the land in the hands of relatively few families was more pronounced in Wales than in England: it has been estimated that in 1877 estates of over 1,000 acres covered just over 60 per cent of the cultivated land in Wales, and just over 50 per cent of that in England. Moreover, the first Agricultural Returns of 1887 reveal that freehold accounted for just 15.5 per cent of cultivated land in England, 12.7 per cent in Scotland and only 10.2 per cent in Wales.[84] Less than a century later, as table 1.1 indicates, almost 70 per cent of Cardiganshire's cultivated land was owned by the occupier, the highest proportion of any county in England and Wales.

Table 1.1 Percentage of holdings and of acreage owned by the occupier

	1887		1909		1941–3		1960	
	holdings	acreage	holdings	acreage	holdings	acreage	holdings	acreage
Cardiganshire	21.6	19.3	18.5	15.9	48	48	71.4	69.4
Wales	10.5	10.2	10.6	10.2	37	39	58.4	57.5
England	16.1	15.5	13.4	12.4	34	33	56.4	47.8

Source: J. Davies, 'The end of the great estates and the rise of freehold farming in Wales', *Welsh History Review*, 7 (1974–5), 212.

THE DECLINE OF LANDED ESTATES

The landed gentry were more than just landlords; they had long been a dominant element in Welsh life. Certainly, in the

---

[82] D. W. Howell, 'The agricultural labourer in nineteenth-century Wales', *Welsh History Review*, 6 (1972–3), 262, 263. Welsh outdoor labourers were generally given their meals at the farms as part of their wages.

[83] R. J. Moore-Colyer, 'Farmers and fields in nineteenth-century Wales: the case of Llanrhystud, Cardiganshire', *National Library of Wales Journal*, 26 (1989–90), 32; J. Davies, 'The end of the great estates and the rise of freehold farming in Wales', *Welsh History Review*, 7 (1974–5), 186–7.

[84] Davies, 'End of the great estates', 187.

case of Cardiganshire, their attitudes and actions profoundly influenced the social, commercial and agricultural development of the county.[85] At the beginning of the nineteenth century most Cardiganshire squires were content to stay at home, managing their estates, hunting and attending to their many local duties including justices of the peace, militia officers and guardians of the poor. To their tenants and to the rural poor, the squire was generally regarded as the leader of local opinion, advisor on all manner of problems and sympathetic patron in times of distress.[86] This, in the main, was a paternalistic society and most landlords saw charity as their Christian duty, often maintaining larger workforces than were necessary rather than throw redundant labourers and their families on the parish, even when the landlords themselves were in dire financial straits. As Thomas Johnes of Hafod wrote: 'I know of no other remedy than feeding, employing and taking care of them', although there were others who disapproved of the 'promiscuous doles' and felt that these should be earned in some way.[87] Nevertheless, charity, however well meaning, failed to address the basic issues of Cardiganshire's rural poverty: inadequate wages, poor housing and lack of employment prospects.

With a few notable exceptions, Cardiganshire's gentry were staunch supporters of the Established Church, although they were not implacable enemies of Nonconformity and often granted leases of land for the building of Nonconformist chapels and meeting houses. This religious tolerance was, however, often tempered with expediency in the cause of political control. Prior to 1872, a landlord could exercise control over the voting behaviour of his tenants but he had none over the freeholders, whom it was therefore in his interests to treat not only with religious tolerance but also with patronage in the matter of local posts and positions. Thus the local squire was confident in his status as the leader in political and administrative matters during the early decades of the nineteenth century.[88]

[85] Ibid.; Moore-Colyer, 'Farmers and fields', 54.
[86] Colyer, 'Gentry and county', 497.
[87] Ibid., 499.
[88] Ibid., 504–6.

Change, however, was in the air. With the growing public awareness of rural poverty and agrarian problems in Wales, as highlighted by the Rebecca riots of 1839–44, a radical press was helping to foster a climate of opinion in which people began to question the established order. In addition, the rapidly growing strength of Nonconformism was providing farmers and cottagers alike with a new sense of values. As the Welsh gentry became increasingly anglicized, they were also becoming less readily identifiable as leaders of Welsh rural society, and the charisma and sincerity of the Nonconformist orators were gradually winning people away from their traditional allegiance to local landed families, so that in time the 'manse had come to replace the mansion' as a focal point for villagers and farmers wishing to discuss their domestic, financial or personal problems.[89] In addition, the electorate was beginning to exhibit a greater degree of political independence. From the 1868 election onwards the reign of Cardiganshire's gentry as the sole political representatives of the people was at an end; and this was just one illustration of the rift that had developed between church-going landlord and chapel-going tenant.

The waning of the political control of Cardiganshire's gentry was paralleled by a progressive decline in their economic fortunes. For many, this had reached crisis proportions by the time of the agricultural depression of the later nineteenth century. Despite the considerable improvements and 'the example of a better system of farming' that had been 'set upon the estates of the larger owners', many estates had become heavily encumbered so that the annual income was no longer sufficient to meet all the charges, annuities and debts, and also to run the estate.[90] Inevitably, further debts accrued. Some of these were owed locally, causing hardship and resentment in the community, a resentment that was compounded by what was perceived as the landlord's increasing inability to carry out his duties, hindered as he was by financial embarassment. The main area of concern was the condition of farmhouses and buildings on tenant farms,

---

[89] Ibid., 513.
[90] *Mr Doyle's Reports*, p. 12.

and not without reason. Official reports of the nineteenth century consistently drew attention to the unsatisfactory condition of Cardiganshire's rural dwellings and farm buildings. During the long farm leases of the eighteenth century, tenants had been responsible for their own repairs; this had resulted in a countryside full of farm buildings in a state of neglect.[91] Nineteenth-century estate records show that landlords attempted to improve the condition of their farms and cottages, providing materials and/or labour for the maintenance of old buildings and the construction of new ones.[92] However, the sheer scale of the problem of maintenance, let alone refurbishment, was causing problems for most landowners, impeded as they now were by financial difficulties. By the end of the century many of the county's small farms had had little capital invested in improvements to either land or buildings by tenant, landlord or owner-occupier.[93]

Thus, in the closing decades of the nineteenth century, Cardiganshire's landed estates were feeling the strain of both social and economic pressures. Estate incomes were increasingly inadequate while taxes were falling more heavily on them than on the growing numbers whose wealth derived from non-landed sources. From the 1870s, some Cardiganshire landowners began to retrench by selling off outlying areas of land, and, despite the recession in agriculture, tenants competed to buy their holdings, fearful of the prospect of their farms' falling into unsympathetic hands. Moreover, ownership of landed estates no longer automatically carried with it political power and the deference and loyalty of the local community. While some of Britain's landlords had justifiably gained a reputation as rapacious, spendthrift hedonists, the Welsh Land Commission of 1894 concluded that many landlords in Wales took their responsibilities to their tenants seriously but were hampered by lack of capital.[94] There is apparently little evidence in the available accounts of Cardiganshire estates to support the

[91] Colyer, 'Gentry and county', 524.

[92] See, for example, K. J. Cooper, 'Rhydhir Uchaf: the history of a Cardiganshire farm', *Ceredigion*, 9 (1982–3), 249–53.

[93] Moore-Colyer, 'Agriculture and land occupation', pp. 31, 36.

[94] Thomas, *Digest*, pp. 211–12.

allegation that landlords gratuitously refused to carry out improvements on their tenants' farms.[95] One disillusioned landowner felt that he spoke for the majority when he commented that

> We who are owners have done our best to act as if in partnership with our tenants and have not been governed by purely mercenary considerations. A change, however, is coming over the scene and those of us who do not possess other sources of income must regulate our affairs accordingly.[96]

The factors involved in the decline of Cardiganshire's landed estates were extremely complex and reflected the changing social, political and economic conditions of nineteenth-century Britain as a whole. In the space of little more than a century, these changes had brought about the eclipse of a class whose influence in Cardiganshire had been profound and far reaching. With the decline of the landed estates, the scene was set in the county for the great flood of land sales that characterized the early decades of the twentieth century.[97] The demise of the great estates and the rise of freehold farming have, in fact, been described as a 'change of the greatest significance' in rural society, not just in Cardiganshire, but in Wales as a whole.[98]

Some idea of the socio-economic structure of Cardiganshire in the second half of the nineteenth century and the changes that were occurring as the century drew to a close can be gained from table 1.2.[99] The major source of male employment in Cardiganshire in 1851 was provided by agriculture followed by general labour and lead mining: numbers in these three categories alone accounted for just under 65 per cent of the occupied males in the registration county. At

---

[95] Colyer, 'Gentry and county', 529.

[96] Ibid., 531.

[97] For a chronology of estate sales in Cardiganshire, 1870–1950, see Colyer, 'Gentry and county', 532–4.

[98] Davies, 'End of the great estates', 186.

[99] Female occupations have been excluded from this table because of problems with the data in the Victorian census. For more on this, see E. Higgs, *Making Sense of the Census: The Manuscript Returns for England and Wales, 1801–1901* (2nd edn, London, 1991), pp. 81–2. Although these statistics are for the registration county, they serve as a useful guide to the occupational structure in the geographical county.

Table 1.2 Selected male occupational trends: 1851, 1871 and 1891[1]

Occupation	1851	1871	1891
agriculture	13331	12564	10943
lead mining	1677	1823	766
general labour	2472	1505	991
building works[2]	1888	2040	1623
professions[3]	566	745	857
innkeeper/lodging house keeper	125	231	418
commerce[4]	65	155	266

Source: Population censuses, 1851, 1871 and 1891.

[1] It should be noted that there was some fluidity of movement between the categories as well as dual occupations.

[2] These occupations include builders, carpenters/joiners, masons, plumbers, glaziers and plasterers.

[3] These occupations include the clergy and those in the legal, medical and education professions.

[4] These occupations include merchants, accountants, auctioneers, agents (e.g. insurance), clerks, commercial travellers and those in banking.

the other end of the scale, commerce and the professions were under-represented. The census for 1871 marked the county's population high point, yet already there was a significant decline in general labourers and also a slight reduction in the agricultural workforce. Numbers employed in all the other categories listed in table 1.2, however, had increased by 1871. The lead-mining industry was obviously thriving, and the rise in the county's population was mirrored by a rise of those in the building trade as rural and urban settlements expanded. By 1891 lead mining was in crisis and employment in the industry had plummeted by almost 60 per cent from 1871 levels. The decade 1881–91 saw the county's greatest percentage loss by out-migration, and the decline of the number employed in agriculture, lead mining and general labouring had obviously made a significant contribution to this population loss. Given these circumstances, the decline of those employed in the building trade was inevitable. By contrast, those occupations associated with urban living – the professions, commerce and hospitality – showed a sustained increase throughout the period, confirming the modest but steady move towards urbanization in the county that was demonstrated in figure 1.4 (above).

Nineteenth-century Cardiganshire did not enjoy a high general standard of living.[100] Despite this, the pauper element was below the average for Wales and only slightly above that for England and Wales combined during the second half of the century.[101] However, contemporary evidence suggests that informal and occasional assistance from local bene-factors almost certainly prevented a greater incidence of pauperism in the county.[102]

Agriculture dominated the employment structure and about half of Cardiganshire's employed males still worked on the land in 1911, compared with less than 12 per cent in Wales as a whole.[103] The county's urban settlements remained few and small, and although the move towards urbanization was apparent as the nineteenth century progressed, the towns remained modest in size and had too narrow a commercial base to absorb much surplus labour from the surrounding countryside where a rising population was putting increasing pressure on the limited employment opportunities.

[100] For a useful survey of the range of sources that may be considered when studying nineteenth-century poverty in Cardiganshire, see Palmer, 'Documentary evidence', 11–29. See also A. M. E. Davies, 'Poverty and its treatment in Cardiganshire' (unpublished MA thesis, University of Wales, 1968).

[101] D. Jones, 'Pauperism in the Aberystwyth Poor Law Union, 1870–1914', *Ceredigion*, 9 (1980), 80.

[102] Palmer, 'Documentary evidence', 23.

[103] J. Williams, 'The move from the land', in T. Herbert and G. E. Jones, *Wales, 1880–1914* (Cardiff, 1988), p. 17.

II

THE ROLE OF THE LEAD-MINING INDUSTRY

The abandoned lead mines of Cardiganshire have so blended into the surrounding countryside that their presence is often overlooked. Nevertheless, the effects of metal mining on the historic landscape have been considerable. Cardiganshire's mines were numerous and widely scattered, and the mining process has impacted on the county's northern uplands in unexpected ways. The mines were almost totally reliant on water power, and the reservoirs, dams and leats that were constructed to serve the mines are still prominent features of the upland landscape, while some of the watercourses and mine tracks have become public footpaths. Moreover, the many scree slopes on the steep valley sides are more likely to be waste tips resulting from metal mining than produced by natural processes. Remains of the mines themselves, their shafts and adits, wheel pits and derelict buildings, though often obscured by vegetation, are also quite widely found.[1] Even less apparent today is the significance of this once wide-spread rural industry in the socio-economic history of the county.

In the nineteenth century, Cardiganshire's metal mines varied greatly in size, productivity and length of time worked. There were at least ninety mines scattered throughout northern Cardiganshire and, although some had very rich deposits, others, despite much effort and expenditure, produced very little ore. There were also many trial shafts in the region that came to nothing at all.[2]

Lead ore is to be found throughout the highland regions of Britain, and has been mined in many of them. The ore is usually associated with other minerals, and in Cardiganshire

---

[1] For some examples, see K. J. Cooper, 'Cardiganshire's rural exodus' (unpublished Ph.D. thesis, University of Leicester, 2008), 56–8.
[2] For an idea of the extent and distribution of the mines, see W. J. Lewis, *Lead Mining in Wales* (Cardiff, 1967), map facing p. 70.

it was most often associated with silver and zinc. Lead, along with copper, silver and gold, was mined in Britain in pre-Roman times and, although the evidence for early workings is scanty, the speed with which the Romans developed the metal mines of Britain suggests that many sites were already well known when they arrived.[3]

Mining skills and the use of lead in Britain declined after the Romans left, but interest revived as a result of the Norman policy of building castles and encouraging urbanization. In Wales, however, there was little lead-mining activity until the thirteenth century and even then nothing to rival the three great lead-mining areas of England: Alston Moor, the Peak District and the Mendips.[4] A further boost to the demand for lead came with the great increase in the building and rebuilding of Britain's great houses from the later sixteenth century. Vast quantities were needed, not only for roofs and windows but also for gutters, downspouts, storage cisterns and pipes. Moreover, Elizabeth I, on her accession, had two urgent needs: munitions to defend the country from the threat of a Spanish invasion and money to replenish the royal coffers. Copper, zinc and silver were, therefore, in great demand and experienced miners were sent to prospect for them in the mineral districts of England and Wales. As a result of this activity the Society of Mines Royal came into being.[5]

Britain's great age of lead mining came in the eighteenth and nineteenth centuries, when, as the world's main producer, it developed new techniques for mining and smelting. New uses for lead evolved, such as its addition to glass to produce crystal and its use in paint and pottery glazes. Meanwhile, the rapid urban and industrial growth meant that lead was now in even greater demand for roofing, water pipes and even ornaments.

---

[3] Ibid., pp. 22, 24.

[4] Ibid., pp. 26, 29.

[5] In a court action brought in 1568 it was adjudged that a mine belonged to the Crown and became a mine royal if the ore contained sufficient gold or silver to pay for the cost of refining. The Society of Mines Royal was established to oversee the locating and working of these mines. Lewis, *Lead Mining in Wales*, p. 38; G. C. Boon, *Cardiganshire Silver and the Aberystwyth Mint in Peace and War* (Cardiff, 1981), pp. 1–2.

Cardiganshire archaeological excavations have demon-strated that opencast lead and copper mining was undertaken at various sites during the Bronze Age, and lead was prob-ably mined there in Roman times, although there is little to suggest that the Romans themselves worked the mines. Not a great deal is known about mining activities in Cardiganshire in the medieval period, although there is slight evidence of lead ore being mined sporadically and on a small scale at a number of locations, and there is certainly evidence of lead working by the Cistercian monks of Strata Florida Abbey, near Pontrhydfendigaid, from the late twelfth century.[6] By the early seventeenth century the potential of the coun-ty's mineral wealth, and in particular its silver content, was attracting attention.[7]

Most of Cardiganshire's lead mines lay within the three large estates of Gogerddan, Nanteos and Trawsgoed which dominated the north of the county. The landowners did not work the mines themselves; they leased the rights to prospect for and work the mines to individuals or companies. By the mid-eighteenth century there were thirty-seven lead mines being worked in the county, with varying degrees of effi-ciency and success, but by the end of the century many of the mines had been in operation long enough to have exhausted the shallower deposits. The majority of mining promoters were concerned only with quick returns and easy profits, making little or no attempt to open new ore-ground. Before the deeper deposits could be worked, considerable capital expenditure was required, but the depressing effects of the Napoleonic wars on the industry made most promoters reluc-tant to invest, and so work stopped at many of the mines.[8]

The nineteenth century saw the last long burst of activity in the county's metal mines. Interest in the mines began to revive in the early 1820s. In 1822 the Alderson brothers took the lease of mines on the Nanteos estate bringing with

[6] Lewis, *Lead Mining in Wales*, pp. 28–9; *Welsh Mines Society Newsletter*, 48 (April 2003), 13–14; S. J. S. Hughes, *The Cwmystwyth Mines* (Sheffield, 1981), pp. 5–6. It is estimated that the monks would have needed about 70 tons of lead for the roof alone.

[7] For more on the history of the individual mines, see D. E. Bick, *The Old Metal Mines of Mid-Wales. Parts 1–3* (Newent, 1974–6).

[8] Lewis, *Lead Mining in Wales*, pp. 106, 115–16.

them mining specialists and working miners from their native Yorkshire. This was soon followed by the beginnings of the so-called 'Cornish invasion' when the Williams family, mining engineers from Gwennap, took the leases of mines on the Trawsgoed and Gogerddan estates. With them came both Cornish expertise and working miners, marking the start of a long association between the mining districts of Cardiganshire and those of Cornwall.[9] Unfortunately, during this decade the price of lead slumped again and, despite their undoubted efficiency, the Aldersons and the Williams Company failed in the early 1830s. The Williams family surrendered their lease to one of their partners, John Taylor, a Cornish mining engineer. Taylor did more for the county's lead mining industry than any other man. Where others had attempted to get rich in the shortest space of time and with the minimum investment, Taylor had the mines carefully surveyed and properly drained, and his company made roads and invested in new machinery. The result was almost fifty years of high productivity for the mines managed by the Taylors and a royalty bonanza for the landlords.[10]

METAL MINING AND THE ECONOMY OF CARDIGANSHIRE

Throughout its history, the metal-mining industry had been subject to substantial fluctuations in output due mainly to market forces and to the technical problems associated with extraction of the ores. For Cardiganshire, these fluctuations were still apparent during the nineteenth century, the era of the industry's final and most successful phase. Statistics for annual output are available from 1845 onwards and excerpts from these returns are reproduced in table 2.1. The rapid rise in productivity from 1845 to the county's peak year for lead ore production of 1856 is striking. This was also the year of the maximum number of mines in operation. Equally apparent from the statistics is the rapidity of the decline of

[9] Ibid., pp. 173–4; W. J. Lewis, 'Lead mining in Cardiganshire', in G. H. Jenkins and I. G. Jones (eds), *Cardiganshire County History*, vol. 3, *Cardiganshire in Modern Times* (Cardiff, 1998), p. 167.
[10] Lewis, 'Lead mining in Cardiganshire', p. 167; G. Morgan, *A Welsh House and its Family: The Vaughans of Trawsgoed* (Llandysul, 1997), p. 222.

Table 2.1 Productivity of Cardiganshire's metal mines for selected years, 1845–1901

Year	Number of mines working	Numbers employed	Lead ore (tons)	Zinc ore (tons)	Silver (ounces)
1845	19	n.a.	5726	–	–
1851	n.a.	1932	7182	–	87135
1856	38	n.a.	8560	1096	38751
1861	24	2039	7755	1807	54989
1871	36	2052	7553	630	46980
1881	28	1824	4598	3453	28755
1891	18	781	2150	3741	14731
1901	8	550	1090	2596	2862

Sources: Lewis, *Lead Mining in Wales*, appendices C and E; J. Williams, *Digest of Welsh Historical Statistics*, 2 vols (Cardiff, 1985), vol. 2, pp. 8–9; population censuses, 1851–1901.

the industry after 1881, although some short-lived partial revivals of mining activity, especially for zinc, kept some metal mines working into the early twentieth century.

The census confirms that lead mining was a major element in Cardiganshire's occupational structure during the middle years of the nineteenth century. Moreover, besides employment for the miners themselves, the mines generated work for supplementary trades such as that of the mason, carpenter and blacksmith, while many of the miners' womenfolk and children were also employed at the mines as ore dressers. In addition to providing employment on a scale second only to agriculture, lead mining boosted the local economy by creating a demand for goods and services to provision the mines and miners. These included clothing, food and draft animals, while local farmers regularly augmented their often subsistence livelihoods by hauling the partially dressed ores down to the port of Aberystwyth for onward shipping to the smelteries.

The carriage of the ore to the nearest smeltery or port was a perennial problem facing lead-mine operators and one that impinged on the transport infrastructure of Cardiganshire from early modern times. Most lead mines were in remote upland areas so that originally the only means of transport was by pack horse. With the growth of the industry in eighteenth-century Britain, horse-drawn wagons were needed to carry the increased ore output, but many mining areas still had no roads suitable for wheeled vehicles. As late as the 1760s, upland Cardiganshire was described as a place where a wheeled cart was never seen. Matters were complicated by the frequent neglect of their duty by the parish officers responsible for such roads as did exist in rural Cardiganshire. Thus, those who worked the county's mines often had to make their own roads, a process that was greatly hampered not only by the remoteness of the mines but by hazards of the terrain such as peat bogs and steep hillsides. The expense of road building and maintenance of these mountain roads continued to be a burden on the industry to the end of its life.[11]

As we have seen, by the nineteenth century Aberystwyth was a port of some consequence, and the lead-mining industry was a catalyst of its development. The great weight and bulky nature of lead ore meant that the cheapest form of transport was by water. The rapid growth in exploitation of the mines in the Aberystwyth hinterland, notably Cwmsymlog, Darren and Esgair-mwyn, from the 1740s, and the closure of the smelting furnaces in the far north of the county, led to the development of the port of Aberystwyth as the main outlet for ore from Cardiganshire.[12] At this time, however, a serious obstacle to the expansion and efficient working of the port was the fact that Aberystwyth was a creek of the port of Aberdyfi, the latter only a settlement of a few houses and a wharf beside the office of the collector of customs. Accordingly, a petition was presented to parliament in 1759 to have the customs house transferred to Aberystwyth:

> The trade of late has become greatly increased, and . . . the same would become still more considerable but for the inconvenience of our having no Customs House within ten miles of the town . . . We are thereby greatly retarded in getting despatches, and consequently prevented from sailing . . . when the wind permits it . . . We further beg leave to represent . . . that the town of Aberystwyth is situated

[11] Lewis, *Lead Mining in Wales*, pp. 295–6.
[12] There were a couple of smelteries established in the county after this date but they were soon abandoned due to bankruptcy. Lewis, *Lead Mining in Wales*, pp. 173, 313.

in the centre of the Port, . . . having from Thirty to Forty Vessels . . .
constantly employed particularly in exporting Lead Ore and Black
Jack [zinc blende], and of the former Commodity there is from Three
to Four Thousand Tons annually shipped Coastwise.[13]

The petition was successful and in 1763 the customs house
was transferred from Aberdyfi to Aberystwyth. As a result, the
port grew rapidly so that the number of ships registered there
rose from one in 1701 to ninety-nine in 1799.[14] The future of
the port as a centre for expanding coastal and overseas trade
and a thriving shipbuilding centre seemed assured.

Records of sailings from Aberystwyth survive for the mid-
nineteenth century only, during which time lead ore still
dominated the exports.[15] The destinations for these ore
shipments are interesting. In 1842 there were fifty-seven
sailings, all to Flint, which remained the sole destination
for Cardiganshire's lead ore until 1847. The smelteries of
Flintshire had long been the main recipients of ore from
Britain's lead mines, but by mid-century Deeside was beginning to lose ground, especially to Bristol and Llanelli, and
this change was reflected in the pattern of lead ore shipments
from Aberystwyth.[16] After 1847 the number of destinations
increased rapidly to include not only Bristol and Llanelli
but also Liverpool, Swansea, Cardiff, Newport, Plymouth,
Falmouth, Truro, London and even Newcastle. This gives
some indication of the geographical extent of commercial
contact between Cardiganshire and the rest of England and
Wales through this export alone when the port of Aberystwyth
was at its zenith, and the significance of this commercial
contact in the context of out-migration will become apparent
later in this book. The main receiving port for the county's
lead ore, however, continued to be Flint during the time for
which the harbour records are still extant.[17]

---

[13] Ibid., p. 301.
[14] Ibid., pp. 301–2.
[15] NLW, Aberystwyth Borough Records. F11. Port of Aberystwyth. (a) Vessels
sailed 1842–51; (c) Vessels sailed 1851–1866, and June–October 1886.
[16] Lewis, *Lead Mining in Wales*, p. 318.
[17] In Cardiganshire's peak year of lead ore production, 1856, 69 of the 135 shipments of the ore were bound for Flint. NLW, Port of Aberystwyth. (a) Vessels sailed
1842–51.

For most of the lead-mining companies of Wales the coming of the railways offered a quicker and more dependable means of transporting lead ore to the smelteries. However, it was also much more expensive, and substantial amounts of Cardiganshire's ore continued to be transported by sea after the extension of the railway network to the county.[18]

As well as boosting the commerce of the port through exports of lead ore and imports of mining supplies, the industry contributed to the commerce of the town. Lead mining generated the need for a range of goods and services in Aberystwyth as well as in the rural neighbourhoods of the mines. One commodity that impinged on the occupational structure of the town in this way was the demand for mining equipment (see figure 2.1). This helped to sustain a number of small-scale iron foundries in Aberystwyth, the largest of which, Green's Foundry of Alexandra Road, manufactured items during the second half of the century, both for home markets and for export.[19]

Changes in population at parish level reflect changes in the socio-economic factors operating in a region and, in order to gain some idea of the effects of lead mining on the local community, the population trends of three parishes within each of four distinct regions of Cardiganshire have been compared for the whole of the nineteenth century.[20] The contrast between the lead mining townships and the parishes of the other three regions – central coastal, Mynydd Bach and Lower Teifi Valley – was immediately apparent.[21] As might be expected, the trend in the lead-mining townships closely mirrored the fortunes of the lead-mining industry, with population numbers rising steeply from the 1820s and

[18] Lewis, *Lead Mining in Wales*, pp. 304–5.
[19] C. R. Lewis and S. E. Wheatley, 'The towns of Cardiganshire, 1800–1995', in Jenkins and Jones (eds), *Cardiganshire County History*, vol. 3, p. 217.
[20] Graphs of these population trends can be seen in Cooper, 'Cardiganshire's rural exodus', 70.
[21] For the purposes of this comparison, the lead-mining townships were Cwmrheidol, Melindwr and Trefeirig, the central coastal parishes were Llanddeiniol, Llanychaiarn and Mefenydd, the Mynydd Bach parishes were Nantcwnlle, Trefilan and Upper Lledrod, and the Lower Teifi Valley parishes were Bangor, Brongwyn and Llandyfriog.

Figure 2.1 Metal ore wagon at Bronfloyd disused lead mine
Photo: K. Cooper

peaking in all three townships in 1871. This date, it will be remembered, was also the population high point for the county. The parishes in each of the other three regions show a much more level graph and, although small local variations are apparent, the general tendency was towards a slight population gain followed by a long slow decline, seven out of the nine sampled parishes containing fewer individuals in 1911 than in 1801. In several of the parishes the decline was already apparent by mid-century, suggesting that significant rural out-migration was already underway in many areas of the county by this time.[22] County-wide statistics often conceal significant local variations, and certainly in the case of Cardiganshire the spectacular rise in numbers in the lead-mining townships up to 1871 was enough to affect

[22] This conclusion is confirmed by notes in the 1851 census population tables which attributed the great increases in northern parishes to in-migration because of the flourishing lead-mining industry, and the decline in some central and southern parishes both to migration to industrial south Wales and to emigration. *Census of Great Britain, 1851. Population Tables. 1. Numbers of the Inhabitants*, vol. II ([1852], 2nd edn, Shannon, 1970), pp. 447, 449, 451.

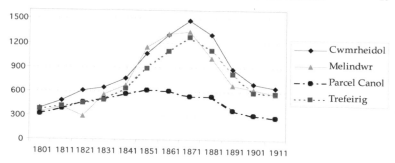

Figure 2.2 Population trends of four townships in northern Cardiganshire, 1801–1911
Source: Population censuses, 1801–1911.

the overall population trend while masking the decreases experienced elsewhere in the county.[23] Figure 2.2 illustrates the contrast between populations in the lead mining townships of Cwmrheidol, Melindwr and Trefeirig, and that in the predominantly agricultural Parcel Canol where the rise was more gradual and a slow decline began from mid-century.[24]

During the industry's final phase metal mining made a major contribution to the economy of Cardiganshire, and exports and imports connected with it continued to boost coastal trade in the second half of the century, incidentally helping to postpone the decline of Aberystwyth's port function. The scattered nature and small scale of the county's mines, however, meant that they did not give rise to any industrial towns and, although the great influx of labour to the mining regions in the early- and mid-nineteenth century expanded existing settlements and created new ones, the landscape remained a semi-agricultural, semi-industrial patchwork.

WORKING AND LIVING CONDITIONS

The chief attraction of lead mining was that it offered unskilled and semi-skilled work at about twice the pay, locally,

---

[23] For an analysis of population trends by registration district, see chapter IV.
[24] Victorian Trefeirig covered a much larger area than present-day Trefeurig.

for agricultural labour. Nevertheless, the miners of mid Wales were among the lowest paid in England and Wales, and this was one of the factors that drew mine investors and operators to the area.[25] The low level of wages, combined with irregularity of employment, meant that the miner's income often had to be augmented by family labour at the mines. Women and children were widely employed in Britain's lead mines to wash and break up the ore for onward transport until the installation of ore-dressing machinery from the 1850s reduced the demand for their labour. In Cardiganshire, however, the operators of the many small mines found it cheaper to continue to employ women and children for these tasks until mining ceased. The wages paid to women in the later nineteenth century were often only 6d. per day, the same as at the beginning of the eighteenth century, although rates of 10d. or 1s. were not unknown.[26] As for the men, there was little improvement in their earnings during the nineteenth century either, miners averaging about 15s. and mine labourers about 11s. per week.[27] Moreover, wages were subject to deductions for items such as candles and gunpowder.[28] Even when the industry was at its height, payment of wages by the smaller mining companies was not always made on a regular basis. The extra burden this placed on families already at or near subsistence level was such that in 1863 petitions were presented to parliament by miners from Cardiganshire complaining of irregular payment going back as far as 1855. In some instances, legal proceedings for recovery of the money were contemplated but abandoned due both to the expense involved and to the risk for the whole community of mining companies' declaring themselves bankrupt; in the event of bankruptcy it was not just the miners who suffered – local tradespeople who regularly extended credit to the mining companies were also losers.[29]

[25] A. K. Knowles, 'The structure of rural society in north Cardiganshire, 1800–1850', in Jenkins and Jones (eds), *Cardiganshire County History*, vol. 3, p. 85; Lewis, 'Lead mining in Cardiganshire', p. 179.

[26] Lewis, *Lead Mining in Wales*, pp. 273–5; D. E. Bick, *The Old Metal Mines of Mid-Wales. Part 2. Cardiganshire – The Rheidol to Goginan* (Newent, 1975), p. 46.

[27] There were 12 old pence to a shilling (now 5p) and 20 shillings to a pound.

[28] Lewis, 'Lead mining in Cardiganshire', pp. 162, 180.

[29] *Minutes of Evidence taken before The Commissioners Appointed to Inquire into the*

A common supplementary source of income for mining families was small-scale farming, and the dual occupation of miner/farmer was a characteristic of the industry in many parts of upland Britain:

the nature of the employment and its unhealthy character making it undesirable to work longer at it [than a 40-hour week] – some of the remaining time was often employed in gardening, in tending small grazing farms and in other modes.[30]

We have already noted the deep attachment to the land that was characteristic of rural Wales and, for many of Cardiganshire's lead miners, mining was merely a means to earn sufficient to pay their rents and so keep possession of their holdings. As production at the mines began to run down from the 1870s, and miners suffered reduction in, or non-payment of their wages, many families experienced difficulties in paying their rents, as is graphically illustrated by a letter of 1892 from the collector of rents to the manager of the Gogerddan estate:

As requested I went round Cwmsymlog, Cwmerfyn, Cwmsebon & Penbont-rhydybeddau yesterday in search for Rent but it was all in vain for I did not receive a single penny . . . Jas Edwards would pay when he would receive wages from Bronfloyd [mine] . . . Two or three other people promised to pay after Saturday as such is the Pay Day of East Darren Mine.[31]

In 1863 a government commission was appointed to look into the conditions in Britain's mines, and the minutes of evidence from the Kinnaird Report give a valuable insight into the working and living conditions of the Cardiganshire miners and their families when the industry was at its height. It was widely acknowledged that the main health hazards caused by work in lead mines, apart from accidents, were dust, bad air and smoke from the gunpowder. The state of underground ventilation was, therefore, a prime concern for the commission but one that gave rise to conflicting

Condition of all Mines in Great Britain (Kinnaird Report) ([1864], 2nd edn, Shannon, 1969), pp. 511–12, 515.
[30] 'Our lead mines and their produce', Mining Journal, 12 May 1877, 501.
[31] NLW, Gogerddan Estate, Box 44. Lead mining letters, R. Owens to Col. Williams, 21 July 1892.

evidence. According to one mine captain, ventilation was sadly inadequate in most of Cardiganshire's mines 'Because we try to save the expense to the Company'. Asked if the miners suffered because of this, his response was:

> When you go in about 20 or 30 fathoms, you will perceive a smell which will almost knock you back, a nasty, filthy, bad smell; that is what kills the miners . . . It affects their lungs . . . Generally [they die from it] about 25 or 30. When a miner gets up about 40 years of age he is not worth a snap of a finger.[32]

The next witness, the captain of the Cwmystwyth mines, did not agree with this opinion. He declared that all the mines in the locality were well ventilated and that the miners' health did not suffer 'except that when they come to get old I think that they get short of breath a little'.[33] This evidence was, in turn, contradicted by the mine doctor who declared that the Cwmystwyth mines were among the more unhealthy ones in the region.[34] He added that lung disease in miners was now more widespread than in former times because 'the mines are worked a great deal more extensively now . . . [and] people have been more underground'. He added that a 'great many die under 40', but he considered that the worst affected were those who had worked in the mines from a young age: 'I think that they die sooner if they go [down the mines] earlier . . . people who have been in agricultural labour til they grow up pretty strong stand it best.'[35]

The commissioners also enquired into the health of the miners as compared with that of the local non-mining population. In response, one doctor declared that although Cardiganshire's miners were 'not a healthy-looking class of people at all . . . the agriculturalists do not look very healthy themselves'.[36] Poor domestic conditions were blamed for this: 'I find them in a great measure causing fever in the houses . . . During the last six years that I have been living here there

---

[32] *Kinnaird Report*, p. 501.

[33] Ibid., p. 503.

[34] Miners had, on average, 6d. per month deducted from their wages to pay for medical care for themselves and their families. This covered illness and accidents. See, for example, *Kinnaird Report*, p. 508.

[35] Ibid., p. 509.

[36] Ibid., p. 505.

has been a constant fever, typhus and typhoid and scarlet fever.'[37] There was also 'a good deal of phthisis', or pulmonary tuberculosis (consumption), among the poorer sector of the community, both mining and non-mining.[38] Whether bacteriological and associated with poor living conditions, or mechanical such as that suffered by miners, this disease was a major cause of death in Europe until well into the twentieth century. In England and Wales, Cardiganshire consistently had one of the highest mortality rates from tuberculosis.[39] The disease has been the subject of much sociological as well as medical research.[40]

In northern Cardiganshire, miners' cottages in the mid-nineteenth century were, according to the witnesses before the 1863 commission, indistinguishable from those of the agricultural labourers, and both were 'generally very small and very dirty too'.[41] Many of the older cottages were earth walled 'because we have no building stone in this country', and they mostly consisted of 'one room, or . . . one room divided by partitions of linen'. Windows usually had 'one small pane or two or three small panes and without any means of opening' so that any ventilation was via the chimney and the door, that usually stood open 'sometimes so much so that it is extremely cold' (see figure 2.3). The floor was 'more often than otherwise of clay, and a sort of bog'. In the larger cottages there was 'a door to go into one room, and then there is a little room at the other end, and then a loft thrown over the building for the children to sleep in'.[42]

All witnesses giving evidence for the Kinnaird Report were unanimous about the squalid living conditions of these dwellings, both inside and out; often 'the cesspool is close

[37] Ibid., p. 511.

[38] Ibid., p. 510.

[39] R. Woods and N. Shelton, *An Atlas of Victorian Mortality* (Liverpool, 1997), pp. 100, 102.

[40] See, for example, E. G. Bowen, 'A clinical study of miners' phthisis in relation to the geographical and racial features of the Cardiganshire lead mining area', in I. C. Peate (ed.), *Studies in Regional Consciousness and Environment: Essays presented to H. J. Fleure* (London, 1930), pp. 189–202; S. Lyle Cummins, 'Tuberculosis as a social disease', *Journal of State Medicine*, 36 (1928), 1–4.

[41] *Kinnaird Report*, pp. 505, 509.

[42] Ibid., pp. 505, 509, 512.

Figure 2.3 Earth-walled cottage in a former lead-mining township, north Cardiganshire
Photo: K. Cooper

to the house, as are also the dungheaps'.[43] However, not all mining families were accommodated in these cottages. In some areas the mining companies erected rows of small terraced housing, with gardens, for the miners to rent. These new dwellings were generally 'kept in very nice order'.[44] Mine proprietors also provided barracks or lodging shops for the more remote mines. Some could house 'perhaps 100 men; they come up on Monday morning and leave on Saturday evening. Those barracks are very healthy.'[45]

[43] Ibid., p. 511.
[44] Ibid., p. 512.
[45] Ibid., p. 512.

CHILD LABOUR

The occupation of children is seriously under-recorded in the Victorian censuses.[46] In most working-class families the contribution of children to the family income was vital; this usually took the form of casual, part-time or seasonal work, or help with the family trade or on the family farm, and as such did not usually appear on the census returns. The most common designation for children in the census schedules was 'scholar'.[47]

At the time of the Kinnaird Report, boys and girls of 9 years of age and upwards worked in the ore-dressing sheds of Cardiganshire's mines along with the women and older men.[48] From about 12 years of age, the boys started work underground, 'learning to mine; they are turning the borer and wheeling stuff'.[49] The young starting age for child labour at lead mines had apparently altered little since the beginning of the century: one of the mine captains giving evidence for the report had started work on the dressing floors of a Yorkshire mine in 1809 at the age of 8 and considered this to be quite unexceptionable.[50]

During the peak period of activity at Cardiganshire's lead mines, young labour was a significant component of the workforce. In 1851, employees under 20 years of age accounted for a quarter of the labour in the mines and dressing sheds, and by 1871 this had risen to over 28 per cent (see table 2.2).

Although the employment of children in Cardiganshire's lead mines seems to have been widespread, a few mine promoters also made provision for some basic education before school attendance became compulsory. For instance, there was a school attached to Cardiganshire's Lisburne mines that was funded jointly by the company and by a

---

[46] For more on this, see E. Higgs, *Making Sense of the Census: The Manuscript Returns for England and Wales, 1801–1901* (2nd edn, London, 1991), pp. 82–5.

[47] Before compulsory elementary education a scholar was defined for census purposes as either attending a school or receiving instruction at home and the scholars listed in the censuses could include those who attended only a Sunday school.

[48] *Kinnaird Report*, pp. 502–4, 508.

[49] Ibid., p. 503.

[50] Ibid., p. 504.

Table 2.2 Numbers employed in Cardiganshire's metal mines, 1851 and 1871

Employees	1851	1871
under 20 years	485	582
20 years and over	1447	1470
% under 20 years	**25.1**	**28.4**

Source: Population censuses, 1851, 1871

deduction of 1d. per month from the miners' wages. Local children from non-mining families also had access to the school on payment of a fee. The education, however, was probably fairly rudimentary because the teacher was apparently 'not one of the certificated masters', but it had the merit of being available when school attendance was still on a voluntary basis.[51]

Compulsory elementary school attendance from 1880 was a severe blow for the income of Britain's working-class families, and truancy in the early decades, supported by parents, was common despite the efforts of school attendance officers. The latter years of the century, however, saw a significant decrease in the levels of child employment, due to the cumulative effects of education and factory legislation and to the rise in men's wages.[52] But for much of the century, despite the census evidence to the contrary, the majority of working-class children would have been making some contribution to the family economy.[53] Indeed, as late as 1877, the *Mining Journal* was quite open about the role of child labour in the lead mines:

> The fact that . . . lead mining is looked to to furnish employment for the bulk of the population [of the lead mining districts], and that, in some of the processes of purification of the ore, children have long been employed, has kept wages down.[54]

[51] Ibid., p. 506.
[52] *Royal Commission on Labour. Fifth and Final Report. Part I. The Report* ([1894], 2nd edn, 1970), p. 223.
[53] Higgs, *Making Sense of the Census*, pp. 82–5.
[54] *Mining Journal*, 12 May 1877, 501.

From the 1870s, the use of child labour at Cardiganshire's mines dropped sharply as the lead-mining industry went into a steep decline and demand for labour of all ages plummeted.

POPULATION MOBILITY

It has been suggested that the most important feature of society in nineteenth-century Britain, after inequality, was its mobility.[55] Indeed, even by 1851, the census noted that 'there is a constant emigration from house to house, parish to parish, and county to county'.[56] It has been estimated that over half the population by this time were no longer living within two kilometres of their stated birthplace.[57]

In Cardiganshire, the census takers noted in the middle decades of the century that a major stimulus to movement within the county was the thriving lead-mining industry in its northern regions.[58] However, the industry also attracted incomers from outside the county. Mention has already been made of the 'Cornish invasion', and to gain an idea of the movement into the county's lead-mining districts from else-where in England and Wales the birthplace data from the manuscript returns for the township of Trefeirig (see figure 2.4) for 1851, 1871 and 1891 were analysed.[59] Some migrants had come from as far afield as Scotland and Ireland, but the majority had come from mining regions in England and Wales – counties such as Montgomery, Glamorgan, Anglesey, Durham and Yorkshire. The main sending area, however, was undoubtedly Cornwall. Cornish mining expertise was in great demand both in Britain and abroad at this time. For instance, one of the witnesses giving evidence for the

---

[55] M. Anderson, 'Recent work on the analysis of nineteenth-century census returns', *Family History*, 11 (1980), 154–5.

[56] *Census of Great Britain, 1851. Population Tables. II. Ages, Civil Condition, Occupations, and Birth-Place of the People*, vol.1 ([1854], 2nd edn, 1970), p. ciii.

[57] M. Anderson, 'The social implications of demographic change', in F. M. L. Thompson (ed.), *The Cambridge Social History of Britain, 1750–1950*, vol. 2, *People and their Environment* (2nd edn, Cambridge, 1993), p. 11.

[58] *1851 Census. Population Tables. 1*, vol. 2, p. 451.

[59] The results have been mapped in Cooper, 'Cardiganshire's rural exodus', 81–3. For a more detailed study of the effects of the rise and decline of lead mining on Cardiganshire communities, see K. J. Cooper, 'Trefeurig, 1851–1891: a case study of a lead mining township', *Ceredigion*, 16 (2009), 81–116.

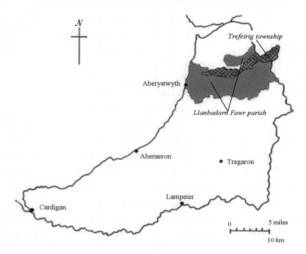

Figure 2.4 Nineteenth-century Cardiganshire showing Trefeirig township in the parish of Llanbadarn Fawr
Based on: Jones, *Statistical Evidence*, pp. 182–3.

Kinnaird Report was Henry Thomas, the general manager of the Lisburne Mines for John Taylor's Company. A Cornish man, he had started work in the tin-mining industry, after which his mining experience had taken him to Ireland, Spain and Anglesey before bringing him to Cardiganshire.[60]

Nevertheless, incomers to Trefeirig from outside Cardiganshire made up only a small proportion of the township's inhabitants. In 1851 they totalled 76, or 8.4 per cent; by 1871 there were 80 incomers, or 6.3 per cent of the population, but 28 of these had already been present at the time of the previous census; and by 1891 the number was down to 62 incomers, of whom 16 were already there in 1881. It is interesting to note that, despite the problems in the lead-mining industry from the late 1870s, migrants were still moving into the township in the 1880s when significant out-migration from northern Cardiganshire was already underway.

---

[60] *Kinnaird Report*, p. 505.

The occupational data of Trefeirig's non-Cardiganshire in-migrants have been analysed to see what was drawing them to Trefeirig, and although a mining connection was discovered for most of them, the data revealed another influence – the presence in the township of Gogerddan mansion, the seat of the Pryse family. Throughout this period much of the domestic labour employed at Gogerddan came from outside Cardiganshire, accounting for the high proportion of this occupational class among the distance in-migrants to Trefeirig. Of the 29 in-migrants in the domestic service category, 25 were employed in the Gogerddan household. These servants came from as far away as York, Kent, the Isle of Wight and Ireland, and it is noticeable that the incomers always held the more prestigious positions such as that of butler, valet and governess. It was not only in the Pryse household, however, that the incomers held the highest positions. Census evidence suggests that, small though their numbers were, migrants from outside Cardiganshire to the county's lead mines tended to hold the more skilled posts such as that of mine agent, manager, engineer and blacksmith.

As noted above, clues to inter-census moves may be gained from the birthplaces of family members as revealed in the enumerators' schedules. Some families had experienced quite high rates of mobility over long distances before arriving in Trefeirig during this period as can be seen from the following examples.

The Reed family, Cwmsymlog Mine Office, 1851

Name	Age	Relationship	Occupation	Birthplace
James Reed	45	head	mine agent	Kenwyn, Cornwall
Anne	43	wife		Workington, Cumb.
Samuel	21	son	lead miner	Mold, Flintshire
James	16	son	lead miner	Loweswater, Cumb.
Mark	15	son	scholar	Loweswater, Cumb.
Anne	13	daughter	scholar	Inerdale, Cumb.
Henry	11	son	scholar	Inerdale, Cumb.
William	8	son	scholar	**Llanbadarn Fawr**

Source: Population census, 1851.
Note: Cardiganshire birthplaces are in bold script.

The Evans family, Horeb Cottage, 1881

Name	Age	Relationship	Occupation	Birthplace
George Evans	35	head	Baptist minister	Cilgerran, Pembs.
Jane Ann	27	wife		Ffestiniog, Mer.
William Samuel	6	son	scholar	Beaumaris, Anglesey
Anne Ellen	4	daughter	scholar	**Llanbadarn Fawr**
(2 more children born in Llanbadarn Fawr parish)				

Source: Population census, 1881.

There were also those who had moved away and then returned as, for example, Margaret Jeffreys, whose husband appeared to no longer be with the family. It is impossible to guess the reason for these long-distance migrations but the birthplaces of the children suggest a mining conection.

The Jeffreys family, Penrhyncoch, 1851

Name	Age	Relationship	Occupation	Birthplace
Margaret Jeffreys	36	head	none given	**Llanbadarn Fawr**
George	8	son		Montgomeryshire
John	6	son		Cornwall
Mary Anne	2	daughter		Devon

Source: Population census, 1851.

Instances of long-distance mobility were, however, the exception in Trefeirig. Although there was much evidence of family mobility, the majority of moves were of a more local nature.

Conventional migration theory holds that for each migration flow there is usually a counterflow, and this was true of Victorian Trefeirig.[61] Contrary to what one might have expected given the demand for young male labour at the lead mines, analysis of the age structure of the township reveals a slight decrease in males in the 21–40 age group over the period 1851 to 1871. This was the time when the industry was buoyant and the population of the township was increasing dramatically – from 887 to 1,273 individuals, and well before

---

[61] C. G. Pooley and J. Turnbull, *Migration and Mobility in Britain since the Eighteenth Century* (London, 1998), p. 12.

the steep decline of 1881 to 1891 when the figure fell to 822 individuals.[62] Further research is needed to reveal how far this pattern was typical of Cardiganshire's other lead-mining townships, but one example of a young lead miner who left while the industry was still expanding was Thomas James. He left Llanfihangel Geneu'r Glyn (Llandre) for London in 1856, aged 24, and he 'possibly followed the Lewis family who also came from Llanfihangel Geneu'r Glyn and had settled in Islington'.[63] Welsh artisans were becoming involved in the rapid expansion of nineteenth-century London, especially from mid-century when the demand for labour in the building trade soared; and building firms owned by Welshmen in areas such as Islington were a particular magnet for Welsh craftsmen.[64] It seems that Thomas was among those taking advantage of this demand; he was employed there as a house painter and grainer. Thomas settled into his new life and married a London girl of Welsh descent in 1862. Sadly, he died in 1876 aged just 44; the cause of death was pulmonary tuberculosis.[65] Could his early life working in the lead mines have been a contributory factor in his final illness?

The demise of the lead-mining industry in late nineteenth-century Britain was inevitable because it could not compete with cheap foreign imports, but the rapidity with which it succumbed was due in no small measure to the widespread financial malpractices of the period. In mid Wales especially, despite the presence of companies such as John Taylor's, the industry acquired a bad reputation among serious investors so that the financial support so necessary at this critical period was not forthcoming.[66] The all too visible result for Cardiganshire was a fossilized landscape of abandoned cottages, shrunken settlements, derelict mine workings and a retreat from cultivation of marginal land as population numbers in the mining regions fell and people were driven to seek employment elsewhere.

[62] By 1911 Trefeirig's population had fallen to 576 individuals.
[63] Family history interview with Daphne Parry, 15 July 2009.
[64] R. Griffiths, 'The Lord's song in a strange land', in E. Jones (ed.), *The Welsh in London, 1500–2000* (Cardiff, 2001), pp. 165–6.
[65] Interview with Daphne Parry, 15 July 2009.
[66] For more details of financial malpractices in the industry, see Lewis, *Lead Mining in Wales*, pp. 194–9.

III

THE DECISION TO MOVE

Rural out-migration and the state of agriculture in late Victorian Britain have generated a considerable literature as well as several government reports. Studies have shown that the principal motives for rural out-migration were economic.[1] Equally, it is recognized that the decision to move is a very complex and personal one; as one nineteenth-century commentator wrote,

> there can be no doubt that many causes contribute their quota, and it may well be that in each locality some one of these contributory causes . . . may, owing to the special circumstances of the country or district, become so important as even to be predominant. Further, . . . the many contributing causes act and re-act upon one another [in a way] which is far from easy to unravel.[2]

The socio-economic background of nineteenth-century Cardiganshire has been considered in some detail, but which are the factors within this background that may have prompted many people to seek employment and a new life elsewhere in the closing decades of the century?

THE AGRICULTURAL DEPRESSION

Research has shown that the phasing of rural out-migration in Victorian Britain varied considerably between regions, and this has led to the conclusion that there was 'no obvious

---

[1] See, for example, C. G. Pooley and J. Turnbull, *Migration and Mobility in Britain since the Eighteenth Century* (London, 1998), p. 12; G. R. Boyer and T. J. Hatton, 'Migration and labour market integration in late nineteenth-century England and Wales', *Economic History Review*, new series, 50 (1997), 731; C. G. Pooley and J. C. Doherty, 'The longitudinal study of migration: Welsh migration to English towns in the nineteenth century', in C. G. Pooley and I. D. Whyte (eds), *Migrants, Emigrants and Immigrants* (London, 1991), p. 168.

[2] G. G. Longstaff, 'Rural depopulation', *Journal of the Royal Statistical Society*, 56 (1893), 413.

connection with the ebb and flow of agricultural prosperity'.[3] Not all historians have agreed with this opinion. Perhaps the most widely cited reason for the movement out of rural areas in the later nineteenth century is agricultural depression. Certainly, contemporary commentators considered that it was 'impossible to avoid the conclusion that . . . the rural exodus is connected with the state of agriculture'.[4] The reasons for the problems in British agriculture in the later nineteenth century were the subject of much debate. Many blamed foreign competition.[5] Others blamed a succession of poor harvests.[6] Certainly, the unfavourable weather affecting the country as a whole in the mid-1870s was a cause for concern in Cardiganshire. The *Cambrian News* reported that '1877 was the third year in succession decidedly adverse to agriculturists', while 1879 had 'absolutely nothing good to be said about it. Neither corn, hay, roots nor garden crops did well, and livestock have been unusually unhealthy.'[7]

Poor harvests meant that markets had to depend more on foreign imports. Free trade policy and improved transportation methods meant that not only imported cereals were flooding British markets but also butter, cheese and meat. Inevitably, the competition meant that the prices obtained by the British farmer 'all have a tendency to fall'.[8] Moreover, other commodities, including wool and lead, that were significant for rural economies such as Cardiganshire's, were being adversely affected by competition from cheaper imports. The following remark summed up contemporary opinion:

> Our great trial is that of having to meet in our own markets every country which has a special superiority in the cheap production of one or two particular commodities.[9]

[3] W. A. Armstrong, 'The flight from the land', in G. E. Mingay (ed.), *The Victorian Countryside* (London, 1981), pp. 119–20.

[4] P. A. Graham, *The Rural Exodus* (London, 1892), p. 10.

[5] For example, ibid., p. 12.

[6] J. S. Nicholson, *The Relations of Rents, Wages and Profits in Agriculture, and their Bearing on Rural Depopulation* (London, 1906), p. 78.

[7] *CN*, 11 January 1878, 3; 31 December 1880, 2.

[8] Graham, *Rural Exodus*, p. 12.

[9] W. E. Bear, 'Advantages in agricultural production', *Journal of the Royal Agricultural Society of England*, 3rd series, 5 (1894), 253.

Farmers also had to contend with increased taxes such as railway tolls that were 'so high that bulky produce will often not yield enough money to cover its conveyance . . . to a central market'.[10] Rural commentators in Cardiganshire as elsewhere in Britain considered that 'the imposition of new rates for highways and national education have materially increased the existing agricultural distress'.[11]

Such was the concern about the state of agriculture in the later 1870s that a government commission was appointed in 1879 to enquire into the condition of farms and farming and to suggest causes and possible remedies.[12] Andrew Doyle, the assistant commissioner reporting on Wales, concluded that, in contrast to the English border counties on which he was also reporting,

> the statements as to the existence of distress [in Wales] are by no means decided or uniform . . . the condition of farmers would seem to vary in different parts of the same county. The tenour [*sic*] of a great deal of the evidence is that the state of the farmers is not prosperous, that they have sustained considerable losses, but that there is *no actual distress amongst them.*[13]

This local variation in conditions was certainly apparent in the evidence of the witnesses for Cardiganshire. The witness from the Aberaeron union, for instance, who was an agent for a fairly large estate in the neighbourhood, was

> not aware of any agricultural distress prevailing or having prevailed in any part of our union. All classes, from the large to the small farmers, are very industrious . . . endeavouring in every possible manner to pay their rents and taxes, and have succeeded in doing so thus far . . . but are generally complaining of bad times.[14]

By constrast, the witness for the Cardigan union considered that agricultural distress had prevailed 'to a considerable

[10] Ibid., 252.

[11] *CN*, 6 February 1880, 2.

[12] Incidentally, agricultural labourers were officially excluded from giving evidence before the commission despite protests from the National Agricultural Labourers Union which, therefore, decided to collect evidence from its members and publish it separately. *CN*, 25 June 1880, 2.

[13] *Royal Commission on Agriculture* (*Richmond Commission*). *Reports of the Assistant Commissioners. Mr Doyle's Reports* ([1882] 2nd edn, Shannon, 1969), p. 10. [My italics.]

[14] Ibid., p. 36.

extent' in his region.[15] Summarizing the evidence of the Cardiganshire witnesses, however, Andrew Doyle concluded that: 'There does not appear to be "agricultural distress" in this county, though complaints of "bad times" have been pretty general.'[16]

These 'bad times' continued to a greater or lesser degree, and evidence from Cardiganshire before the second Royal Commission reporting on agricultural depression, appointed in 1894, indicated that farmers, in addition to reduced profit margins because of foreign competition, were now experiencing the added burden of high labour costs. It was felt that these conditions bore hardest on the small farmers of between 50 and 150 acres, coincidentally the largest class of farmers in Cardiganshire. On the other hand, farm workers were benefiting from increased wages, and were 'better off now than they have ever been during the memory of the oldest people in the neighbourhood'.[17] The commission's final report of 1897 concluded that:

> In Wales, which is mainly a pastoral country . . . agricultural depression has, relatively speaking, been generally of a mild character . . . Welsh agriculture has not been exposed to those depressing influences which have so seriously affected the arable districts of England.[18]

The agricultural depression is often cited as a major factor in the later nineteenth-century rural exodus from Cardiganshire.[19] However, the above evidence does not lend specific support to this theory.[20] On the contrary, a 'land hunger' persisted in the county throughout the nineteenth century, even in times of agricultural hardship. Indeed, in 1882 the *Cambrian News* reported on the dilemma facing many tenant farmers who were having difficulty paying their rents:

[15] Ibid., p. 28.

[16] Ibid., p. 12.

[17] *Royal Commission on Agriculture. Minutes of Evidence*, vol. 4 ([1896], 2nd edn, Shannon, 1969), p. 379.

[18] *Royal Commission on Agriculture. Final Report* ([1898], 2nd edn, Shannon, 1969), p. 19.

[19] For example, J. W. Aitchison and H. Carter, 'The population of Cardiganshire', in G. H. Jenkins and I. G. Jones (eds), *Cardiganshire County History*, vol. 3, *Cardiganshire in Modern Times* (Cardiff, 1998), pp. 4, 14.

[20] Although the move away from crop and cereal cultivation would require less labour.

If landlords do resist the request for lower rents, are the tenants prepared to leave their farms? . . . they know that they cannot go on much longer without substantial relief, but they are afraid that if they left their farms there are men who would take them.[21]

MECHANIZATION IN AGRICULTURE

It has been claimed that a significant contributory factor in Cardiganshire's rural population decline was the transition to labour-saving farm machinery.[22] The use of mowing and reaping machines was already widespread in England by the mid-nineteenth century.[23] However, in Wales, although the gentry farmers tended to follow current trends, the backward state of much of the agriculture and the general reluctance to adopt new practices and technological improvements were apparent even in the early 1880s when Andrew Doyle commented that

it is impossible for agriculture to make any decided advance in a district where the holdings are so small as to make it unprofitable for the occupier to employ the ordinary mechanical aids which increase the produce of a farm . . . Some of the formidable hindrances to an improved state of agriculture in Wales are the want of capital and of agricultural education and enterprise.[24]

For much of the nineteenth century there was an abundance of agricultural labour in most districts of England and Wales, and some farm work was either part time or seasonal.[25] However, by the late 1870s, some districts were reporting a scarcity of agricultural labour, especially in areas close to industrial centres.[26] Certainly, by this time the scarcity of labour was already being felt in parts of Cardiganshire.[27]

[21] *CN*, 3 March 1882, 5.
[22] For example, Aitchison and Carter, 'Population of Cardiganshire', p. 4; G. W. Williams, 'The disenchantment of the world: innovation, crisis and change in Cardiganshire, *c.*1880–1910', *Ceredigion*, 9 (1983), 312.
[23] Armstrong, 'Flight from the land', p. 120.
[24] *Mr Doyle's Reports*, p. 7.
[25] *Report on the Decline in the Agricultural Population of Great Britain, 1881–1906* (London, 1906), p. 9; R. J. Moore-Colyer, 'Agriculture and land occupation in eighteenth- and nineteenth-century Cardiganshire', in Jenkins and Jones (eds), *Cardiganshire County History*, vol. 3, p. 42; Nicholson, *Relation of Rents*, p. 127.
[26] *Royal Commission on Labour. Fifth and Final Report. Part I. The Report*, p. 218.
[27] *Mr Doyle's Reports*, p. 58.

However, it seems that not only was industrial south Wales attracting a steady stream of former agricultural workers but the higher wages were forcing up the rates of pay for labourers generally, including farm workers.[28] Accordingly, the Royal Commission on Labour of 1894 concluded that increasing mechanization had become as much a consequence as a cause of rural out-migration, since the farmer 'was compelled by the scarcity and dearness of labour to adopt additional machinery'.[29] The government report of 1906 on the decline of the agricultural population endorsed this view, concluding that mechanization had indeed become the farmer's main means of controlling the ever-increasing cost of labour; but, although mechanization had led to greatly reduced demand for farm labourers, this was paralleled by a reduced supply, because: 'Alongside the influences affecting demand, and more than keeping pace with them, has been the increasing desire of the labourers to leave the land.'[30]

Farm mechanization came late to Cardiganshire, where the agriculture was largely pastoral, and farmers were reluctant to innovate. Indeed, farming methods were generally of an almost medieval simplicity up to the closing decades of the nineteenth century.[31] The widespread adoption of farm mechanization probably occurred between about 1890 and 1910, and as late as 1899 one eyewitness recorded that

> lately, reaping machines are commonly in use and within the last two years reaping and binding machines have begun to be used in some farms in the parish, and a sowing machine is also in use in one or two places.[32]

As noted, Cardiganshire experienced the steepest population decrease between 1881 and 1891, thus contemporary evidence suggests that mechanization in agriculture was unlikely to have been a major factor in this decline.

---

[28] *Royal Commission on Labour. Fifth and Final Report. Part I. The Report*, p. 218.
[29] Ibid., p. 218.
[30] *Decline in the Agricultural Population*, pp. 14–5.
[31] Williams, 'Disenchantment', 310–11.
[32] Ibid.

FARM TENANCIES AND THE RISE OF FREEHOLD

For most of the eighteenth century Welsh farm leases had generally spanned a period of three lives and many were merely verbal agreements. The life-lease system meant that, in general, farm rents could not be reviewed until the death of the final life. As these leases expired they tended to be replaced by written leases, for seven, fourteen or twenty-one years, that contained clauses requiring the tenants to follow good husbandry practices. In time, these leases were themselves gradually superseded by renewable annual tenancies.[33]

In Cardiganshire, the annual tenancy agreement was initially considered to be 'practically as safe as a lease', and the regular increases in rents were met by improved agricultural production backed up by rent abatements in times of crisis.[34] Moreover, the longer-term leases had committed tenants to carry out their own repairs, which they no longer had to do under the annual tenancy agreement.[35] By the 1880s, however, the annual tenancies were generating feelings of discontent and insecurity in Cardiganshire as farmers struggled with low prices and high labour costs:

> The difficulties under which farmers now labour cannot be met by a reduction in rents. Nothing will meet the case but increased production ... [but] yearly tenants cannot be expected to farm in ways calculated to increase the productive power of the soil.[36]

This sense of insecurity was further emphasized by the knowledge that 'as soon as trade improves there will then be that competition for farms ... and offers will be made ... at increased rentals'.[37] Mention has already been made of the land hunger, that persisted throughout the century in Cardiganshire, despite the problems in agriculture, and there was 'at all times, however great the agricultural depression, an abundance of applicants for any farm that may be let'.[38]

[33] R. J. Colyer, 'Some aspects of land occupation in nineteenth-century Cardiganshire', *Transactions of the Honourable Society of Cymmrodorion* (1981), 80–3.
[34] *CN*, 3 March 1882, 5.
[35] Colyer, 'Aspects of land occupation', 86.
[36] *CN*, 3 March 1882, 5.
[37] Ibid.
[38] D. Ll. Thomas, *The Welsh Land Commission: A Digest of its Report* (London, 1896), pp. 141, 142.

Indeed, the level of competition achieved such notoriety that the Welsh Land Commission expressed concern about the 'injurious effect' that it 'produced upon the character of the tenantry', for there was 'no real spirit of . . . co-operation among farmers . . . each man fights for himself . . . trying to cut one anothers' throats by competing and bidding against sitting tenants when they try to get their rents reduced'.[39]

The level of farm rents was the subject of numerous complaints from Cardiganshire tenants to the Welsh Land Commissioners. One witness, who reported that his family had migrated to Swansea in 1880, claimed that they 'left the farm because the rent was too high . . . rents were advanced in good times, but not reduced during bad times'.[40] Yet another declared of the increase in his farm rent that

> Nothing but sheer necessity compelled me to promise the exorbitant price . . . I had no place to turn to, and besides, I had paid for all the repairs on the understanding that the amount expended would be repaid in rent.[41]

Problems associated with the Welsh annual tenancy agreement received much official attention in the later nineteenth century. One major concern was the tenant's feeling of insecurity arising from a fear of unfair eviction, although the Welsh Land Commission reported that this fear was, in the main, unfounded:

> most of the large estates as well as many other small ones also, are able to show a remarkable record of family succession in the occupation of holdings . . . If I were asked . . . whether capricious or vindictive eviction is often resorted to I should say no . . . but the power to resort to it is enough.[42]

However, impoverished landowners were beginning to retrench by selling off outlying portions of their estates and this added to the tenant farmers' anxiety. The craving for security of tenure was thus a major catalyst in the move towards acquiring freeholds, not only in Cardiganshire, but in Wales as a whole.

[39] Ibid., pp. 140, 143.
[40] Ibid., p. 227.
[41] Ibid.
[42] Ibid., p. 137.

The long periods of depression that afflicted agriculture during the first half of the nineteenth century produced 'a most marked diminution' in the number of small owner-occupiers in Wales, as former freeholders swelled the ranks of those migrating from rural areas to the developing industrial regions, and also, as in the case of Cardiganshire, of those emigrating to North America.[43] However, as hard-pressed landowners started to sell off outlying portions of their estates in the latter decades of the century, there was a move towards acquiring freeholds again; and these farm sales, while aggravating the tenants' sense of insecurity, also provided them with the opportunity of purchasing their holdings. The Welsh Land Commission found that the majority of freeholders of the 1890s were first-generation owner-occupiers, although these freeholders still formed a very small proportion of the total number of occupiers.[44] In some instances, of course, the new freeholders had merely replaced other small owners, and thus Cardiganshire, for instance, actually saw a drop in numbers of owner-occupiers between 1887 and 1909 from 21.6 per cent to 18.5 per cent (see above, table 1.1). Despite this slight dip, however, both the number of holdings and the acreage held by owner-occupiers were considerably higher for Cardiganshire than the national average and remained so into the second half of the twentieth century.

The perceived insecurity of tenure induced by the renewable annual tenancy agreement only added to the tenant farmer's desire to purchase his holding. This craving became more and more apparent as the nineteenth century drew to a close. Tenants competed against each other at sales so that holdings often went for inflated prices, and the buyers frequently had to borrow large sums of money with the result that they ended up paying more in interest charges than they would have done in rent.[45] The fact that economically the small freeholder would probably end up in a worse position than when he was a tenant farmer did little to deter the farming community in their urge to possess their holdings. Indeed, such was the passion induced by farm sales at this

[43] Ibid., p. 330; see, for example, *Carnarvon and Denbigh Herald*, 8 May 1847, 3.
[44] Thomas, *Digest*, p. 330.
[45] Ibid., pp. 330–1.

time that Welsh salerooms regularly witnessed 'the curious phenomenon ... where neighbours cheered themselves hoarse when a tenant bought his holding'.[46]

Despite the evident hardship of life for a farmer in Cardiganshire, the agricultural labourer often aspired to a tenancy also, and acquiring a smallholding was a first step.[47] Indeed, the competition for tenancies was such that farmers' sons often had to serve as farm servants on neighbouring holdings, or leave the area altogether.[48] On at least one large estate during the 1880s, when the county's rural exodus was well underway, 'every vacated farm was applied for by at least a dozen good men'.[49] By the closing years of the century little had altered; the Welsh Land Commission reported that 'many newly married couples cannot get farms'.[50]

RURAL TRADES AND CRAFTS

In his report of 1882 to the Richmond Commission, Andrew Doyle observed that: 'The younger members of Welsh families of the agricultural class never hesitate to seek employment away from home; they emigrate and migrate freely and without hesitation.'[51] The nineteenth-century rural exodus, however, was more than just a move from the land: it involved the rural community as a whole, not just those engaged in agriculture. For generations, the rural neighbourhood was more than a social unit; it was also an interdependent economic entity. Certainly, in the case of Cardiganshire, the scattered rural communities were largely self-sufficient for much of the nineteenth century. Some idea of the range and importance of rural trades and services in the local economy of the county in the second half of the century can be gained from table 3.1. Stonemasons, boot and shoe makers, tailors and blacksmiths featured prominently in

[46] J. Davies, 'The end of the great estates and the rise of freehold farming in Wales', *Welsh History Review*, 7 (1974–5), 210.
[47] D. W. Howell, 'The agricultural labourer in nineteenth-century Wales', *Welsh History Review*, 6 (1972–3), 262; *Mr Doyle's Reports*, p. 66.
[48] *CN*, 31 March 1882, 5.
[49] *CN*, 3 March 1882, 5.
[50] Thomas, *Digest*, p. 138.
[51] *Mr Doyle's Reports*, p. 8.

Table 3.1 Selected male occupations in Cardiganshire in 1851 and 1871[1]

Occupation	1851	1871	% change
farmer	4546	4780	**5.1**
agricultural labourer	2176	2305	**5.9**
farm servant	3709	3012	−18.8
carrier	159	96	−39.6
saddler	69	68	−1.4
carpenter/joiner	1079	1131	**4.8**
mason	685	703	**2.6**
plumber/painter/glazier	70	99	**41.4**
weaver	480	387	−19.4
tailor	763	626	−18.0
boot/shoe maker	923	671	−27.3
clog maker	48	79	**64.6**
butcher	135	170	**25.9**
miller	239	174	−27.2
tanner	43	49	**13.9**
currier	50	39	−22.0
cooper	152	87	−42.8
lead mine worker	1677	1823	**8.7**
lime burner	14	8	−42.9
slate quarrier	94	53	−43.6
blacksmith	575	530	−7.8
general labourer	2472	1505	−39.1

Source: Population censuses, 1851 and 1871.

[1] A very small percentage of the craftsmen will have been urban based. These statistics are for the registration county.

the occupational structure though the carpenter/joiner was by far the most numerous and widespread craftsman. Rural communities depended on their local carpenters and joiners not only for the building of, and repairs to, their farmhouses and cottages, but also for farm equipment and tools, for gates and horse-drawn ploughs and even for furniture, while the county's major industries of lead mining and shipbuilding also involved large numbers of carpenters. Inevitably, the rise in the county's population up to 1871 generated an increase in the various craftsmen associated with the building trade, but despite this population increase many rural trades and crafts were already in decline by this date. The railway

Table 3.2 Males employed in Cardiganshire's main maritime occupations, 1851–1911

Occupation	1851	1871	1891	1911
boat builder	145	92	45	20
fisherman	84	69	59	51
mariner	810	816	539	244

Source: Population censuses, 1851–1911.

network had finally reached Cardiganshire in the 1860s, but the nation's railways impacted on rural economies in conflicting ways. While it opened up wider markets for farm produce, the network led to a centralization of industry and to the mass-production of goods. As these latter became ever more widely available and the rural populace more mobile, the demand for rural crafts and services declined, thereby reducing employment opportunities in the countryside while increasing the demand for labour in the towns and industrial centres.[52]

As noted above Cardiganshire's coastal economy had given rise to a variety of occupations besides providing employment for fishermen and mariners. Flourishing shipbuilding centres with all their ancillary industries, which included foundries, rope works, smithies and sail lofts, had developed along the coast and were a significant element in the county's economy, providing work for skilled craftsmen and unskilled labourers. Table 3.2 shows the numbers employed in the county's main maritime-related occupations in the second half of the nineteenth century and also demonstrates the dramatic downward trend in these occupations in the closing decades of the century. As the size of ships increased with the transition from sail to steam, activity at the numerous small ports along Britain's coastline declined, and the extension of the railway network to Cardiganshire in the 1860s merely hastened the demise in the county of both coastal trade and shipbuilding with all the associated employment opportunities.

[52] Longstaff, 'Rural depopulation', 414; J. Williams, 'The move from the land', in T. Herbert and G. E. Jones (eds), *Wales, 1880–1914* (Cardiff, 1988), p. 33.

The decline of lead mining

We have seen the important role played by the lead-mining industry in the economic development of early modern Cardiganshire. The production of ores and the number of working mines fluctuated over time, but towards the middle of the nineteenth century demand for lead was so great that money and miners 'poured into the mines of mid-Wales'.[53] The metal mines of Cardiganshire were scattered throughout the northern uplands of the county and this, more than any other single factor, explains the tremendous boost to the populations of many of the townships in the Aberystwyth and Tregaron registration districts between 1841 and 1871. We have already noted the contrast in the population trends of primarily agricultural parishes compared with lead-mining townships. This leads to the inescapable conclusion that lead mining was a major factor in the nineteenth-century chronology of both the increase and the decline of Cardiganshire's population.

The significance of the lead-mining industry in the socio-economic history of nineteenth-century Cardiganshire cannot be over-emphasized. In the 1860s the Lisburne Mines Company alone paid out between £60,000 and £70,000 per year in miners' wages, and between £30,000 and £40,000 per year to local tradesmen and ancillary workers.[54] There were more people employed in Cardiganshire's lead mines in the later nineteenth century than in those of any other county in England and Wales.[55] The dramatic decline of the industry from the late 1870s, therefore, affected not only the miners and their families but the whole region. In its heyday the industry had generated a valuable income for landowners through leases of land to the mining companies, and it provided employment on a scale second only to, and often supplementing, agriculture in rural north Cardiganshire.[56]

---

[53] W. J. Lewis, 'Lead mining in Cardiganshire', in G. H. Jenkins and I. G. Jones (eds), *Cardiganshire County History*, vol. 3, *Cardiganshire in Modern Times* (Cardiff, 1998), p. 168. The ore field extended into neighbouring Montgomeryshire.

[54] Lewis, 'Lead mining', p. 169.

[55] *Census of England and Wales. 1891. Vol. IV. General Report* ([1893], 2nd edn, Shannon, 1970), p. 55.

[56] Lewis, 'Lead mining', p. 167.

Village settlements had grown up or expanded within reach of the mines, and some woollen factories had been established primarily to produce flannel for the miners.[57] Mining had also boosted the local agricultural economy, which was often barely subsistent, by creating a demand for draft animals and for provisions for those animals and for the miners. Moreover, as we have seen, the shipping of lead ore had made a significant contribution to the early development of the port of Aberystwyth, and it had long been the county's main export. Thus, the failure of the industry was not only disastrous for the economy and society of rural north Cardiganshire; it dealt a serious blow at county level, and was undoubtedly the major economic impetus in the county's rural exodus in the late nineteenth century. The decision to move, however, was a complex one and economic motives, although highly significant, were by no means the only ones.[58]

RURAL WORKING AND LIVING CONDITIONS

In his report of 1882 to the Richmond Commission, Andrew Doyle concluded that, in Wales, not only were most of the small farms 'occupied by men who really belong to the labouring classes', but that the farm labourers were actually better off than the farmers, and were able to 'command more of the comforts of life'.[59] In addition, he noted that 'the peasant farmers are not only obliged themselves to work harder than ordinary labourers, but are obliged also to make their children work at a very early age'.[60]

Farm workers fell into two categories: unmarried farm servants, both male and female, and married outdoor labourers who rented cottages on the farms or in nearby hamlets. The farm servants were usually hired for the year

---

[57] J. G. Jenkins, 'Rural industries in Cardiganshire', in Jenkins and Jones (eds), *Cardiganshire County History*, vol. 3, p. 146.

[58] C. G. Pooley and J. Turnbull, 'Migration and urbanization in north-west England: a reassessment of the role of towns in the migration process', in D. J. Siddle (ed.), *Migration, Mobility and Modernization* (Liverpool, 2000), p. 187.

[59] *Mr Doyle's Reports*, p.7.

[60] Ibid.

and boarded on the farm. Unlike in England, this remained the dominant form of hired labour on Welsh farms in the later nineteenth century. Farming in Wales was predominantly pastoral, and the livestock could require attention at any time. Moreover, most farmers possessed little capital and found it easier to pay for labour with board and lodgings. This economy also applied to outdoor labourers in Wales who were generally given meals as part of their wages.[61] Until the later nineteenth century farm servants worked from early morning to late in the evening and the agricultural labourer's average day was from 5 a.m. to 8.30 p.m.[62] Gradually, these working hours were reduced to between twelve and a half and thirteen and a half hours for the farm servants, but included Sunday working for stockmen, while the agricultural labourers worked between ten and a half and eleven and a half hours in summer and from dawn to dusk in winter. At the same time, hours in factories, mines and workshops were generally being reduced to between fifty-four and fifty-six per week, so that by the 1880s farm workers were becoming increasingly unsettled not only by the arduous nature of their employment but also by the long working hours.[63]

During the later nineteenth century conditions for Britain's farm labourers were improving slightly.[64] It is difficult to gauge accurately the earnings of these labourers in Wales because of payments in kind and meals as part of wages.[65] However, a significant increase in rates of pay coincided with the expansion of the railway networks from mid-century when labour for their construction affected the labour markets generally. Meanwhile, the earning potential in industrial south Wales continued to influence the labour market and agricultural pay rates increased on a regular basis. Nevertheless, agricultural wages were still low considering the excessively long hours that were expected.

---

[61] Howell, 'Agricultural labourer', 263.

[62] Ibid., 269.

[63] Armstrong, 'Flight from the land', p. 121.

[64] See, for example, *Royal Commission on Agriculture. Minutes of Evidence. Vol. VI*, p. 379; T. E. Kebbel, *The Agricultural Labourer* (2nd edn, London, 1887), pp. xiv–xv.

[65] *Royal Commission on Labour. Fifth and Final Report. Part I. The Report*, p. 221; Howell, 'Agricultural labourer', 271.

In the 1870s, Cardiganshire shared the lowest weekly wage rate with its neighbouring counties of Carmarthenshire and Pembrokeshire (between 9s. and 11s. 6d.), and by 1898 Cardiganshire had the lowest average weekly pay rate (14s.) except for Radnorshire (13s.).[66] Allowing for regional variations, industrial wage rates were generally almost 50 per cent higher than agricultural rates in this period, and for a much shorter working day.[67] When the lead-mining industry was in the ascendant, Cardiganshire's agricultural labourers did not have to migrate far for higher pay and shorter hours. Lead mining offered unskilled and semi-skilled work in the rural uplands at about twice the daily pay, locally, for farm labour, and for a shorter working day – an eight-hour shift. However, as noted above, working conditions in the mines were very harsh and were generally regarded as shortening a man's life expectancy.[68]

As regards domestic arrangements, commentators were unanimous about the atrocious domestic conditions of the rural poor in much of Wales throughout the nineteenth century. Much of the blame for the poor housing lay in two main areas. First, there were the economic problems facing landlords with increasingly encumbered estates; but also there was a deficiency in Wales of good building materials. At the beginning of the century a traveller reporting to the Board of Agriculture had found little to commend in the rural accommodation in Cardiganshire. In his diary he noted that

> Farmhouses and offices very bad – in low situations . . . Barns mere hovels, . . . [and for cottages] you have here a bank of mud about 5 feet high – and over that a deep roofing of straw – the chimney of twigs – making an obtuse angle with the mud walling of the gable end.[69]

It was not unknown for the cottager's animals to share the living accommodation, a practice that continued in some areas to the end of the century:

[66] Howell, 'Agricultural labourer', 272–3.
[67] Armstrong, 'Flight from the land', p. 121.
[68] See, for example, *Kinnaird Report*, pp. 505, 509.
[69] NLW, 1759B1 Agriculture, material relating to agriculture in South Wales collected by Walter Davies during journeys undertaken for the Board of Agriculture (early nineteenth century).

She occupied one end of the house, the cow the other, and the pig resided in the passage, whose warm breath in the winter answered the purpose of a stove. The fowls had the run of the whole house.[70]

Even in the second half of the nineteenth century, a typical rural Cardiganshire cottage consisted of one room with a fireplace, a small window that did not open and a clay floor, although roofs were now usually slated rather than thatched. Many dwellings were not weathertight, living conditions were cramped and very dirty and sanitation non-existent.[71] The Public Health Act of 1875 enabled the newly created sanitary districts to exercise considerable powers over the condition and sanitary arrangements of Britain's old and new cottages.[72] By the 1890s, however, while many English landowners were making efforts to improve the condition of their cottages, very little was being done in Wales, so that 'bad as the cottage accommodation is in some parts of England, it is far worse in Wales'.[73] In both England and Wales, however, it was recognized that the sanitary authorities faced a dilemma, because 'the result of energetic action on their part would be in many places to make a large number of families homeless'.[74] In Wales, many of the old one-roomed cottages, in which the whole family lived, cooked and slept, were still in use, although there were now more stone-built dwellings with from two to five rooms. Nevertheless, living conditions in rural Britain remained generally unsatisfactory; dwellings were often overcrowded and not provided with privies, refuse and dung heaps were in close proximity to the cottages and the water supply was often contaminated.[75]

The beginning of the twentieth century does not seem to have seen any great improvement in rural living conditions. A government report of 1906 concluded that the problem in Britain's rural areas was not a scarcity of cottage accommodation but a 'lack of cottages which satisfy the more exigent requirements of the labourers in these times, or comply with

[70]   *CN*, 10 June 1901.
[71]   See, for example, *Kinnaird Report*, pp. 505, 511.
[72]   Howell, 'Agricultural labourer', 279.
[73]   *Royal Commission on Labour. Fifth and Final Report. Part 1*, pp. 220–1.
[74]   Ibid., p. 224.
[75]   Ibid., p. 220.

the demands of vigilant sanitary authorities'.[76] Although the situation of Britain's agricultural labourers had by now improved as regards working conditions and rates of pay, their living conditions were still a 'most pressing subject for reform'.[77]

If the accommodation available to agricultural labourers in nineteenth-century Wales was appalling, that provided for the farm servants was 'apparently still worse'.[78] Moreover, it actually deteriorated as the century progressed.[79] Some servants were lodged in the farmhouse but with no privacy or effective segregation of male and female quarters. More generally, the male servants slept 'over the stable or cow house', where a bed might be

> the body of an old cart filled with straw; and where beds are provided, the bed-clothes are sometimes washed only once in six months; no sanitary utensils are supplied; and the men often went to bed in their working clothes, without taking even their boots off.[80]

These appalling living conditions were certainly widespread in Cardiganshire, even in the late nineteenth century. In 1882, a report in the *Cambrian News* on the prosecution of a farm servant recorded that he both slept and kept his few possessions in a hayloft, a circumstance that was, apparently,

> common in Cardiganshire . . .[It is] not a desirable sleeping apartment. The rats and the draughts are strong, whilst points of cleanliness are few and weak . . .The way male and female servants are housed in many farms in Cardiganshire is disgusting, not only from the moral but physical points of view.[81]

As far as the farmers on the smaller farms typical of Cardiganshire were concerned, their domestic situation was often little better than that of their labourers:

> The Welsh farmer presents a stronger contrast than even the Welsh labourer to the same class in England . . . [He] is but little removed either in his mode of life . . . his dwelling or his habits from the day

---

[76] *Decline in the Agricultural Population*, p. 15.
[77] *Royal Commission on Labour. Fifth and Final Report. Part 1*, p. 223.
[78] Ibid., p. 221.
[79] Howell, 'Agricultural labourer', 278.
[80] *Royal Commission on Labour. Fifth and Final Report. Part 1*, p. 221.
[81] *CN*, 17 November 1882, 5.

Table 3.3 Number of persons living more than two per room in 1891 as a percentage of the county/country populations

	% of population
Anglesey	8.8
Breconshire	4.8
Cardiganshire	**9.4**
Carmarthenshire	8.7
Carnarvonshire	8.4
Denbighshire	11.4
Flintshire	9.4
Glamorgan	7.9
Merioneth	5.9
Monmouthshire	9.3
Montgomeryshire	5.1
Pembrokeshire	14.3
Radnorshire	2.8
Wales (incl. Monmouthshire)	8.2
England	14.3
England and Wales	11.2

Source: D. Ll. Thomas, *Bibliographical, Statistical and other Miscellaneous Memoranda, being Appendices to the Report of the Royal Commission on Land in Wales and Monmouthshire* (London, 1896), p. 296.

labourers ... feeding on brown bread, often made of barley, and partaking but seldom of animal food.[82]

Commenting on the state of both farms and farming in Cardiganshire, the *Cambrian News* reported, in 1882, that many farmers were 'poor and hard-pressed ... their houses and farm buildings are little better than sheds'.[83] Official reports of the nineteenth century consistently drew attention to the unsatisfactory condition of Cardiganshire's rural dwellings and farm buildings, and even by the beginning of the twentieth century many of the small farms had had little capital invested in improvements to either land or buildings by landlord, tenant or owner-occupier.[84]

Poor living conditions were of particular concern in nineteenth-century Britain in both rural and urban areas, and

[82] *Mr Doyle's Reports*, p. 8.
[83] *CN*, 31 March 1882, 5.
[84] Moore-Colyer, 'Agriculture and land occupation', pp. 31, 36.

overcrowding was a significant aspect of these conditions. The Royal Commission on Labour of 1894 reported that, in rural Wales, 'overcrowded dwelling-houses unprovided with privies . . . seem to be the characteristics of almost every village described'.[85] Statistics in the 1891 census, however, reveal that overcrowding was by no means confined to rural Wales. In Wales as a whole 8.2 per cent of the total population was living more than two to a room, whereas the average for England was a hefty 14.3 per cent. Cardiganshire's rate of 9.4 per cent, therefore, though higher than the all-Wales figure, was significantly less than that for England, as table 3.3 demonstrates.

COMMUNICATIONS

Some of the greatest advances in the Victorian era were in the field of communications, and these in turn impinged on migration. Improving levels of literacy and the spread of ideas and information encouraged a growing awareness of the contrasts in an individual's situation as compared with that of others, and a major factor in the improving literacy levels was the introduction of compulsory elementary education from 1880. Even at this late stage of the nineteenth century poverty and comparative remoteness meant that many of Cardiganshire's older rural inhabitants were 'bound to the soil by their language and do not know how to help themselves'.[86] Many illiterate parents, however, became very proud of their educated children and encouraged them in their efforts to improve themselves.[87] Even a basic elementary education had the potential for raising the individual's personal expectations, and for Cardiganshire's young people education in English not only increased their knowledge

---

[85] *Royal Commission on Labour. Fifth and Final Report. Part I. The Report*, p. 220.

[86] *CN*, 31 March 1882, 5. Cardiganshire was part of the predominantly Welsh-speaking region that covered most of west Wales and, although some areas such as Aberystwyth were becoming more anglicized towards the end of the century, over 90 per cent of the county's population spoke Welsh and over 50 per cent were monoglot Welsh. D. Jones, *Statistical Evidence relating to the Welsh Language, 1801–1911* (Cardiff, 1998), p. 330; J. W. Aitchison and H. Carter, 'The Welsh language in Cardiganshire, 1891–1991', in Jenkins and Jones (eds), *Cardiganshire County History*, vol. 3, p. 573.

[87] *CN*, 11 August 1882, 2; *Decline of the Agricultural Population*, p. 32.

of employment opportunities elsewhere but also improved their ability to seek these out, while the expansion of the railway networks and cheaper fares provided the means for changing his or her situation.[88] Migrants returning home for visits 'generated unease' with tales of the attractions of urban life and demonstrated that there was 'a whole new world only a rail journey away'.[89] As one descendant of a Cardiganshire migrant commented about his ancestor, who left Llandysul for London in about 1851:

> I would think that adventure and work opportunities were the main driving forces . . . I have also surmised that the 1851 Exhibition may have been an attraction. Perhaps an intended visit became permanent.[90]

Contemporary commentators were quick to make a connection between compulsory elementary education and rural depopulation.[91] Education was blamed for fostering in the rural poor a distaste for life on the land: 'The school master has been busy . . . kindling the desire of a wider life . . . [and the] most noticeable result has been to create a certain loathing of farm-work.'[92] In Cardiganshire, where a shortage of agricultural labour was being experienced in the 1870s, there were 'those who advocate ignorance as the only means of keeping the country supplied with workmen'.[93] A report in the *Cambrian News* of November 1878 warned that 'As education spreads in Wales the people will be less and less willing to live on poor farms'.[94]

Some Victorian authors and artists tended to sentimentalise farm work and rural life, but many people held it in low esteem. Not only did agriculture necessitate a 'frugal way of living and the most unwearied industry', but 'complaint is made of the gross and palpable dullness of lower class . . . country life' and its comparative isolation.[95] But Britain's

---

[88] *Royal Commission on Labour. Fifth and Final Report. Part I*, p. 110.
[89] Williams, 'Disenchantment', 309.
[90] Interview with Mike Thomas, 12 July 2009.
[91] See, for example, Graham, *Rural Exodus*, pp. 73–6.
[92] Ibid., pp. 25–6.
[93] *CN*, 4 January 1878, 4.
[94] *CN*, 22 November 1878, 4.
[95] Graham, *Rural Exodus*, pp. 204, 69–70; *Royal Commission on Labour. Fifth and Final Report. Part 1*, pp. 220–1.

farm workers were beginning to recognize the dependence of their lives, the lack of any reasonable prospect of advancement, and to 'revolt against it'.[96] They were 'stimulated by all they hear and read of town life', and were becoming ever more aware of alternatives to agricultural labour.[97] The range of trades and occupations available in urban/industrial Britain presented 'innumerable temptations for men to quit husbandry', while urban life provided far greater opportunities for social contact and leisure-time activities.[98] Through newspapers, magazines and word of mouth, then, the rural populace were increasingly made aware of life beyond the narrow confines of their neighbourhood, and new horizons with their economic, commercial and social attractions constantly beckoned. The effect of this was:

> aroused ambitions, which never can . . . be stilled again. Let a man love the land ever so much, when once he is educated . . . it is utterly impossible that he should drudge and drudge at farmwork with no outlook save that which is bounded by the workhouse. He must see that, provided he have the requisite ability and industry, there is a career before him by which he can at least be assured that the children who follow him will have a more favourable starting-point than fell to his share.[99]

It has been shown that females in Victorian Britain were more internally mobile than males and for Britain's female rural migrants there was a particular incentive in moving to the towns.[100] At this time, economic prospects for single women were very poor, and almost no women's wages were sufficient to support them adequately alone. Marriage was thus seen as essential to escape penury, and women were becoming aware that a move from the country to the town greatly improved their marriage prospects. Domestic service was the main female occupation in Victorian Britain, and female migrants were attracted to urban destinations with

---

[96] *Decline of the Agricultural Population*, p. 15; Graham, *Rural Exodus*, p. 25.

[97] T. Stirton, 'Small holdings', *Journal of the Royal Agricultural Society of England*, 3rd series, 5 (1894), 87.

[98] Graham, *Rural Exodus*, pp. 204–5.

[99] Ibid., p. 209.

[100] D. Baines, *Migration in a Mature Economy* (Cambridge, 1985), pp. 235–6; Pooley and Turnbull, *Migration and Mobility*, p. 12.

their large and growing demand for servants.[101] Town life offered a wider social life and far more opportunities to meet prospective husbands, while the demands of domestic service appeared less daunting than agricultural drudgery, and the board and lodging provision offered the chance to accumulate savings for a dowry.

MIGRATION NETWORKS

In addition to economic and social considerations, the existence of family or cultural links would have influenced the potential migrant's decision to move and the choice of destination. Support networks were vital components of the migration process as was communication. This latter conclusion is endorsed by family histories: 'How did they choose where to go? It was by word-of-mouth, always by word-of-mouth.'[102] The prospect of arrival in a strange place would not be so daunting if the newcomers could be sure of help with adjusting to the new environment; and, as we shall see, kinship networks and chapel contacts in Welsh immigrant communities actively recruited from home with offers of help in finding both work and accommodation. In general, rural out-migrants from the same geographical origins tended to cluster together wherever possible in urban Britain, forming communities that grew 'in geometric ratio by the importation of friends and relations'.[103] Interviews with descendents of migrants tend to confirm this trend:

> David went to London where he had an older brother and a younger sister in the dairy trade.[104]

> Thomas possibly followed the Lewis family who also came from Llanfihangel Geneu'r Glyn and had settled in Islington.[105]

> He went to London to join his sister and brother-in-law.[106]

---

[101] Boyer and Hatton, 'Migration and labour market integration', 706.
[102] Interview with E.J., 21 February 2009.
[103] Armstrong, 'Flight from the land', p. 128; K. Bartholomew, 'Women migrants in mind', in C. G. Pooley and I. D. Whyte (eds), *Migrants, Emigrants and Immigrants* (London, 1991), p. 185.
[104] Interview with A.R., 27 April 2009.
[105] Interview with Daphne Parry, 15 July 2009.
[106] Interview with E.D., 25 February 2009.

Sophia probably went to Paddington to accompany her brother as housekeeper and dairymaid.[107]

Edward had a brother John and a sister Diana also living in London.[108]

John was related, through his sister Sarah's marriage, to some Lloyds who came to Islington. A number of their contemporaries went to the same part of Islington.[109]

Thomas went to St Luke's [London] between 1851 and 1854 ... A cousin of his is recorded in St Luke's in the 1851 census in the house of a Cardiganshire family ... I have been told that there were many from Cardiganshire in the area.[110]

In some cases, migrant destinations were the result of trading links and seasonal movements. In the case of Cardiganshire, maritime trade was the chief means of contact with the outside world until the arrival of the railways in the county in the 1860s and this was responsible for long-standing commercial links especially with the other ports of Wales and the western seaboard of England, with London and even with western Europe and North America. Of particular significance were the maritime connections between Cardigan and Bristol and between Aberystwyth and Liverpool.[111] Overland links would also have been forged between Cardiganshire and the Midlands and south-eastern England through the cattle-droving trade and through the seasonal movement of females to London and Kent to work in the market gardens and hop fields, and also as a result of farm hands seeking harvesting work in the border counties and the Vale of Glamorgan. The significance of these links for Cardiganshire's migrants will become clear in later chapters.

The Royal Commission on Labour of 1894 recognized that there were many causes for migration 'besides actual deficiency of employment or lowness of wages'.[112] Lack of

---

[107] Interview with A.R., 27 April 2009.
[108] Interview with Joan Paparo, 3 July 2009.
[109] Interview with S.B., 20 July 2009.
[110] Interview with Mike Thomas, 12 July 2009.
[111] M. I. Williams, 'Commercial relations', in Jenkins and Jones (eds), *Cardiganshire County History*, vol. 3, pp. 205–8.
[112] *Royal Commission on Labour. Fifth and Final Report. Part I*, p. 110.

employment prospects at home, the perceived potential to improve one's situation, or simply the urge for a
change, each fuelled the restless spirit that characterized
nineteenth-century Britain. In the case of Cardiganshire
it was undoubtedly the demise of the lead-mining industry
and its knock-on effect on the mining communities that
provided the major economic impetus for the dramatic
rural exodus of the 1880s, but this was by no means the full
picture. Contemporary evidence has shown that there were
many other factors in the social and economic background
of Cardiganshire, some particular to the county and some
operating more broadly, that provided powerful incentives for seeking a new life elsewhere in the later decades of
the nineteenth century, while the expanding rail network
and cheaper travel were putting hitherto inaccessible and
undreamt-of destinations within the reach of more people.

IV

RURAL OUT-MIGRATION TRENDS:
THE CENSUS EVIDENCE

It is generally accepted that much of our current knowledge about migration in the recent past is derived from the
census.[1] Possibly the most significant fact to emerge from
the 1851 census is the great natural increase in the population of Great Britain over the previous century despite the
continuous flow of emigrants to 'all the temperate regions
of the world'.[2] Of perhaps equal importance is the evidence
for the growing urbanization of Britain. Not only were rural
and urban populations 'equally balanced' for the first time,
but it was revealed that a large proportion of the population
of the 'market towns, the county-towns, the manufacturing
towns, and the metropolis' had been born in rural areas.[3]
This appears to have been the first time that out-migration
from the countryside had received any official attention,
for, according to the census report, the 'constant flow of
the country population into the towns . . . went on unno-
ticed by the earlier writers, and it has never yet been clearly
exhibited'.[4] Thus, the inclusion of birthplace data in the
census from 1851 onwards meant that it was now possible to
'determine its extent and character'.[5]

Population movements received only slight attention in
the census reports for 1861 and 1871 and do not appear
to have given particular cause for concern: 'there is a
constant migration from one part of England [and Wales]
to another'.[6] In fact, the move from country areas was looked

---

[1] C. G. Pooley and J. Turnbull, *Migration and Mobility in Britain since the Eighteenth Century* (London, 1998), p. 23.

[2] *Census of Great Britain, 1851. Population Tables. 1. Numbers of the Inhabitants, Vol. 1* ([1852] 2nd edn, Shannon, 1970), p. lxxxii.

[3] Ibid., p. lxxxiv.

[4] Ibid., p. lxxxiii.

[5] Ibid.

[6] *Census of England and Wales, 1861. Vol. III. General Report* ([1863] 2nd edn, Shannon, 1970), p. 40.

upon as an inevitable result of the general improvement in health of the rural population and of the reduction in infant mortality rates:

> As agricultural labourers enjoy good health and . . . rear many children, while the food the land produces . . . is necessarily limited, migration is a necessary part of the present economy of rural parishes.[7]

By 1881 the contrast in population trends in the various parts of Britain was attracting much more attention as urban populations continued to grow at a far greater rate than rural ones. Moreover, thirteen counties had actually declined in numbers since the previous census; Cardiganshire was one of these, having decreased by over 4 per cent (see above, p. 11 figure 1.2).[8] The census report concluded that, because of the excess of births over deaths in each county in the previous decade, the reduction in the populations of the declining counties must have been due either to out-migration or to emigration.[9] Furthermore, it seemed that the movement was mainly from the country into the towns and industrial regions, because it was the primarily agricultural counties that were declining.[10] This appeared to be borne out by the fall of nearly 10 per cent since 1871 in the numbers of agricultural labourers, that was apparently 'not due to any falling off in the amount of land under cultivation'.[11]

County-wide statistics conceal significant local variations because of the complex patterns of urban, industrial and rural areas, and some commentators consider that registration districts give a more accurate picture of population movements.[12] Certainly, the statistics for the registration districts of Cardiganshire (for a map of these see figure 4.1) suggest that different influences were affecting the various

[7] *Census of England and Wales, 1871. Vol. IV. General Report* ([1873] 2nd edn, Shannon, 1970), p. xxi.

[8] *Census of England and Wales, 1881. Vol. IV. General Report* ([1883] 2nd edn, Shannon, 1970), p. 8. The census noted that Cardiganshire's population had declined by 2.8 per cent but this figure was for the registration county.

[9] Ibid., p. 50.

[10] Ibid., p. 51.

[11] Ibid., p. 37.

[12] See, for example, L. L. Price, 'The census of 1891 and rural depopulation', *Journal of the Royal Agricultural Society of England*, 3rd series, 5 (1894), 53; G. G. Longstaff, 'Rural depopulation', *Journal of the Royal Statistical Society*, 56 (1893), 383.

Figure 4.1 Nineteenth-century registration districts of Cardiganshire
Based on: D. Jones, *Statistical Evidence relating to the Welsh Language, 1801–1911* (Cardiff, 1998), pp. 182–3.
Note: Ysgubor y coed township is in the geographical county of Cardiganshire but in the registration district of Machynlleth, Montgomeryshire.

regions of the county. For instance, between 1851 and 1871, as table 4.1 indicates, some areas were declining in numbers while others were increasing dramatically, with the result that by 1871 the county's population had reached a level that would not be attained again until the year 2001. The bulk of the increase was concentrated in the Aberystwyth and Tregaron registration districts, where the lead mines lay.[13] Aberayron and Lampeter registration districts showed a small gain, but the populations of Cardigan and Newcastle Emlyn districts were declining.[14]

The 1891 census gives a much more dramatic picture of rural decline, with twelve English and eight Welsh counties showing a population decrease in their rural areas since the previous census, although only thirteen of these counties

---

[13] Aberystwyth town itself also showed a substantial increase in this period.
[14] More than a third of the decrease in Cardigan district was in Cardigan town. See above, figure 1.3.

Table 4.1 Cardiganshire population trends by registration district, 1851 to 1871

District	1851	1871	loss/gain
Cardigan*	7595	6613	−982
Newcastle Emlyn*	9601	8986	−615
Lampeter*	5626	5714	88
Aberayron	13224	13377	153
Aberystwyth	23753	27439	3686
Tregaron	10404	10677	273
*Ysgubor y coed***	*593*	*635*	*42*
Total	**70796**	**73441**	**2645**

Source: Population censuses, 1851 and 1871.
*Only parishes which fall within the geographical county of Cardigan are included in these statistics.
**This township lies within the geographical county of Cardigan although it is in the registration district of Machynlleth, Montgomeryshire.

showed an overall decrease in numbers.[15] Of these latter, Cardiganshire had the second greatest decline, with a loss of 10.9 per cent since 1881.[16] Table 4.2 demonstrates how the different registration districts of the county contributed to the period of its greatest decline. The northern districts were demonstrably experiencing major losses.

Rural out-migration continued into the twentieth century. In the 1911 census, thirty-eight counties showed losses by migration since the previous census, eighteen of which recorded a loss of more than 5 per cent.[17] Of these eighteen, six were Welsh counties, but Cardiganshire was no longer among the highest losers. After the 1880s the exodus from Cardiganshire moderated considerably, although this more gradual decline continued until the 1950s.[18]

Is it possible to identify which sectors of the rural population were leaving Cardiganshire in the later nineteenth century? Comparison of the census occupational data would be an obvious approach, but unfortunately the recording

[15] *Census of England and Wales, 1891. Vol. IV. General Report* ([1893] 2nd edn, Shannon, 1970), pp. 11, 8.

[16] The greatest was Montgomeryshire with 11.7 per cent.

[17] *Census of England and Wales, 1911. Vol. IX. Birthplaces* (London, 1913), p. v.

[18] B. R. Mitchell, *Abstract of British Historical Statistics* (Cambridge, 1962), pp. 20, 22.

Table 4.2 Cardiganshire population trends by registration district, 1881 to 1891

District	1881	1891	loss/gain
Cardigan*	6721	6319	–402
Newcastle Emlyn*	8822	8848	**26**
Lampeter*	5785	5735	–50
Aberayron	12543	11595	–948
Aberystwyth	25606	21102	–4504
Tregaron	10272	8613	–1659
Ysgubor y coed	*521*	*418*	*–103*
total	70270	62630	–7640

Source: Population censuses, 1881 and 1891.
*Only parishes which fall within the geographical county of Cardigan are included in these districts.

unit changes towards the end of the period: the 1851–91 statistics are for the registration county, while those for 1901 onwards are for the smaller, administrative county.[19] Nevertheless, an indication of the trends in rural occupations during the period of the county's greatest population decline can be gained by comparing statistics for 1871 with those for 1891 (see table 4.3).

Female occupations in the Victorian census were notoriously under-recorded but inclusion of the female data in this table reveals some interesting trends. Immediately apparent is the massive increase in both males and females employed in the woollen industry. This was mainly due to the mill villages that were becoming established along the Teifi Valley and that attained considerable prosperity between 1860 and 1920.[20] Unfortunately for the economy of Cardiganshire, most of this industrial complex fell into the geographical county of Carmarthen. The drop in numbers of farm workers of both sexes between 1871 and 1891 is particularly marked. Reference to table 3.1 (see p. 72) shows that numbers of male agricultural labourers increased by 5.9 per cent between 1851 and 1871 at a time when the county's population was

[19] The registration county of Cardigan included parts of Pembrokeshire and Carmarthenshire.
[20] J. G. Jenkins, 'Rural industry in Cardiganshire', *Ceredigion*, 6 (1968–71), 113.

Table 4.3 Main occupations of Cardiganshire's rural population, 1871 and 1891

Occupation	1871	1891	% change
males			
farmer/grazier	4780	4354	–8.9
farmer's son etc	1997	1885	–5.6
farm servant or agric. labourer[1]	5317	4261	–19.9
general labourer	1505	991	–34.2
lead mine worker	1823	766	–58
woollen industry worker	387	876	**126.4**
females			
farmer/grazier	947	1102	**16.4**
farmer's daughter etc[2]	2582	n/a	**n/a**
farm servant or agric. labourer[3]	1557	869	–44.2
general labourer	120	36	–70
lead mine worker	229	15	–93.4
woollen industry worker	134	242	**80.6**
domestic servant	6445	6336	–1.7

Source: Population censuses, 1871 and 1891.

[1] The 1891 census occupational tables do not differentiate between farm servant and agricultural labourer.
[2] There are no statistics for farmers' female relatives in the 1891 census.
[3] The 1891 census occupational tables do not differentiate between farm servant and agricultural labourer.

also increasing, but, perhaps surprisingly, male farm servants over the same period decreased by 18.8 per cent. On the other hand, table 3.1 indicates that numbers of male general labourers had decreased by a massive 38 per cent over the same period, and table 4.3 shows that this steep decline was continuing: numbers of these labourers had fallen from 2,472 in 1851 to 991 in 1891. The female data for farm and general labour shows an even more marked decline, perhaps indicating the growing disinclination of women for manual labour. Not surprisingly, table 4.3 illustrates that the crisis in the lead-mining industry had led to the greatest employment decline in any category between 1871 and 1891: a loss of 58 per cent of male labour and almost 94 per cent of female labour.[21] Interestingly, although domestic service was by far the most common female occupation throughout the period, numbers in this category also declined over the two decades. The domestic servant, however, featured prominently in the occupational structure of Cardiganshire's female out-migrants, as will become clear. A further point of note revealed by table 4.3 is the increase in numbers of female farmers that effectively counterbalanced the decrease in numbers of male farmers over the period. Reference has already been made to the increase in the proportion of females among Cardiganshire's farmers in the second half of the nineteenth century, and this trend will be discussed further in chapter V.

A similar picture of decline emerges from the statistics for males employed in rural trades and crafts over the same period, as can be seen in table 4.4; but as noted earlier many rural trades and crafts were already in decline by 1871, even when the county's population was still increasing.

Cardiganshire's population levels continued to fall between 1901 and 1911, but perhaps surprisingly the decline during this decade was in the number of females: the total male population actually increased very slightly from 26,887 to 26,918, while the number of males recorded in employment rose from 16,775 to 17,420. The accelerating trend towards urbanization in the county would at first seem to account for this upturn in the male labour market but, significantly, the early years of the twentieth century also saw a rise in those employed in agriculture. Elsewhere in rural Cardiganshire the employment situation was bleak, with continuing decreases in the main rural industries, trades and services (see table 4.5).[22]

Cardiganshire had started the nineteenth century with a marked deficit of males in the population, the sex ratio (males per 100 females) being 90.5. Reference to figure 1.2 (see p. 11) confirms that from the 1820s the gap steadily widened so that by 1851 the ratio had fallen to 87.1 and by

---

[21] Although, as noted above, women's employment statistics in the Victorian census are notoriously unreliable.

[22] Unfortunately, the 1901 employment statistics cannot be compared with those of 1891 because the census recording unit altered between the two dates.

Table 4.4 Numbers of males employed in Cardiganshire in the main rural trades and crafts in 1871 and 1891[1]

Occupation	1871	1891	% decrease
blacksmith	530	458	–13.6
carpenter/joiner	1131	852	–24.7
stonemason	703	571	–18.8
tailor	626	574	–8.3
boot, shoe and clog maker	750	465	–38
miller	174	139	–20.1

Source: Population censuses, 1871 and 1891.

[1] A very small proportion of the craftsmen will have been urban based.

Table 4.5 Main male occupations of Cardiganshire's rural population in 1901 and 1911

Occupation	1901	1911	% increase or decrease
Workers on the land			
farmer/grazier	2905	3029	**4.3**
farmer's son etc	1516	1684	**11.1**
farm bailiff	39	45	**15.4**
farm servant or agric. labourer	2531	2944	**16.3**
shepherd	112	82	–26.8
Rural industries and trades			
lead mine worker	548	463	–15.5
blacksmith	299	272	–9.0
carpenter/joiner	759	601	–20.8
stonemason	545	427	–21.6
woollen industry worker	296	237	–19.9
tailor	386	342	–11.4
boot and shoe maker	208	165	–20.7
miller	82	63	–23.2

Source: Population censuses, 1901 and 1911.

1911 it was down to 81.7, at a time when that for England and Wales as a whole was 93.6.[23] Comparison of the age profiles from the censuses for 1851 to 1911 reveals that females outnumbered males in all but the 0–14 age group, a fact that

[23] J. Saville, *Rural Depopulation in England and Wales, 1851–1951* (London, 1957), p. 90.

is suggestive of high male out-migration. The data also reveal gradual changes to the age structure of the county's population over this period. The significant improvement in the life expectancy of both sexes is apparent – although female life expectancy, as might be expected, remained above that of males, and this in turn was altering the generational ratios.[24] The situation was compounded by the extremely low sex ratio due to high male out-migration; the growing excess of females meant that a significant proportion of them would not marry, and this progressively lowered the rate of natural increase in the county, leading to an ageing population.[25]

Destinations of Cardiganshire's migrants

Although the decline in Cardiganshire's total population did not start until the 1870s, natural increase, combined with inward movement into the lead-mining districts, masked the outward trend already under way from various regions of the county by mid-century. We have seen that Cardiganshire had some long-established seasonal migratory traditions, such as the summer movements of female labour to the market gardens of London and the hop fields of Kent and the harvesters who made regular trips to the Vale of Glamorgan and the English border counties.[26] There is no systematic evidence for studying migration to and from Cardiganshire in the early nineteenth century, but two outward trends were remarked upon in the 1851 census as taking place from the registration districts of Cardigan, Newcastle Emlyn and Aberayron: the move to the iron works and coal mines of south Wales and emigration.[27] This was by no means the full picture, however, for the birthplace data of the 1851 census

---

[24] M. Anderson, 'The social implications of demographic change', in F. M. L. Thompson (ed.), *The Cambridge Social History of Britain 1750–1950*, vol. 2, *People and their Environment* (2nd edn, Cambridge, 1993), p. 18.

[25] For charts of these trends, see K. J. Cooper, 'Cardiganshire's rural exodus' (unpublished Ph.D. thesis, University of Leicester, 2008), 114.

[26] A. K. Knowles, 'The structure of rural society in north Cardiganshire, 1800–1850', in G. H. Jenkins and I. G. Jones (eds), *Cardiganshire County History*, vol. 3, *Cardiganshire in Modern Times* (Cardiff, 1998), p. 89; W. J. Lewis, 'The condition of labour in mid-Cardiganshire in the early nineteenth century', *Ceredigion*, 4 (1963), 333.

[27] *1851 Census. Population Tables. 1. Vol. II*, pp. 35, 37 and 39.

indicate that there were Cardiganshire natives living in every county of England and Wales by that date.

There is disagreement in the literature about the main destinations of nineteenth-century migrants from rural Wales. One school of thought, based on Brinley Thomas's calculations, is that up to 1880 most went either to England or overseas, while between 1880 and 1914 most of the Welsh rural exodus stayed in Wales, being principally absorbed by the industrial south.[28] On the other hand, Dudley Baines considered that Brinley Thomas had misinterpreted the census data and he calculated that industrial south Wales (Glamorgan and Monmouthshire) drew migrants in any numbers from only four rural Welsh counties – Brecon, Carmarthen, Cardigan and Pembroke – and that even these counties had more migrants living outside Wales than in Glamorgan and Monmouthshire in 1901.[29] He calculated that Welsh rural migrants throughout the second half of the nineteenth century, taken altogether, were about twice as likely to go to England as to Glamorgan.[30] The census data for Cardiganshire, however, do not support either of these viewpoints: the county's migrants were at least three times more likely to stay in Wales from 1851 to the end of the century, after which time the trend had slowed to just over two-and-a-half times.[31] Figures 4.2 to 4.5 give an overview of their distribution in England and Wales between 1851 and 1911. The picture gained from figure 4.2 is one of considerable short-distance movement into Cardiganshire's neighbouring counties while longer-distance migration centred on major industrial and commercial centres. This trend is, in fact, consistent with conventional migration theory.[32] However, it is apparent from figures 4.3 to 4.5 that

[28] J. Williams, 'The move from the land', in T. Herbert and G. E. Jones (eds), *Wales, 1880–1914* (Cardiff, 1988), pp. 21, 25 and 38.

[29] D. Baines, *Migration in a Mature Economy* (Cambridge, 1985), pp. 277–8.

[30] Ibid., pp. 276–8.

[31] In 1851, there were 2,935 Cardiganshire migrants living in England and 10,419 living in Wales. In 1911, there were 9,134 Cardiganshire migrants living in England and 24,757 living in Wales.

[32] See, for example, P. Joyce, 'Work', in F. M. L. Thompson (ed.), *The Cambridge Social History of Britain, 1750–1950*, vol. 2, *People and their Environment* (Cambridge, 1990), p. 140.

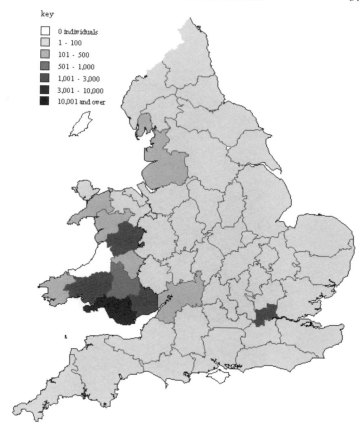

key
- ☐ 0 individuals
- ☐ 1 - 100
- ☐ 101 - 500
- ☐ 501 - 1,000
- ☐ 1,001 - 3,000
- ☐ 3,001 - 10,000
- ■ 10,001 and over

Figure 4.2 Residential distribution of Cardiganshire migrants in 1851 as recorded in the census

as the century progressed and communications improved and different motivations came into play, the movement from Cardiganshire to England gathered momentum.

The pattern of migration in nineteenth-century England and Wales differed across the decades. From 1841 to 1881 rural to urban migration rates were high and emigration rates were low. In the 1880s rural to urban migration, especially to the northern cities, declined, while emigration increased sharply. Internal migration picked up again in the 1890s and

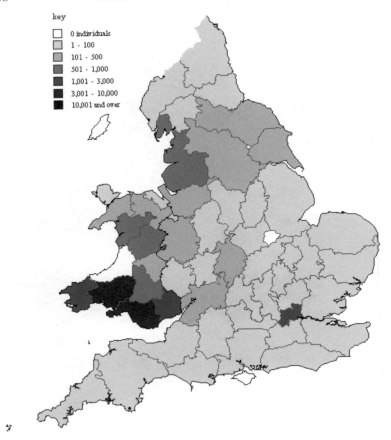

Figure 4.3 Residential distribution of Cardiganshire migrants in 1871 as recorded in the census

emigration declined to a very low level, only to revive again in the early years of the twentieth century, at the same time as some English and Welsh towns began to experience net out-migration.[33] Cardiganshire's outward movement diverged significantly from the national trends. Although emigration

[33] G. R. Boyer and T. J. Hatton, 'Migration and labour market integration in late nineteenth-century England and Wales', *Economic History Review*, new series, 50 (1997), 706.

key

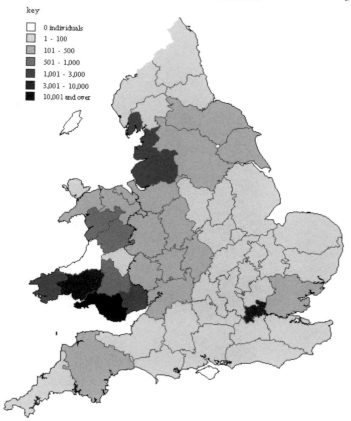

☐	0 individuals
☐	1 - 100
▨	101 - 500
▨	501 - 1,000
▩	1,001 - 3,000
■	3,001 - 10,000
■	10,001 and over

Figure 4.4 Residential distribution of Cardiganshire migrants in 1891 as recorded in the census

from the county was possibly at its highest in the 1840s, out-migration rates to other parts of Britain were fairly low until after 1871.[34] The major exodus occurred between 1881 and 1891, and thereafter the outward movement continued at a

[34] See, for example, B. Owen, 'Ymfudo o Sir Aberteifi (Emigration from Cardiganshire), 1654–1860. III. 1795–1860', *Ceredigion*, 2 (1952–5), 230. For more on this, see below, chapter VIII. There are no county statistics for emigration from England and Wales in the nineteenth century. For county estimates for 1861 to 1900, see Baines, *Migration*, pp. 141–77.

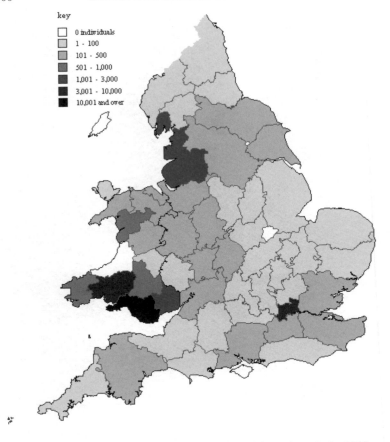

key

☐ 0 individuals
▨ 1 - 100
▨ 101 - 500
▨ 501 - 1,000
▨ 1,001 - 3,000
▨ 3,001 - 10,000
■ 10,001 and over

Figure 4.5 Residential distribution of Cardiganshire migrants in 1911 as recorded in the census

much slower rate until the 1950s. As regards major destinations, however, the county's migrants conformed much more closely to the national patterns. In England the county's main migrant destinations were London followed by the north-west (Lancashire and Cheshire).[35] South Wales, however, was

---

[35] The main migrant destinations in England between 1841 and 1881 were London followed by Manchester and Liverpool. Boyer and Hatton, 'Migration and labour market integration', 706.

consistently the major attraction and Glamorgan the main destination by a massive margin throughout the period.[36] Indeed, the presence there of large numbers of migrants from Cardiganshire was noted by Andrew Doyle in his report of 1882 to the Richmond Commission.[37] It is impossible to overestimate the significance of this destination for Cardiganshire's nineteenth-century migrants: in the decades surrounding the turn of the twentieth century almost half of them (47 per cent) were living in Glamorgan.

The trends for Cardiganshire's other top migrant destinations are compared in figure 4.6. The growth in popularity of London throughout the period, and to a lesser extent the north-west of England, is apparent. Perhaps rather more surprising is the sustained popularity of Carmarthenshire throughout the period, while movement to industrial Monmouthshire steadily declined from mid-century.

Conventional migration theory holds that females in the nineteenth century were more migratory than males, and research has shown that in twenty-nine out of the thirty-four rural counties of England and Wales women were more likely to move internally than were men.[38] Cardiganshire, however, was one of the five exceptions, males being the more likely to move throughout the period.[39] Some destinations did, however, consistently attract more female than male migrants from Cardiganshire, notably London, the north-west and the south midlands in England, and the Welsh counties of Carmarthen, Pembroke and Merioneth.

The census evidence has demonstrated that of all the counties of England and Wales, Cardiganshire had, proportionally, one of the most dramatic population declines in the later nineteenth century due to out-migration. Both the timing and the volume of the outward movement, however, varied considerably from region to region within the county,

---

[36] Of the nine colliery regions of England and Wales, Glamorgan attracted the most migrants in the period 1841 to 1911. Boyer and Hatton, 'Migration and labour market integration', 706.

[37] *Royal Commission on Agriculture* (*Richmond Commission*). *Reports of the Assistant Commissioners. Mr Doyle's Reports* ([1882] 2nd edn, Shannon, 1969), p. 8.

[38] See, for example, Pooley and Turnbull, *Migration and Mobility*, p. 12.

[39] Baines, *Migration*, p. 236. The others were Breconshire, Carmarthenshire, Pembrokeshire and Cumberland.

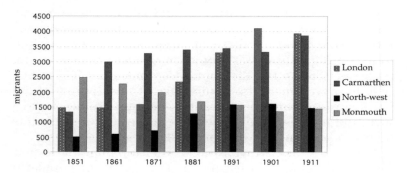

Figure 4.6 Cardiganshire's main migrant destinations, excluding Glamorgan, 1851–1911
Source: Population censuses, 1851–1911.

as did the popularity of destinations, reflecting not only the complex interaction of socio-economic factors that influence the decision to move, but also demonstrating the problems associated with drawing conclusions from county-based statistics.

V

THE MOVE TO SOUTH WALES

For Europe, the nineteenth century was a time of unprecedented population growth despite considerable emigration. In Wales, between 1801 and 1911, the population increased from just over half a million to almost 2.5 million; and this increase was accompanied by a substantial redistribution of the people: a movement southwards. In 1801 less than 20 per cent of the people lived in the two southern counties of Glamorgan and Monmouthshire but by 1911 this proportion had risen to almost 63 per cent.[1] Not surprisingly, there were six Welsh counties whose populations in 1911 were smaller than in 1851: Anglesey, Breconshire, Cardiganshire, Montgomeryshire, Pembrokeshire and Radnorshire.[2] The agricultural character of these losing counties and the rapid industrialization of south Wales confirm that a significant feature of the population redistribution was a movement away from the land.

An indicator of the accelerating urbanization of Wales in the second half of the century is that in 1851 more than 35 per cent of males were still employed in agriculture while by 1911 the proportion had dropped to less than 12 per cent.[3] The census indicates that much of this decline was in the number of farm workers rather than in the number of farmers.[4] But why were so many people leaving rural Wales while others apparently chose to stay? The decision to move, as we have seen, was a complex one, but contemporary opinion was in no doubt as to who was leaving nineteenth-century

---

[1] J. Williams, 'The move from the land', in T. Herbert and G. E. Jones (eds), *Wales, 1880–1914* (Cardiff, 1988), pp. 11–14.

[2] B. R. Mitchell, *Abstract of British Historical Statistics* (Cambridge, 1962), pp. 20, 22.

[3] Williams, 'Move from the land', pp. 17, 30.

[4] Ibid., p. 18; R. Lawton, 'Rural depopulation in nineteenth-century England', in R. W. Steel and R. Lawton (eds), *Liverpool Essays in Geography* (London, 1967), pp. 248–9.

Cardiganshire and why: 'The farmers are unable to keep the best labourers, and they consequently leave this district for Glamorganshire, where they get better wages.'[5] Reference to tables 4.3 and 4.4, however, confirms that in the case of Cardiganshire the decline between 1871 and 1891 was not just in farm workers, it also embraced all the main rural trades and industries with the notable exception of the woollen industry.

By the time of the 1881 census, the first in which the population of Cardiganshire showed a decrease on the previous one, there were almost 18,500 Cardiganshire natives enumerated outside the county but still in Wales. The migrants were following the general movement southwards: 75 per cent of them were to be found in Carmarthenshire, Glamorgan and Monmouthshire. These three counties were consistently the main destinations within Wales for migrants from Cardiganshire during the second half of the century and figure 5.1 illustrates the relative trends. Glamorgan was the top destination throughout the period but with a most pronounced increase in numbers between 1881 and 1891. The movement to Carmarthenshire maintained a fairly steady pace throughout the period, while that to Monmouthshire dwindled from mid-century.

Migration networks between Cardiganshire and south Wales probably evolved through trade and seasonal movements. Long before the arrival of the railways in Cardiganshire there were established commercial and social links with south Wales. This was mostly as a result of maritime trade but also through the network of drovers' routes from mid- and south Cardiganshire that connected to those from Carmarthenshire and Pembrokeshire on the way to England via Herefordshire.[6] Moreover, the seasonal migration of male labour to help with the harvests in the fertile Vale of Glamorgan was already a well-established practice by the early nineteenth century.[7] Inevitably, some temporary

[5] *Royal Commission on Agriculture (Richmond Commission). Reports of the Assistant Commissioners. Mr Doyle's Reports* ([1882] 2nd edn, Shannon, 1969), p. 58.

[6] R. J. Colyer, *The Welsh Cattle Drovers* (Cardiff, 1976), p. 141.

[7] A. K. Knowles, 'The structure of rural society in north Cardiganshire, 1800–1850', in G. H. Jenkins and I. G. Jones (eds), *Cardiganshire County History*, vol. 3, *Cardiganshire in Modern Times* (Cardiff, 1998), p. 89.

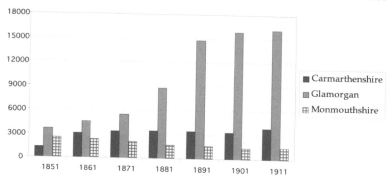

Figure 5.1 Cardiganshire migrants enumerated in Carmarthenshire, Glamorgan and Monmouthshire, 1851–1911
Source: Population censuses, 1851–1911.

and seasonal moves gave rise to more permanent ones and migration networks were formed. Indeed, the census reveals that by mid-century the movement out of Cardiganshire was well underway; but what else can the census tell us about key issues of the migration process, and in particular about the movement to the two major destination counties of Glamorgan and Carmarthen?

THE MOVE TO CARMARTHENSHIRE

Along much of its northern boundary Carmarthenshire shares the Teifi valley with Cardiganshire.[8] The two main urban centres, Carmarthen and Llanelli, had very different characters and economic bases. Carmarthen was the county town and possibly the oldest town in Wales.[9] It provided a wide range of goods and services, not only for the towns-people but also for the agricultural hinterland.[10] By contrast,

---

[8] Ten of Carmarthenshire's parishes on this boundary fell within the registration districts of Newcastle Emlyn and Lampeter and were thus in the registration county of Cardiganshire. J. Williams, *The Digest of Welsh Historical Statistics*, 2 vols (Cardiff, 1985), vol. 1, p. 43; D. Jones, *Statistical Evidence relating to the Welsh Language, 1801–1911* (Cardiff, 1998), p. 178.

[9] Roman Moridunum.

[10] *Kelly's Directory of Monmouthshire and the Principal Towns and Places in South Wales* (London, 1884), pp. 311–12.

Llanelli was a Victorian boom town and port. In 1801 there were about two thousand inhabitants in Llanelli, similar in size to Aberystwyth, but by 1881 there were nearly twenty thousand.[11]

Much of nineteenth-century Carmarthenshire was given over to agriculture although the thirty-five miles of coast-line supported considerable fishing and coastal trade. There were, however, some rapidly developing pockets of industry. The woollen-mill villages of the Teifi Valley attained notable prosperity between about 1860 and 1920, but it was in the south-eastern parishes of the county that the main industrial activity was concentrated. The town of Llanelli developed as a port and a centre for heavy industry, notably tinplate production, while the mining of anthracite coal in the Amman and Gwendraeth valleys gave rise to industrial towns and villages almost overnight. The vast majority of the workforce in these industrial regions was drawn initially from the surrounding agricultural districts.[12] Thus, despite considerable rural out-migration, the rapid growth in the industrial sectors of Carmarthenshire ensured a steadily increasing population.[13]

In the second half of the nineteenth century Carmarthenshire ranked second only to Glamorgan as a destination for Cardiganshire's migrants until the former was overtaken by London in the 1901 census. Contrary to conventional migration theory that females were more migratory than males, Cardiganshire lost more males by out-migration during this period.[14] The movement to Carmarthenshire, therefore, is particularly interesting because it was one of the few in which Cardiganshire's migrant females consistently outnumbered males.[15] Data from the census enumerators' books for Carmarthenshire for 1881 was analysed to shed light on this and other key features of the migration process.

---

[11] Williams, *Welsh Historical Statistics*, vol. 1, p. 62.

[12] M. A. Williams, 'Secret sins', *Victorian Studies*, 42 (2000), 344.

[13] R. Davies, *Secret Sins: Sex, Violence and Society in Carmarthenshire, 1870–1920* (Cardiff, 1996), pp. 3, 14–15.

[14] D. Baines, *Migration in a Mature Economy* (Cambridge, 1985), pp. 235–6; C. G. Pooley and J. Turnbull, *Migration and Mobility in Britain since the Eighteenth Century* (London, 1998), p. 12.

[15] For a chart of this trend, see K. J. Cooper, 'Cardiganshire's rural exodus' (unpublished Ph.D. thesis, University of Leicester, 2008), 129.

The study of the 1881 census has included all the Cardiganshire natives enumerated in the two principal towns of Carmarthen and Llanelli, together with a 25 per cent random sample from the remainder of the county. According to the census, there were 3,388 Cardiganshire natives living in Carmarthenshire at this time, but only just over 15 per cent of the migrants were living in the two principal towns: 269 in Carmarthen and 249 in Llanelli. In total, the sample contained 1,236 individuals – 567 males and 669 females.[16] Comparatively few of the children in this study population were born in Cardiganshire, suggesting that many of these migrants had left Cardiganshire as childless young adults.

MIGRANT ORIGINS AND RESIDENTIAL DISTRIBUTION

Mention has already been made of the problems arising from the birthplace data in the Victorian censuses. Among the more common problems in the Welsh data are: a farm name rather than a parish being given as a birthplace, and the county of birth recorded but with no town or parish specified. Moreover, many long names were truncated, for example, Llanbadarn Fawr or Llanbadarn Odwyn became simply Llanbadarn, making geographical identification impossible. Bearing these limitations in mind, the birthplace data from the 1881 census study population has been analysed and useable data identified for 1,037 of the 1,236 individuals. As far as this sample population is concerned, although there were migrants from most areas of Cardiganshire, key sending areas were concentrated in the Teifi Valley, and in particular in Cardigan, Llandysul, Llanwenog, Lampeter, Cellan and Llanddewi Brefi.[17] This accords well with the population loss experienced by Cardiganshire's southern registration districts of Cardigan and Newcastle Emlyn from mid-century onwards.[18]

---

[16] This represented almost 37 per cent of Cardiganshire's migrants enumerated in Carmarthenshire in 1881.

[17] For a distribution map, see Cooper, 'Cardiganshire's rural exodus', 131.

[18] See above, chapter IV.

Migration theory accepts the significance of geographical origins in the 'residential clustering of the newly arrived'.[19] The place-of-residence data from the 1881 census sample has been analysed to see whether tendencies to residential clustering could be identified among Cardiganshire's migrants. Although they were to be found throughout Carmarthenshire, the majority had gathered along the south of the Teifi, with sizeable communities in Cenarth, Llanfihangel ar Arth, Llanllwni, Pencarreg and Cynwyl Gaeo.[20] More than this: close links were indicated between some sending parishes and certain destinations, such as Llandysul with Llanfihangel ar Arth, Llanwenog with Llanllwni, and Cellan with Llanycrwys, suggesting that chain-migration was operating here.

OCCUPATIONAL PROFILE

What employment opportunities, then, were drawing so many Cardiganshire migrants to Carmarthenshire in the later nineteenth century? As far as the two major towns were concerned, the 1881 census study population reveals that the male occupations, while reflecting the range of commercial opportunities available in both Carmarthen and Llanelli, also provided some surprises. There were very few in the professional classes, although the clergy were well represented, nine of whom, perhaps surprisingly, were Anglican.[21] As might have been expected, heavy industry was a major source of employment in Llanelli: 38 out of the 113 employed males in the census sample were labourers in the various foundries, factories and tinplate works. In Carmarthen town the range of male migrant occupations was much wider, although that of draper dominated. There was

[19] P. Joyce, 'Work', in F. M. L. Thompson (ed.), *The Cambridge Social History of Britain 1750–1950*, vol. 2, *People and their Environment* (Cambridge, 1990), p. 141.

[20] For a distribution map, see Cooper, 'Cardiganshire's rural exodus', 133.

[21] Nineteenth-century Cardiganshire was a stronghold of Nonconformity, in particular Welsh Calvinistic Methodism. However, there was a theological college at Lampeter (St David's College) which trained men for the Church, and which consistently took many more students from Cardiganshire than from any other county during the nineteenth century. D. T. W. Price, *A History of Saint David's University College Lampeter*, 2 vols (Cardiff, 1977), vol. 1, appendix IV.

also a grim twist to the Cardiganshire-born in Carmarthen town. Only 60 of the 119 males aged 14 years and over were in employment. Of the remainder, 2 were retired, one was unemployed, 9 were students at either the training college or the theological college.[22] Three were in prison.[23] One was an inmate of the workhouse, and the rest, totalling 43, were in the Joint Counties Lunatic Asylum for Carmarthenshire, Cardiganshire and Pembrokeshire.

The proportion of employed female migrants was very small: 38 of the 131 aged over 14 years in Carmarthen, and 29 of 114 in Llanelli. This comes as no surprise because female employment in the Victorian censuses is notoriously under-recorded. Women, especially at the lower end of the social scale, often worked on a casual or part-time basis and this labour frequently did not find its way into the census returns. In addition, there was the problem of how to treat the work of women in the home, especially if, as was common in the nineteenth century, the home was a place for the production of goods for sale and the provision of services.[24] The range of female occupations in both towns was very limited and domestic service dominated. Within this migrant group, one female (in Llanelli) was in receipt of outdoor poor relief, and one (in Carmarthen) was in prison. In addition, 38 females were inmates of the Joint Counties Lunatic Asylum. This brings the total of Cardiganshire-born in the asylum to 81, or 30 per cent of the county's natives enumerated in Carmarthen town at this date.

It seems clear that the provision of goods and services rather than heavy industry was drawing Cardiganshire migrants to Carmarthenshire's two main towns in the later nineteenth century, but what of the situation elsewhere in the county? A brief trawl of the main settlements in the coal-mining region

---

[22] These colleges were the South Wales and Monmouthshire Training College for elementary education, and the Presbyterian College, a non-denominational college 'for the education of young gentlemen for the ministry'. *Kelly's Directory*, p. 311; *Worrall's Directory of South Wales* (Oldham, 1875), p. 121.

[23] Her Majesty's Prison for the Counties of Carmarthenshire, Cardiganshire and Pembrokeshire.

[24] For instance, lodging houses, shops and inns. For more on this, see E. Higgs, *Making Sense of the Census: the Manuscript Returns for England and Wales, 1801–1901* (2nd edn, London, 1991), pp. 81–2.

in the south-east of the county reveals only one Cardiganshire native who was a collier. The census sample for the rest of Carmarthenshire reflects a similar range of employment of both males and females in the retail and service industries as was apparent in Carmarthen town. The professional classes, with the exception of the clergy, were again under-repre-sented.[25] Several dual occupations were noted, for instance, Calvinistic minister/farmer, shoemaker/barber. There were also some less common occupations such as that of jockey, architect, umbrella mender and clockmaker. It was agricul-ture, however, that dominated the employment structure of the migrants in this sample, accounting for 123 of the 240 employed males and 107 of 236 employed females. The other main female occupation was domestic service, accounting for a further 89 females.[26] Throughout the nineteenth century this latter occupation constituted the largest single class of employment for women in England and Wales.[27] In the closing decades of the century, however, prospects were beginning to open up as women moved into spheres such as clerical, shop and factory work and even teaching, and there was evidence in the occupational data of this widening of female employment opportunities. Only 2 males and 5 females were in receipt of outdoor poor relief and 2 females were workhouse inmates.

Evidently, for the majority of migrants in the 1881 sample, the move to Carmarthenshire was not initially a move from the land. A similar rural-to-rural movement has recently been identified in south-east Shropshire.[28] In that instance, the main cause of the migration was considered to have been the agricultural depression, but even so the men had responded by leaving home rather than abandoning agricul-ture. We noted that the majority of Cardiganshire migrants in the census sample had not moved very far, merely crossing

---

[25] Here again Anglicans predominated: only 3 of the 14 clergy were Nonconformist.

[26] One of these was an 11-year-old general servant.

[27] Higgs, *Making Sense*, p. 82. Female domestic service will be discussed in more detail in chapter VII.

[28] G. Nair and D. Poyner, 'The flight from the land? Rural migration in south-east Shropshire in the late nineteenth century', *Rural History*, 17 (2006), 167–86.

the river Teifi. So, why had they moved? Nineteenth-century agriculture in both counties was predominantly pastoral, but the rich alluvial soils in Carmarthenshire's river valleys were particularly suited to dairying. The growing industrialization of south-east Wales and the consequent rise in population resulted in an increased demand for milk, butter, cheese and meat that could not be met by local agriculture. The opening of the railway network in Carmarthenshire in 1853 provided the county's dairy produce with a buoyant market, not only in these industrial regions but as far afield as London where it was also in great demand. In addition, the increasing acreage devoted to hay suggests that Carmarthenshire farmers were raising their cattle at home rather than sending them to England to be fattened for market there.[29] Despite the demand for their produce, it seems that the native agricultural population was forsaking rural Carmarthenshire for industrial south-east Wales.[30] Farmers and farm labourers were moving in from neighbouring Cardiganshire to take their places, driven out of their own county, perhaps, by the land hunger and 'competition for farms' at home, and lured into Carmarthenshire by the prospect of improved fortunes in the thriving dairying industry.[31] Research has revealed that a west-to-east movement of the agricultural labour force across south Wales towards the industrial districts of east Carmarthenshire, Glamorgan and Monmouthshire had been going on at least since mid-century.[32] The data from the 1881 census sample suggest that farmers and farm workers from Cardiganshire formed part of this stage-migration.

CULTURAL ISSUES AND SOCIAL CONDITIONS

Most of the migrants in the 1881 census sample had not moved far. This supports conventional migration theory

[29] Davies, *Secret Sins*, p. 35.

[30] The number of males engaged in agriculture in Carmarthenshire fell from nearly 13,000 in 1851 to just over 9,000 in 1881. Williams, 'Move from the land', p. 31.

[31] *CN*, 31 March 1882, 5. For more on land hunger in Cardiganshire, see above, chapter I.

[32] S. Thomas, 'The agricultural labour force in some south-west Carmarthenshire parishes in the mid-nineteenth century', *Welsh History Review*, 3 (1966–7), 72.

that most moves were short-distance. The river Teifi may have formed the boundary between the two counties, but from medieval times the valley shared a common history.[33] The people of south Cardiganshire would have been more familiar with north-west Carmarthenshire than with the northern regions of their own county, and more at home in, say, Newcastle Emlyn than in Aberystwyth. Migration for these individuals would, therefore, have brought no culture shocks, since the communities on the banks of the Teifi would have had much in common in terms of traditional values and attitudes and shared religious beliefs and language. Nineteenth-century Carmarthenshire, like Cardiganshire, was a stronghold of Nonconformity.[34] Chapel was at the heart of the community, providing for a full social life and sponsoring cultural events. Nonconformity also played a major role in promoting the Welsh language at a time when the linguistic balance in Wales was beginning to shift towards English.[35] Thus, at the close of the nineteenth century, although administrative, commercial, industrial and market centres were becoming increasingly anglicized, Carmarthenshire, like Cardiganshire, was still overwhelmingly 'Welsh in speech and culture'.[36]

Whether the move improved the quality of life for the migrants is difficult to assess. Evidence before the Richmond Commission reveals that during the agricultural depression of the late 1870s, Carmarthenshire was not nearly so adversely affected as many rural areas of England.[37] On the contrary:

> The small farmers live from hand to mouth, save nothing . . . but they and their children dress and live better than they did . . . The labourers have better wages than they used to, but there is no saving, they live better, send their children to school, and clothe them better.[38]

[33] For more on the historic landscape, see *http://www.dyfedarchaeology.org.uk/*
[34] Davies, *Secret Sins*, p. 187.
[35] K. D. M. Snell and P. S. Ell, *Rival Jerusalems* (Cambridge, 2000), p. 205.
[36] Jones, *Statistical Evidence*, pp. 212–3, 333; Davies, *Secret Sins*, p. 18; P. N. Jones, *Mines, Migrants and Residence in the South Wales Steamcoal Valleys: the Ogmore and Garw Valleys in 1881* (Hull, 1987), p. 71.
[37] *Mr Doyle's Reports*, p. 463.
[38] Ibid., p. 471.

Nor was there any shortage of work for 'good labourers', because 'when the coal and iron works go on well, the best men, as a rule, leave'. They were drawn to south-east Wales, not only by better wages but also by the prospect of improved housing because rural landlords allowed their cottages 'to get into a dilapidated condition'.[39] Comment has already been made about the atrocious living conditions of the rural poor in much of Wales throughout the nineteenth century. As regards Carmarthenshire, the report of 1870 on the employment of women and children in agriculture found that:

> The state of cottages throughout is most disgraceful . . . generally badly ventilated, and as badly lighted, damp and unhealthy floors and walls, the former of earth . . . overcrowding is . . . universal. Privies are very unusual and oftener than not the piggery is attached to the dwelling.[40]

The appalling living conditions, however, were not confined to rural Carmarthenshire. Indeed, there were areas of overcrowded housing and basic or non-existent sanitation in all the growing centres of population. In Carmarthenshire, although improvements to housing, sewage and water services were being made, their implementation was slow and patchy.[41] Even in the early twentieth century, workers' houses in Carmarthen town were described by one medical officer as 'squalid hovels' and 'hot beds of disease', while the *South Wales Sentinel* considered that the slums of Llanelli were possibly the worst in Britain: 'we never saw anything like the awful, evil-stinking and devitalising conditions of Llanelly's little "hell-holes"'.[42]

Despite these conditions, there is nothing to suggest that the Cardiganshire migrants had not, on the whole, improved their situation by moving. Information and feedback about employment opportunities and social amenities were important factors in migration networks, and the conditions in which the migrants found themselves in Carmarthenshire were apparently sufficiently encouraging for this destination to continue to exert a strong 'pull' for people from Cardiganshire throughout the period.

[39] Ibid., pp. 477, 493, 496.
[40] Davies, *Secret Sins*, pp. 62–3.
[41] Ibid., p. 67.
[42] Ibid., p. 65.

THE MOVE TO GLAMORGAN

Early eighteenth-century Glamorgan has been described thus:

> ye North Part is full of Steep, High and Barren Hills, abounding with Woods, in ye South more plain, rich and fertile . . . it is called for its fruitfullness [sic] ye Garden of Wales . . . The Cheif [sic] Comodities are Corn and Cattle.[43]

Its population in 1750 is estimated to have been about 55,000, and by 1911 it had reached 1,120,910.[44] Glamorgan was thus one of the most dynamic growth regions in the Victorian era, and as such has an exceptional place in the history of internal migration in Britain. The county's explosive economic expansion of the second half of the nineteenth century occurred as a direct result of the exploitation of the coalfields, and the county was among those showing the highest gains by migration in each decade up to 1911. Coal mining then experienced a long slow decline and the inward flow to the coalfields went into reverse.[45]

Until the nineteenth century, the south Wales valleys were lightly inhabited and noted for their natural beauty. Running roughly parallel north to south, the series of valleys stretched from eastern Carmarthenshire, through Glamorgan and into western Monmouthshire and contained abundant seams of iron ore and coal. Small iron works and coal pits had long dotted the landscape, and the coal was originally exploited to fuel the iron industry. This latter became centred on the village of Merthyr Tydfil from the 1750s and an industrial town quickly evolved. A century later this town's population of over 46,000 consisted 'entirely of Ironmasters, . . . their agents and workmen; and Such professional men and tradesmen as are necessary for supplying the wants of the former', so that 'the whole locality abounds with the heaped and smouldering refuse of the works'. Merthyr was

[43] *Britannia Depicta; or Ogilby Improv'd* (London, 1720), on Glamorgan.
[44] Williams, *Welsh Historical Statistics*, vol. 1, pp. 6, 17.
[45] D. Friedlander and J. Roshier, 'A study of internal migration in England and Wales: part 1', *Population Studies*, 19 (1966), 263; P. N. Jones, 'Some aspects of immigration into the Glamorgan coalfield between 1881 and 1911', *Transactions of the Honourable Society of Cymmrodorion*, 1970, 92.

the largest town in Wales in the eighteenth and nineteenth centuries until finally overtaken by Cardiff in the 1870s.[46]

Cardiff in 1800 was 'a sleepy market town'. Its economic development accelerated from about 1840 as a result of three interacting factors: the opening of the first docks, the arrival of the railways and the expansion of output in the adjacent coalfields.[47] With the spread of steam-powered factories, trains and ships, the high quality Welsh steam coal was in great demand, being the fuel of choice for boilers, and by the second half of the century coal had displaced the iron industry as the dominant element in the economy of Glamorgan. New collieries were rapidly opened up throughout the valleys, and the coal, about half of which was for the export trade, was transported by train, or by ship through Cardiff, Swansea and Newport (Mon.) docks. The region experienced a massive influx of workers and their families who flocked to the coalfield from all parts of Britain, giving rise to 'a "frontier" society . . . working, singing, praying and playing in two languages'.[48] They were accommodated in hastily constructed streets of terraced housing that, due to the local topography, filled the valley bottoms and rose, tier upon tier, up the steep slopes.[49] At the heart of the coal industry were the Rhondda valleys, whose transformation from rural backwater to centre of the Welsh coalfield was meteoric.[50] C. F. Cliffe, a traveller visiting south Wales in the late 1840s, wrote of the Rhondda: 'The people of this solitudinous and happy valley are a pastoral race, almost entirely dependent on their flocks and herds for support . . . the air is

[46] Williams, *Welsh Historical Statistics*, vol. 1, p. 63; H. Carter and S. Wheatley, *Merthyr Tydfil in 1851* (Cardiff, 1982), pp. 1, 8–9; B. Thomas, 'The migration of labour into the Glamorganshire coalfield (1861–1911)', *Economica*, 10 (1930), 276.

[47] A. M. Williams, 'Migration and residential patterns in mid-nineteenth-century Cardiff', *Cambria*, 6 (1979), 3.

[48] J. May, *Rhondda 1203–2003* (Cardiff, 2003), p. 5; Thomas, 'Migration of labour', 277; I. G. Jones, *Explorations, and Explanations: Essays in the Social History of Victorian Wales* (Llandysul, 1983), p. 233.

[49] T. M. Hodges, 'The peopling of the hinterland and the port of Cardiff', *Economic History Review*, 17 (1947), 66.

[50] The valleys of the Rhondda *Fawr* and Rhondda *Fach* rivers. Before the creation of the Rhondda Urban District in 1894 most of this area constituted the ancient parish of Ystradyfodwg and this is the name used in all the censuses up to 1901. To avoid confusion, however, the name Rhondda will be used in this chapter.

aromatic with wild flowers and plants.'[51] By 1911, the population of Rhondda Urban District had reached almost 153,000,
and mining villages formed an almost continuous urban
strip along the valley floors, with coal mining and its ancillary
trades virtually the sole industry.[52]

Early immigrants to the coalfield encouraged relatives
and friends to leave their homes and take advantage of the
mining boom.[53] Mine owners competed with each other,
offering high wages and other incentives such as free supplies
of household coal.[54] This attracted not only raw labour from
the countryside but also the experienced workers from other
mines and industrial areas.[55]

Meanwhile, the economy of the coastal region was also
expanding, especially at Cardiff and Swansea, and to a lesser
extent at Neath, Port Talbot, Bridgend and Barry, providing
a counter-attraction for migrants to the county. Coastal and
coalfield Glamorgan, however, displayed profound socio-
economic differences. Much of the work in the coalfields
required low skill levels and provided a very narrow range
of employment opportunities. The industrial hinterland
also had some of the worst housing conditions of anywhere
in Britain. Overcrowding, poor sanitary conditions and
disease prevailed; the taking in of boarders and relatives and
the part-letting of dwellings due to the extreme shortage of
housing merely exacerbated these conditions. Houses on
the coalfield usually had only four or five small rooms, and it
was not uncommon for beds to be occupied day and night by
men on different shifts.[56] By contrast, the coastal towns, such
as Cardiff and Swansea, offered a broad range of employment opportunities and many possibilities for personal
advancement, that in turn generated the wide stratum of

[51] May, *Rhondda*, p. 14.

[52] Williams, *Welsh Historical Statistics*, vol. 1, p. 63.

[53] See, for example, M. J. Davies, 'Population mobility 1835–1885: rural and
urban perspectives' (unpublished Ph.D. thesis, Wales, Swansea, 1986).

[54] S. Eckley and E. Jenkins, *Rhondda* (Bath, 1994), p. 119.

[55] Hodges, 'Peopling of the hinterland', 66–7.

[56] E. D. Lewis, *The Rhondda Valleys* (London, 1959), p. 203; D. Jones, 'Counting
the cost of coal: women's lives in the Rhondda, 1881–1911', in A. V. John (ed.), *Our
Mothers' Land: Chapters in Welsh Women's History, 1830–1939* (Cardiff, 1991), pp. 115,
120.

society typical of Victorian urban Britain. There was also a cultural divide between the two regions. Welsh counties consistently sent the majority of their migrants to the coal-fields, and Rhondda in particular became a destination of 'inordinate importance' to rural Welsh migrants. By contrast, movement into coastal Glamorgan was dominated by non-Welsh migrants, although by 1911 non-Welsh outnumbered Welsh migrants in the coalfield too.[57] The cultural separate-ness was reinforced by the tendencies of migrants, both Welsh and English, to residential clustering by geograph-ical origin, where numbers were numerous enough to make this possible. People originating from the same areas thus formed communities of mutual help and support and insti-gated further chains of migration.[58]

The impact of industrialization on Welsh society has received much attention from scholars. David Williams concluded that it caused irreparable damage to Welsh cultural life, while Brinley Thomas believed that Welsh culture was saved by being transferred from rural to indus-trial Wales.[59] Dudley Baines considered that the statistical evidence does not support this latter theory. He calculated that in 1861 rural Welsh migrants into Glamorgan accounted for just under 16 per cent of the county's total population, while by 1901 they made up less than 12 per cent.[60] Thus, in Baines's opinion, although south Wales could be consid-ered a centre of Welsh culture by the late nineteenth century it could not have been transferred there 'by the weight of numbers of rural Welsh migrants'.[61] Perhaps the reality lies somewhere between these opposing viewpoints. Philip Jones has demonstrated that the volume of rural Welsh migrants moving to industrial south Wales was not sufficient to 'counter the vast flood' of non-Welsh immigration, the inevi-table result of which was the 'cultural submergence' of the

---

[57] Jones, 'Immigration into the Glamorgan coalfield', 87, 89, 95.

[58] Jones, *Mines, Migrants and Residence*, p. 72.

[59] Jones, 'Immigration into the Glamorgan coalfield', 82; Williams, 'Move from the land', pp. 25–6.

[60] He excluded those from Monmouthshire, because very few Monmouthshire people were Welsh-speaking at this time. For more on this, see Baines, *Migration*, pp. 276–8.

[61] Ibid., p. 277.

Welsh element in the new population by the beginning of the twentieth century.[62] Nevertheless, Jones recognized Brinley Thomas's argument as a valid one to the extent that the movement of Welsh migrants from rural Wales to the industrial south, rather than to England or abroad, 'immensely strengthened the fabric of urban Welsh cultural life in the nineteenth century'.[63]

Glamorgan had been drawing migrants from Cardiganshire at least since the early decades of the nineteenth century, and it was consistently the top destination between 1851 and 1911.[64] It is impossible to exaggerate the significance of Glamorgan for Cardiganshire's migrants; in the decades around the turn of the twentieth century almost half of them were living in Glamorgan.[65] The expansion of the south Wales coalfield was greatest between 1881 and 1890 and again between about 1900 and 1911.[66] Fortuitously for Cardiganshire, the first of these two decades coincided with the collapse of the lead-mining industry. Thus, not only was an alternative source of employment available for the redundant lead-mine workers and their families, but improved transport links had put it within easier reach of northern Cardiganshire. Moreover, farm workers and general labourers were also making moves to improve their situation. Cardiganshire's local newspaper, the *Cambrian News*, reported in 1882 that only drastic improvements to their appalling living conditions could stem the flow of the county's labourers 'down to the iron works and coal mines of South Wales, where, at any rate, the people as a rule, sleep in moderately well-constructed houses and live with some regard to elementary decency'.[67] Figure 5.2 illustrates the steep rise in migration from Cardiganshire to Glamorgan between 1881 and 1891; the link between the large proportion of male migrants, the boom in the coal industry and the failure of lead mining is inescapable.

---

[62] Jones, 'Immigration into the Glamorgan coalfield', 87–92.

[63] Ibid., 92–3.

[64] *1851 Census. Population Tables. 1.Vol. II*, pp. 447, 449.

[65] In 1891, of the 30,890 Cardiganshire natives enumerated outside the county, 14,737 were living in Glamorgan; in 1911 there were 16,108 of the county's 33,891 out-migrants living in Glamorgan. Population censuses, 1891 and 1911.

[66] Baines, *Migration*, p. 266; Thomas, 'Migration of labour', p. 284.

[67] *CN*, 17 November 1882, 5.

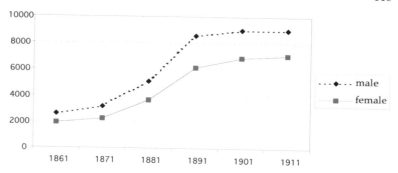

Figure 5.2 Cardiganshire migrants by gender enumerated in Glamorgan, 1861–1911

Source: Population censuses, 1861–1911.

Note: There is no breakdown by gender in the census birthplace tables for 1851.

Even before the demise of the lead-mining industry, the movement of Welsh migrants south-eastwards was attracting official attention. Andrew Doyle reported to the Richmond Commission that: 'The mining population of Glamorganshire . . . is largely recruited from the rural population of Cardiganshire and Carmarthenshire.'[68] Certainly, research has confirmed the presence of large numbers of Cardiganshire migrants in the coalfield communities, especially in the second half of the century.[69] But what other locations and opportunities in Glamorgan were attracting Cardiganshire's migrants before the boom coal-mining years of the 1880s? To answer this question and to test some of the assumptions about the Cardiganshire migration, a 20 per cent random sample (comprising 1,750 individuals) of the Cardiganshire natives enumerated in Glamorgan in 1881 has been extracted from the census enumerators' books.[70]

MIGRANT ORIGINS AND DESTINATIONS

The birthplace data from the 1881 census sample were first analysed to discover how widespread the influence of

[68] *Mr Doyle's Reports*, p. 8.

[69] See, for example, Baines, *Migration*, p. 257; Jones, 'Immigration into the Glamorgan coalfield', 89, 95.

[70] The census total of Cardiganshire migrants in Glamorgan in 1881 was 8,766.

Glamorgan as a migrant destination was in Cardiganshire up to 1880. Although useable data were identifiable for only 1,132 of the 1,750 individuals in the sample, some interesting trends may still be identified. The early decades of the century had seen population declines in Cardiganshire's southern registration districts of Cardigan and Newcastle Emlyn. At this time numbers were increasing and the economy was flourishing in the northern regions of the county due to the expansion of Aberystwyth town and the thriving lead-mining industry. It might, therefore, be expected that the key sending areas to Glamorgan up to 1881 would have been concentrated in the south of Cardiganshire. The census sample, however, indicates that this was not the case. The pull of Glamorgan was apparently felt throughout Cardiganshire, even before the collapse of lead mining; moreover, the county's main urban centres, Aberystwyth, Cardigan, Tregaron, Lampeter and New Quay, were prominent sending areas.[71]

Studies of the migration from rural Wales to Glamorgan in the later nineteenth century have understandably focused on the movement into the coalfield, but this was by no means the full picture.[72] The census sample indicates that Cardiganshire natives were living throughout Glamorgan in 1881.[73] Inevitably, the heaviest concentrations were in the industrial hinterland, especially in the Rhondda, Merthyr Tydfil, Aberdare, Llanwonno and Gelligaer, but the urban coastal regions were also well represented, particularly Cardiff, Swansea and Roath. This comes as no surprise. The decision to move is an individual one, influenced by a complex range of factors, and people do not necessarily react to similar circumstances in the same way. Take, for example, the Lloyd family of Brynhope Farm, Tregaron. Thomas and Elinor Lloyd, born in the 1820s, had ten children of whom seven survived to adulthood. In the 1880s the family

---

[71] For a map of the sending areas, see Cooper, 'Cardiganshire's rural exodus', 150.

[72] For example, Thomas, 'Migration of labour'; Jones, 'Immigration into the Glamorgan coalfield'; Jones, *Mines, Migrants and Residence*; P. N. Jones, 'Population migration into Glamorgan 1861–1911: a reassessment', in P. Morgan (ed.), *Glamorgan County History*, vol. 6, *Glamorgan Society, 1780–1980* (Cardiff, 1988).

[73] For a map of the destination areas, see Cooper, 'Cardiganshire's rural exodus', 151.

lost the tenure of the family farm and Thomas and his children had to seek a living elsewhere. All left not only farming but Cardiganshire as well, but for several different destinations and occupations. Perhaps the first to go was Diana Lloyd. She went to London where she married and settled in Leytonstone. Her brother John also moved to London, where he married an English girl and worked as a car man on his father-in-law's dairy round. Thomas Lloyd himself, now a widower, went with his son Morgan, his daughter, Catherine, and granddaughter, Emily, to Llanwonno, where Catherine worked as a dressmaker and Morgan went down the mines. Thomas's married daughter Margaret and her family also moved to Glamorgan, but to Maesteg where her husband John, who had been a farmer in Cardiganshire, also became a collier. Meanwhile, Thomas's youngest son, Edward, trained as a draper, settling for a while in Cardiff before moving on to London to join his brother John.[74]

OCCUPATIONAL PROFILE

Analysis of the occupational data revealed interesting trends too. The sample contained a total of 1,009 males and 741 females. Of the 933 males aged 12 and over, more than 96 per cent were in employment.[75] Of 671 females aged 13 and over, less than 19 per cent were recorded with paid employment.[76] Rhondda was the main migrant destination in the sample, so it is not surprising that coal mining dominated the male occupational structure. Colliers were to be found at seventeen of the migrant destinations, and accounted for over 46 per cent of employed males. The second largest occupational group among the male migrants, at 13 per cent, was made up of labourers. The majority were classed as general labourers, but there were also dock, quarry and factory workers.[77] Although Merthyr was the second most popular destination

[74] Interviews with Joan Paparo, 3 July 2009, 5 December 2009.
[75] The youngest employed males were aged 12.
[76] The youngest employed female was aged 13; this total excludes a further 24 females listed as servants in their own homes. For more on the problems with female occupational data in the Victorian census, see Higgs, *Making Sense*, pp. 81–2.
[77] At this time general labourers were second in number only to coal miners in the population of Glamorgan as a whole. Hodges, 'Peopling of the hinterland', 69.

in our sample, very few of the males were employed in the iron and steel manufacturing that dominated the town. As a whole, the male migrants in the sample were heavily represented in the unskilled classes and under-represented in all other groups, particularly among the professional classes which contained only 3 accountants, 4 GP/medical assistants and 24 clergy.[78] Nevertheless, there was a wide range of urban trades and crafts within the group, particularly in the coastal towns, and in these the carpenter/joiner dominated with 63 individuals. Seafaring was also well represented – mariners, ship's chandlers, sail makers – accounting for 50 individuals. Less common occupations included those of musician, undertaker, upholsterer, picture framer, police constable, bookseller and customs officer.

Most of the adult females in the sample were married, which accounts, in part, for the very low proportion with paid occupations. The range of female employment opportunities generally at this time was not very diverse, but in the mining communities it was negligible.[79] Almost half of the employed females in the group were in domestic service, but here again, as was apparent in the Carmarthenshire sample, there is evidence of the widening of opportunities that was occurring towards the end of the nineteenth century: the second most common form of employment was in the clothing trade – dressmakers and milliners – and there were also a few factory workers, two school teachers and a midwife.

SOCIAL AND CULTURAL ISSUES

Analysis of the Victorian census data reveals that females were more migratory than males.[80] However, this was not the case for Cardiganshire migrants. Indeed, the sex ratio (males per 100 females) of the county's migrants to Glamorgan was particularly unbalanced, as can be seen from table 5.1. It is worth noting that in 1881, when the sex ratio of the

[78] Here, as in the Carmarthen sample, Anglicanism dominated: only 7 out of the 24 clerics were Nonconformist.

[79] Jones, *Mines, Migrants and Residence*, p. 18; Jones, 'Counting the cost', pp. 113, 131.

[80] Baines, *Migration*, pp. 235–6.

Cardiganshire migrants in Glamorgan was 140.7, that for the population of Glamorgan as a whole was 105.5, while the figure for England and Wales was 94.8.[81] Table 5.1, however, also indicates that the proportion of males among the Cardiganshire migrants in Glamorgan began to decrease slightly from the 1890s.

Table 5.1 Male/female sex ratio of the Cardiganshire migrants in Glamorgan, 1861–1911[82]

	1861	1871	1881	1891	1901	1911
sex ratio	134.7	140.8	140.7	139.9	130.9	126.5

Source: Population censuses, 1861–1911.

The gender imbalance is not particularly surprising given that coal mining dominated Glamorgan's economy in the later nineteenth century. In all the mining regions at this time the demand for a young male labour force inevitably resulted in a high proportion of males in the population, and Glamorgan, Monmouthshire and Durham consistently appeared at the top of the county tables for high male/female sex ratios.[83] The contribution of the coal-mining communities to this high sex ratio can be seen by comparing the ratios of Cardiganshire's migrants in Cardiff, Swansea and the Rhondda in 1881 (see table 5.2).

Table 5.2 Comparison of male/female sex ratio of Cardiganshire migrants in Cardiff, Swansea and Rhondda in 1881

Urban sanitary district	Sex ratio
Cardiff	131.9
Swansea	114.9
Rhondda	176.1

Source: Population census, 1881.

The demand for young male labour in the coal-mining communities led to an imbalance in the age structure as well as in the sex ratios. Studies have revealed that the imbalance

[81] Jones, *Mines, Migrants and Residence*, p. 17.
[82] There is no breakdown by gender in the census birthplace tables for 1851.
[83] Jones, 'Counting the cost', p. 113

was particularly marked in the 15–34 age group.[84] The data from the 1881 census sample have been analysed to see how far the Cardiganshire migrants in Glamorgan conformed to these patterns. Two age profiles were charted, one for the whole sample, which included the coastal towns, and one for only those of the study population who were living in the Rhondda, to see if any variations were apparent in a coalfield community. The results can be seen in figures 5.3 and 5.4. The excess of males over females in the 15–34 age group is very striking in both charts but particularly so in the case of the Rhondda, where it also continued into the 35–54 age group. A possible explanation of the marked increase in the proportion of females over the age of 55 is that female life expectancy then, as now, was above that of males, and this was particularly true for coal-mining families.[85] The charts reveal an imbalance in the age structure of the populations in both samples. The national average for the 15–44 age group at this time was 44.7 per cent of the population.[86] However, this age group accounted for 66.2 per cent of the census sample as a whole and for a massive 73.7 per cent of those living in the Rhondda. While these statistics are highly suggestive, only an age profile of the whole of the Cardiganshire-born element in Glamorgan at this time could give the true picture. One further point of note to emerge from the age profiles is the low proportion of Cardiganshire-born children, which suggests that many of the migrants were leaving Cardiganshire as childless young adults and confirms that migration rather than natural increase dominated demographic growth in the coalfields at this time.[87]

Within the pioneering coal-mining communities the lodger population was of enormous importance.[88] They formed a significant proportion of the primary male workforce,

[84] Jones, *Mines, Migrants and Residence*, p. 17; Jones, 'Counting the cost', p. 113.

[85] M. Anderson, 'The social implications of demographic change', in F. M. L. Thompson (ed.), *The Cambridge Social History of Britain 1750–1950*, vol. 2, *People and their Environment* (2nd edn, Cambridge, 1993) , p. 18.

[86] Jones, *Mines, Migrants and Residence*, p. 17.

[87] For more on the social aspects of the evolution of mining communities, see ibid., pp.78–9.

[88] In the Victorian census, enumerators attempted to distinguish between the boarders, who shared a common table with the household, and the lodgers who ate

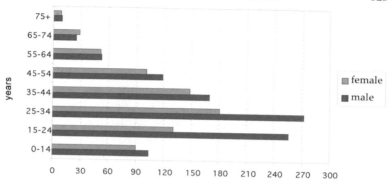

Figure 5.3 Age profile of the Cardiganshire migrants in the 1881 Glamorgan census sample
Source: Population census, 1881.

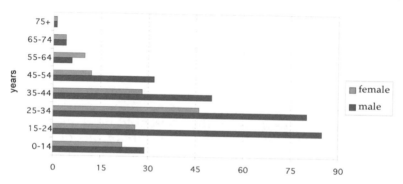

Figure 5.4 Age profile of the Cardiganshire migrants in the 1881 Glamorgan census sample living in the Rhondda
Source: Population census, 1881.

demonstrating not only the mobility of the mining population but also the lack of adequate housing provision. This
was a perpetual problem in the mining valleys, and one that
had not been resolved even by 1914.[89] Studies have shown
that a high proportion of households in the coalfield took
in boarders who thus made a valuable contribution to the

---

separately and constituted their own household, but the distinction was not always
clear in the returns. For more on this, see Higgs, *Making Sense*, pp. 60–2.
    [89] Jones, *Mines, Migrants and Residence*, p. 20; Hodges, 'Peopling of the hinter-
land', 66.

family income for, although wage rates were high, earnings were uncertain due to piece-work pay that could be affected by a range of factors such as injury, restricted output and the fluctuating demand for coal.[90]

The sample from the 1881 census contains a high proportion of male boarders. Of the 904 male migrants aged 14 and over, 348 (over 38 per cent) were boarders. However, the boarders were by no means confined to the industrial heartland but were also to be found in the towns of the coastal region. Only 57 per cent of the male boarders in the study population were colliery workers, the rest being engaged in a wide range of occupations such as those of curate, dock labourer, stonemason and labourer at the iron and steel works, while some, such as the drapers' and tailors' assistants, boarded at their place of work. Census studies have demonstrated among the migrant population in the Glamorgan coalfield a tendency towards residential segregation by geographical and cultural origin, and many groups were also associated through closer ties.[91] The data from the 1881 census sample have been analysed to see how far the Cardiganshire-born boarders in Glamorgan conformed to this pattern. Almost three-quarters (72 per cent) lived in co-residing groups in which the household head and/or his wife originated either from Cardiganshire or one of the two neighbouring counties of Carmarthen and Pembroke. Over half (54 per cent) boarded in households where heads and/or spouses originated from Cardiganshire itself and, of these, 23 per cent came from the same village, parish or town as their household head. Many households in the census sample also contained close family relations, such as niece, brother and grandson. This supports the conclusions reached by other researchers concerning the enduring significance of households in which heads, kin and boarders shared a common birthplace and cultural background, not only in the social structure of the migrant communities of industrial south Wales but also in the migration process itself.[92] Further

[90] Jones, 'Counting the cost', p. 113.
[91] Jones, *Mines, Migrants and Residence*, p. 59; Jones, 'Counting the cost', p. 120.
[92] See, for example, Jones, *Mines, Migrants and Residence*, p. 59.

evidence from the 1891 and 1901 censuses suggests that these co-residing groups were an enduring feature of these communities. The following are just a few examples.

The Morris family, 15 Regent Street, Ystradyfodwg (Rhondda), 1881

Name	Age	Position in household	Occupation	Birthplace
Evan Morris	49	head	collier	Gwnnws
Eluned	48	wife		Gwnnws
David	22	son	collier	Gwnnws
Anne Davies	15	niece	general servant	Tregaron
John Rees	31	boarder (married)	collier	Tregaron
Thomas James	26	boarder	collier	Gwnnws
David Edwards	25	boarder	collier	Gwnnws
Richard Edwards	23	boarder	collier	Gwnnws
David Morris	19	boarder	collier	Gwnnws

The Jones family, 9 George Street, Cardiff St. Mary, 1881

Name	Age	Position in household	Occupation	Birthplace
Ann Jones	29	wife of head	master mariner's wife	New Quay
Ellen Thomas	24	boarder (married)	master mariner's wife	New Quay
Margaret Thomas	3 mths	boarder	daughter of Ellen	New Quay
David Richards	40	boarder	mariner	Cards.
Mary Davies	32	boarder (married)	master mariner's wife	New Quay
Wm. Edwards	32	boarder	mariner	Pembs.
Mary Dace	19	boarder	none given	New Quay

The Rees family, 7 Victoria Street, Merthyr Tydfil, 1891

Name	Age	Position in household	Occupation	Birthplace
Joseph T. Rees	24	head	coal miner	Llandysiliogogo
Elizabeth Rees	28	wife		Llanychaiarn
Thomas Davies	26	brother-in-law	coal miner	Llanychaiarn
Thomas Jones	31	boarder (married)	coal miner	Llandysiliogogo
Thomas Evans	32	boarder (married)	coal miner	Llandysiliogogo
Daniel Rees	28	boarder	coal miner	Llandysiliogogo

The Davies family, 41 Sherwood Terrace, Llwynypia, 1901

Name	Age	Position in household	Occupation	Birthplace
David Davies	35	head	colliery timberman	Pontrhydfendigaid
Ann Davies	34	wife		Pontrhydfendigaid
Morgan Rees	28	boarder (married)	colliery foreman	Lledrod
Evan Rees	25	boarder	timberman	Lledrod
John Rees	14	boarder	collier	Pontrhydfendigaid

The analysis of the boarders data from the 1881 sample reveals that over a quarter of them (26.4 per cent) were married but very few were enumerated with their wives. There could, of course, have been numerous reasons for this, but one of significance is to be found in the evidence of a witness from Tregaron in Andrew Doyle's report of 1882: 'numbers go to the coal and iron works; but as a rule do not take their families with them, hoping, I believe, to get employment again at home'.[93] The deeply rooted sense of identity with the land, that has already been mentioned, and that was a characteristic of rural west Wales, made many reluctant to abandon completely their farms and smallholdings, even when they were in grave financial difficulties.[94] However, a way out of this dilemma was presented by the type of agriculture that

[93] *Mr Doyle's Reports*, p. 495.
[94] See, for example, Moore-Colyer, 'Agriculture and land occupation in eighteenth- and nineteenth-century Cardiganshire', in G. H. Jenkins and I. G. Jones

predominated in Cardiganshire. The mainly pastoral nature of the farming meant that women could be left in charge while their menfolk went to the industrial south to supplement the family finances. The incidence of men from rural west Wales going alone to work in the south Wales coalfield, but returning for a few weeks each summer, was common enough to attract the attention of Lleufer Thomas when reporting on Wales to the Royal Commission on Labour of 1894:

> In some parts of the country there are men who move temporarily from one district to another, . . . and those who have left agriculture for the 'works' [the iron works and coalfields] frequently return to their former homes for the harvest.[95]

This arrangement, however, was not without its problems. Inevitably, many of the men became settled into the work pattern and social life of their new communities in the coalfield, and Cardiganshire people still tell of the conflict in families when men wanted to relocate permanently to south Wales while their womenfolk wished to remain on the family farm.[96]

The 1881 census analysis demonstrates in the coalfield element of the sample the main characteristics that have been shown to exist in nineteenth-century mining communities.[97] It was predominantly youthful, had a highly unbalanced male/female sex ratio in the teenage and adult age groups, was exceptionally occupationally specialized and had a prominent male boarder component. By contrast, the sex ratio, age profile and occupational structure of the migrant group in coastal Glamorgan conformed more closely to those typical of Victorian urban England.

For all the migrants, however, the move from rural Cardiganshire to urban industrial Glamorgan would have

(eds), *Cardiganshire County History*, vol. 3, *Cardiganshire in Modern Times* (Cardiff, 1998)', p. 26; Thomas, *Digest*, p. 330.

[95] *Royal Commission on Labour. Fifth and Final Report. Part I. The Report*, p. 226. See also *Report on the Decline in the Agricultural Population of Great Britain, 1881–1906* (London, 1906), pp. 94–5.

[96] Interview with M.L., 26 February 2008.

[97] Jones, *Mines, Migrants and Residence*, p. 22; D. Friedlander, 'Occupational structure, wages, and migration in late nineteenth-century England and Wales', *Economic Development and Cultural Change*, 40 (1992), 303.

taken them into quite a different social, economic and cultural environment.[98] Within the coal-mining communities the main preoccupation was the struggle to survive and to improve the basic facilities of life, and to this end incomers from the same geographical and cultural backgrounds tended to cluster together forming distinct communities of mutual help and support. Urban coastal Glamorgan was characterized by the broad social and cultural spectrum of thriving Victorian Britain; and a wide range of entertainment venues, retail outlets, employment opportunities and possibilities for personal advancement was on offer. At the heart of the Welsh immigrant community, however, for those who wished to stay within it, was the Nonconformist chapel that provided not only a unifying force but became the main focus of social as well as religious life. For Cardiganshire's migrants in the later nineteenth century, the strength of the attraction of Glamorgan, and to a lesser extent of Carmarthenshire, is undeniable. For those wishing to leave home for a new life, however, there were destinations beyond Wales that were becoming ever more accessible.

[98] Jones, *Mines, Migrants and Residence*, p. 31.

VI

THE LURE OF LONDON

From the later Middle Ages, the number of Welsh people living in London increased steadily. By the mid-eighteenth century there were more Welsh merchants and shopkeepers living in the metropolis than in any town in Wales; and London was becoming a focus for Welsh intellectuals, writers and antiquaries who came to play a significant part in increasing the awareness of a Welsh identity and the attendant revitalization of Welsh culture and language.[1] One commentator noted in the London of the 1770s that 'the Welch are very numerous in and about town at this time and many of them tho' they understand a little – yet not English a nough to understand a sermon'.[2]

The numbers of London Welsh were regularly boosted by seasonal and temporary inward movements. The upper echelons of society divided their time between their estates in the country and their town houses in London, while communities in the depths of rural Wales were kept in touch with life in the capital through commercial links. Undoubtedly the most significant and long standing of these was the droving trade. Since well before the first documentary evidence appears in the thirteenth century cattle had been walked from their breeding grounds in upland western counties such as Cardiganshire, through the rich grasslands of central England on their way to the markets of London and the south-east. This trade was not confined only to cattle, but included sheep and horses – Smithfield itself began as a horse fair. The trade in Welsh wool and woollen goods provided another commercial link with London. Although flannel was the main product, home knitting, particularly of stockings,

---

[1] For example, the London Welsh founded the Eisteddfod in its modern form. E. Jones, 'The age of societies', in E. Jones (ed.), *The Welsh in London, 1500–2000* (Cardiff, 2001), p. 76.

[2] A. K. Knowles, *Calvinists Incorporated* (Chicago, 1997), p. 71.

was the most important domestic industry. Stockings were an easily transported and readily saleable commodity, and it was said that George III preferred Welsh bed socks. The stocking merchants probably followed the same routes as the drovers, as did the young women – *merched y gerddi* (garden girls) – who went seasonally to work in the rapidly expanding market gardens along the Thames and in the hop fields of Kent. Most of these itinerant female workers came from Cardiganshire and Carmarthenshire. Agriculture in these Welsh counties was mostly of a pastoral nature and large families meant that there was more female labour than was needed on the farms. The long journeys followed by the harsh living and working conditions were accepted by these young women not only as a welcome change from their home circumstances where poverty was rife, but also because they could earn a better rate in London and Kent than male agricultural labourers could at home. In addition, they returned home with new gardening skills, all of which made a valuable contribution to the domestic economy. Eventually, the *merched y gerddi* were replaced by the flood of Irish girls fleeing from the effects of the potato famine, but by then there were less onerous and more rewarding opportunities, such as that of milk seller or domestic servant, to draw Welsh girls to London.[3]

Between the prosperous elite and the itinerant workers was a stratum of permanent migrants to London about whom little is known. These would have included skilled, semi-skilled and unskilled workers and those seeking apprenticeships or other opportunities for self-improvement. Towards the close of the eighteenth century a succession of poor harvests in Wales meant that Welsh people were moving to London in ever increasing numbers, and this movement was further boosted from the early nineteenth century by agricultural workers from Cardiganshire whose traditional seasonal migrations to the harvests of Herefordshire

---

[3] Jones, 'Age of societies', pp. 56, 57, 60; Knowles, 'Structure of rural society in north Cardiganshire, 1800–1850', in G. H. Jenkins and I. G. Jones (eds), *Cardiganshire County History*, vol. 3, *Cardiganshire in Modern Times* (Cardiff, 1998), p. 89; W. J. Lewis, 'The condition of labour in mid-Cardiganshire in the early nineteenth century', *Ceredigion*, 4 (1963), 333; J. W. Davies, 'Merched y gerddi: a seasonal migration of female labour from rural Wales', *Folk Life*, 15 (1977), 12–23.

and Shropshire were being undermined by Irish labourers willing to accept even lower wages than the Cardiganshire labourers.[4]

Studies have shown that Welsh migration to England in the nineteenth century conformed to conventional rural–urban migration theory: proximity and employment opportunities being the main controlling factors. Thus, English towns close to the Welsh border attracted the greatest volume of people leaving Wales except where more distant centres offered particular opportunities. Indeed, the only long-distance destination to attract significant numbers of migrants from all parts of Wales was London.[5] Nineteenth-century London was the largest city and foremost commercial centre in the world, and the hub of an immense and growing empire. It was the 'notion of wealth and commerce completely stupendous' that attracted such a constant stream of migrants and immigrants to the metropolis, although the reality for many would prove to be a life of privation in the squalid, disease-ridden, overcrowded districts of the capital so vividly portrayed in the Victorian novel.[6]

Research on the distribution of Welsh natives in London during the seventeenth, eighteenth and early nineteenth centuries has suggested a dispersed settlement pattern with no marked concentrations in any district except for a notable Welsh presence in Clerkenwell, which was the location of the first Welsh Nonconformist chapel in London.[7] It is only after 1851 that we can gain a clearer idea of how the Welsh were distributed throughout the capital. The census tells us that there were 17,575 Welsh natives living in London at that date, or 0.7 per cent of its total population.[8] However,

---

[4] R. Griffiths, 'The Lord's song in a strange land', in E. Jones (ed.), *The Welsh in London, 1500–2000* (Cardiff, 2001), p. 163; Knowles, *Calvinists Incorporated*, p. 77.

[5] C. G. Pooley, 'Welsh migration to England in the mid-nineteenth century', *Journal of Historical Geography*, 9 (1983), 291, 293.

[6] J. Barclay, *Barclay's Complete and Universal English Dictionary* (London, 1842), on London.

[7] It later transferred to Jewin Crescent in nearby Islington. Knowles, *Calvinists Incorporated*, pp. 77, 83; E. Jones, 'The early nineteenth century', in E. Jones (ed.), *The Welsh in London, 1500–2000* (Cardiff, 2001), p. 96.

[8] C. G. Pooley, 'The residential segregation of migrant communities in mid-Victorian Liverpool', *Transactions of the Institute of British Geographers*, new series, 2 (1977), 366.

although they were more numerous in some districts than in others, there were no areas that were either predominantly or even distinctively Welsh.[9] Indeed, evidence from the census supported by that from chapel lists suggests that the London Welsh did not show any tendency towards residential clustering by geographical origins as was apparent among migrants in, for example, the south Wales coal valleys.[10]

It is generally accepted that the process of urbanization leads to a more sophisticated but more uniform lifestyle, and that rural-to-urban migrants inevitably become involved in this social change. Migrants with a distinctive culture, however, are able to resist this change to some extent, and it has been suggested that rural Welsh migrants to English towns were often able to live in two distinct cultural worlds for much of the nineteenth century, 'preserving those elements of a rural culture which they sought to maintain but at the same time fitting easily into the Victorian urban environment'.[11] Certainly, the London Welsh, though scattered throughout the capital, were nevertheless able to create a sense of community and preserve a cultural identity by membership of their many societies.[12] It was the chapels, though, that were at the centre of Welsh life. More than just places of worship, they provided members with a full social programme, and it may have been this that was the attraction for some chapel-goers while they settled into their new lives.

As the London Welsh community grew, their chapels proliferated so that by the late nineteenth century religious services were held in Welsh each Sunday at more than forty different centres in the capital.[13] Meanwhile, the continually

---

[9] This was in contrast to the districts colonized by, for instance, Irish and Jewish immigrants. For a distribution map of the Welsh in London in 1851, see Jones, 'Early nineteenth century', p. 97.

[10] Knowles, *Calvinists Incorporated*, p. 77; Jones, 'Early nineteenth century', p. 99.

[11] Pooley, 'Welsh migration', 288.

[12] One such society formed in the early twentieth century was the Cymdeithas Ceredigion Llundain or Cardiganshire London Society. Some Welsh natives who rose to positions of power and authority in London used their influence for the benefit of Wales; for instance, it was through the efforts of the London Welsh that the University of Wales was established. E. Jones, 'Victorian heyday', in E. Jones (ed.), *The Welsh in London, 1500–2000* (Cardiff, 2001), p. 115.

[13] J. Williams, 'The move from the land', in T. Herbert and G. E. Jones (eds), *Wales, 1880–1914* (Cardiff, 1988), p. 36.

expanding railway network made regular visits to and from Wales ever easier, and strong bonds were thus maintained with 'home'. Return migration was not uncommon. Some migrants returned to Wales to live because of ill health, home-sickness or to retire on the proceeds of the businesses they had built up in London, while others made provision in their wills to be returned to their homeland for burial.[14] Making a new life away from family and friends, however, inevitably brings with it a variety of stresses and conflicting emotions. Migrants aiming for success in an English-speaking world saw fluency in that language as a prime necessity.[15] Furthermore, there were those who considered it preferable to conceal their Welsh origins:

> It was certainly the case in my family that being from Wales was something one didn't make known and it is only through my beloved grandmother that I heard such a lot about it. Perhaps as a small child I was the one person she could tell about her childhood without feeling she had to cover up her humble origins.[16]

Inevitably, perhaps, many Welsh migrants rapidly became anglicized, immersing themselves completely in the cosmopolitan life of the city, and these may have been in the majority, for it has been suggested that only about one in five of the Welsh in London regularly attended chapel.[17]

CARDIGANSHIRE'S LONDON MIGRANTS

As far as the Cardiganshire migrants were concerned, London was consistently the main destination for those leaving Wales in the second half of the nineteenth century. Well-established channels of communication, coupled with extensive employment opportunities, were overcoming issues of proximity, underlining the willingness of Welsh migrants to travel long distances given the appropriate incentives. The trend

[14] Interviews with E.J., 21 February 2009, E.D., 25 February 2009, Shân Hayward, 27 February 2009. See also, Ceredigion County Library, Aberystwyth, Local History Section, *Monumental Inscriptions with Indexes* (typescript, 1994–ongoing).

[15] M. Jones, 'Welsh immigrants in the cities of north-west England, 1890–1930: some oral testimony', *Oral History*, 9 (1981), p. 39.

[16] Interview with Anon., 27 March 2009.

[17] Jones, 'Victorian heyday', p. 116.

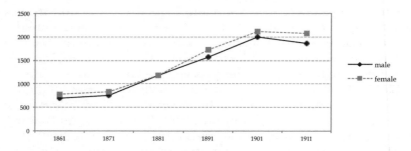

Figure 6.1 Cardiganshire migrants enumerated in London, 1861–1911
Source: Population Censuses, 1861–1911.

of migration to London from Cardiganshire between 1861 and 1911 can be seen in figure 6.1.[18] One striking feature is that females consistently outnumbered males, except in 1881 when the sexes were evenly matched. This is consistent with conventional migration theory that holds that females were more migratory than males but, as we have noted, it was a trend that was exceptional for Cardiganshire.

The 1851 census tells us that, of the 17,575 Welsh natives living in London, 1,488 had been born in Cardiganshire.[19] This was equivalent to just over 2 per cent of that county's 1851 inhabitants, and the relative sparseness of its population meant that Cardiganshire was one of the Welsh counties most affected by loss through migration to London.[20] The greatest percentage increase in the number of Cardiganshire migrants to London in the second half of the nineteenth century occurred between 1871 and 1881, a rise of nearly 48 per cent (from 1,591 to 2,352 individuals). The cause of this dramatic increase is not immediately apparent. Certainly, this was the first decade in which Cardiganshire's population had begun its long decline, but, as we have seen, it was during the following decade that the county experienced its most dramatic population loss. The move to London continued and the Cardiganshire-born in

---

[18] There is no breakdown by gender in the 1851 birthplace tables.
[19] *1851 Census. Population Tables. II. Vol. 1. Division 1. London*, pp. 31–5. Of these Welsh natives, 4,524 did not specify a county of origin, so the Cardiganshire figure could be higher.
[20] Pooley, 'Welsh migration', 293–5.

the London Welsh community in 1891 showed an increase of 40 per cent on the previous decade (from 2,352 to 3,299). After this, the trend started to slow down, although the census of 1901 marked the high point for the number of the county's natives living in London – 4,112 individuals. Indeed, the proportion of natives settled in London at this time was higher for Cardiganshire than for any other Welsh county.[21] In 1911 the Cardiganshire Welsh living in London experienced a drop of almost 5 per cent on the previous decade – down from 4,112 to 3,928 – with the greater decrease being in numbers of male migrants. This gradual decline in migration to London was not limited to Cardiganshire. The registrar general reported in 1913 that 'the proportion of natives in the total population of London has risen at each successive census since 1881' and he concluded that the 'diminution in the stream of immigration has been coincident with a decline in the rate of growth of the population [of Britain]'.[22] Certainly, in the case of Cardiganshire's inhabitants, the growing excess of females in the second half of the nineteenth century meant that many of them would not marry, and this, combined with an ageing population, resulted in a fall in the birth rate; although migration from the county continued, the pool of potential migrants was necessarily constantly shrinking.

DISTRIBUTION OF THE MIGRANTS

The census tells us that Cardiganshire migrants were dispersed throughout London although they were more numerous in some districts than in others, which, as we have seen, was typical of the Welsh community in the capital. Comparison of the census data for 1851 and 1861 reveals several significant trends, and the most obvious one is that, although the total number of Cardiganshire migrants in London was fairly static between the two dates, the individuals were quite mobile. Twenty-one districts had fewer Cardiganshire natives in 1861

[21] *Census of England and Wales, 1901. County of London. Area, Houses and Population* (London, 1902), table 36. Of the Welsh counties, only Glamorgan, with 7,838, and Monmouthshire, with 5,092, had more natives in London at this census. See also Williams, 'Move from the land', p. 37.

[22] *Census of England and Wales, 1911. Vol. IX. Birthplaces* (London, 1913), p. xi.

than in 1851, and some districts, such as Marylebone, St Luke,
City, St Olave, Bermondsey and Lambeth showed significant
losses. Conversely, fifteen districts showed a gain in their
Cardiganshire populations: Kensington, St George Hanover
Square, and St Saviour Southwark being notable. The greatest
change, however, was in the Islington district where the population increased from 46 to 141 between 1851 and 1861. The
reasons behind these various fluctuations are not immediately
apparent, but evidently Islington was increasingly becoming a
focus for Cardiganshire people moving to London.

The 1861 census is of particular interest because it is the
first to give a breakdown by gender in the birthplace tables.
This allows us an insight into the areas of London that were
particular magnets for Cardiganshire's female migrants.
Of the thirty-seven registration districts, twenty-one had
more female than male Cardiganshire Welsh, and of these,
Kensington and City had particularly high proportions of
females. Conversely, Islington, the district with the greatest
increase in Cardiganshire migrants during the decade, had
significantly higher proportions of males. The succeeding
Victorian census tables do not give a breakdown by registration district of birthplaces of the people enumerated in
London so it is not possible to make statistical comparisons of
population trends by registration district for the remainder
of the nineteenth century.

The census tables for 1911, however, give birthplace statistics for London's population by metropolitan
borough.[23] This affords the best picture of the distribution
of Cardiganshire natives in London since the 1861 census,
but the boundary changes make statistical comparisons with
former registration districts impossible. Nevertheless, several
trends can be identified. Cardiganshire natives were still
scattered throughout the capital and, overall, females still
outnumbered males, the sex ratio (males per 100 females)
being 89.2. Of the twenty-nine boroughs, sixteen had more
than 100 migrants from Cardiganshire although the highest
concentration (393) was still in Islington. Females, though,

---

[23] *1911 Census. Vol. IX. Birthplaces*, pp. 43–60. The administrative county of
London was created from parts of Middlesex, Surrey and Kent and was divided, for
administrative purposes, into metropolitan boroughs.

were now dominant there also: the sex ratio having fallen to 88.9 from the remarkably high one of 161.1 in 1861. Kensington was still significantly female dominated in 1911 as were Lambeth and Westminster, which had approximately six male migrants for every ten female migrants.

MIGRANT ORIGINS

The dispersed residential distribution in London is striking. The question arises as to whether there were parts of Cardiganshire that were particularly influential as sending areas. In order to throw some light on this issue, the birth-place data of all Cardiganshire natives living in each of four London districts in 1881 were analysed. The districts selected for the sampling were Islington, north of the river, and Lambeth, south of the river – areas consistently attracting the greatest proportions of the county's migrants – and Kensington and Westminster in which the female migrants significantly outnumbered males. It was immediately apparent that the birthplace data were subject to the short-comings mentioned above. For almost one-third (134) of the individuals located in the four districts, only the county of birth was recorded, and where villages/parishes were given they were often misspelt or ambiguous, making identifica-tion problematical. Altogether, useable birthplace data were obtained for only 278 of the 440 individuals and, although by no means conclusive, they are certainly suggestive of a strong tradition of migration to London from the northern regions of Cardiganshire and especially from the Aberystwyth area.[24] However, it is also clear from this 1881 census sample, and further confirmed by the register of members of the *Cymdeithas Ceredigion Llundain* (Cardiganshire London Society) at its founding in 1933, that all parts of the county felt the influence of London as a migrant destination in the later nineteenth and early twentieth centuries.

One of the issues addressed by nineteenth-century census takers was the proportion of the population deemed to be urban and that considered to be rural. The urban

---

[24] For a distribution map, see K. J. Cooper, 'Cardiganshire's rural exodus' (unpublished Ph.D. thesis, University of Leicester, 2008), 172.

population, for census purposes, was defined as 'the inhabitants of the chief towns and their immediate neighbourhood', while the rural population 'includes the inhabitants of the smaller towns as well as of the strictly country parishes'.[25] The obvious flaw in this definition is that

> The rural population ... as determined by this method includes the inhabitants of a very large number of places which, though not of sufficient magnitude to rank as 'chief towns', are yet of such a size that their inhabitants can scarcely be considered as living under rural conditions.[26]

Nineteenth-century Cardiganshire was a rural county with no large towns, and thus, for census purposes, all of its inhabitants would have been classed as rural and the movement from Cardiganshire to London would have been seen as rural to urban. The sample taken from the 1881 census, despite the shortcomings of the data, clearly showed Aberystwyth, with over 36 per cent of individuals with identifiable origins, as a major sending area to the four London districts at this time, but it is unlikely that these migrants would have considered themselves as being from a rural background, despite the small size of the town (just over 7,000 inhabitants in 1881). This movement out of Aberystwyth is all the more surprising because by the later nineteenth century the town was the main thriving urban centre in Cardiganshire and was itself attracting a considerable volume of in-migration.

AGE PROFILE AND MARITAL STATUS OF THE MIGRANTS

In each of the four London districts the age profiles of the Cardiganshire migrants in 1881 were broadly similar. Almost 57 per cent (248 of the 440 migrants) fell within the 21–40 age group, although it was the 21–30 age group that contained by far the highest proportion of migrants (170 individuals). These figures suggest that Cardiganshire was losing significant numbers of its young adult population by out-migration, which in turn would have had an adverse effect on the remaining population in terms of its reproductive

[25] *1881 Census. General Report*, p. 8.
[26] Ibid., p. 9.

rate. It seems likely that the marital fertility of the London migrants would have been affected also. Each of the four sampled districts had a high proportion of young unmarried adults, suggesting that late marriages were common at this time. Indeed, the predominance of females in a community tends to be associated with relatively late female mean age at first marriage. Almost three-quarters of those in the 16–30 age group in the 1881 study population were unmarried, and the sex ratio of this group was as low as 74.6. In the 31–40 age group the majority of both males and females were married, although this was a much smaller migrant group.

One measure of the social segregation of a migrant group is the extent of intermarrying within that group rather than outside it. Notwithstanding any desire to retain their cultural identity, daily life in London brought the migrants into constant contact with people outside the Welsh community, and a gradual move towards assimilation within the host society was inevitable. In the case of the Cardiganshire migrants in the 1881 census study population, only half of the married females had partners from their home county and the remainder were more than twice as likely to marry non-Welshmen. Of the married male migrants, even fewer – 38 per cent – had partners from their home county, and here again the remainder were more than twice as likely to marry non-Welsh wives.[27] These data are suggestive of a fair degree of social integration in the host community.

Some of Cardiganshire's migrants had evidently arrived in London as married couples, and birthplaces of children can be useful clues as to both the timing and stages of family movements. For example, Isaac Jones (aged 34), cow keeper, and his wife Margaret (aged 32), living in Dawlish Street, Lambeth, in 1881, were apparently new arrivals: their three children aged 4, 3 and 6 months had all been born in Cardiganshire. Incidentally, their general servant, Elizabeth Mason (aged 13), was also born in their home village of Llanbadarn Fawr, so she probably accompanied the family when they moved to London. Another apparently newly

---

[27] There were 7 married males and 6 married females in the sample whose spouses were not enumerated with them and who were, therefore, excluded from this calculation.

arrived family was that of William Morgans (aged 38), a plasterer from Llansanffraid (Llanon), and his wife Ann (aged 41) from Bow Street. They were living in Palmerston Road, Islington, in 1881 but had evidently arrived via south Wales: three of their children, aged 13, 10 and 7, had been born in Aberystwyth, a daughter aged 4 was born in Glamorgan and a daughter aged 2 months was born in Islington. Lodging with this family were Abraham Wright, a carpenter, and Edward Pierce, a plasterer, both originating from the Aberystwyth area, and possibly employed by William. Yet another family demonstrates the long distances that nineteenth-century migrants were sometimes prepared to travel. Thomas Davis (aged 34) and his wife Jemima (aged 31), both from Llangranog (southern coastal Cardiganshire), had a farm dairy in Islington in 1881. Their eldest child, Lizwith [sic] (aged 7), was born in Aberystwyth, the next two children, aged 5 and 3, were born in Durham, while the youngest children, aged 2 and 10 months, were born in Islington. Despite their travels, they had obviously maintained strong links with 'home'. Thomas's unmarried brother James (aged 27), also from Llangranog, lived with them in Islington and worked in the dairy; and their general servant, Margaret Jones (aged 26) and two unmarried boarders, George Williams (aged 23), a carpenter, and John Lewis (aged 20), a grocer, all came from Cardiganshire.

Migrant occupations

The study population of the four London districts contained individuals who spanned the social and economic spectrum, ranging from indoor pauper to landowning MP. The occupational data have been analysed to discover which particular employment opportunities were drawing people from Cardiganshire to the metropolis in increasing numbers in the closing decades of the nineteenth century, and to assess the impact on the migration process.

Females

London, as noted earlier, was one of the few migrant destinations in England and Wales in the second half of the nineteenth century in which females from Cardiganshire consistently outnumbered males. The report from the 1881 census concluded that 'women are on the whole rather more migratory than men, probably in consequence of the demand in towns for domestic servants from the country'.[28] This conclusion certainly applied to the female migrants in the 1881 census sample. Of the 97 females with stated occupations, 77 were in domestic service.[29] This occupation constituted the largest single class of employment for women in England and Wales throughout the nineteenth century.[30] In the closing decades of the century, however, prospects were beginning to open up as women moved into spheres such as clerical, shop and factory work, but there is little evidence of this new trend among the employed females in the 1881 study population, although Islington, which had the greatest concentration of Cardiganshire migrants, showed a slightly wider female occupational range, including a governess, several dressmakers, a waitress and a hospital nurse. In Kensington and Westminster, which were among the wealthiest residential areas of the metropolis, the Cardiganshire female migrant employment was exclusively in domestic service apart from one dressmaker in Westminster. There were also 5 female paupers in the group, 2 in Islington and 3 in Lambeth.

Males

As might be expected, the range of occupations of males in the 1881 census study population was far wider than that of females. There were 179 employed males and they spanned the social and economic spectrum. The group was dominated, however, by three types of employment: the building trade, the dairy business and drapery outlets. The professional classes were significantly under-represented; there were just 2 army officers, 3 barristers and/or JPs, 2 GPs, 2 MPs and 4 schoolmasters/tutors. There were also 2 students,

---

[28] *1881 Census. General Report*, p. 51.
[29] Almost 70 per cent of these domestic servants were employed in non-Welsh-headed households, indicating a high degree of social and economic integration in the host society among this group.
[30] Domestic service will be discussed in more detail in chapter VII.

12 men with no stated occupations, and only 1 man (in Lambeth) in receipt of indoor poor relief.[31]

Cardiganshire people living in London in the nineteenth century are traditionally associated with the milk trade, and the occupation of cow keeper/dairyman was certainly much in evidence among the migrants in Islington, and to a lesser extent in Lambeth, in 1881; yet, surprisingly, it was ranked only second among male occupations in the study population (27 out of 179 employed males). The involvement of the Welsh in London's milk trade was widespread and long standing, and towards the end of the nineteenth century Charles Booth noted that: 'Common report and our own observations lead us to suppose that they number considerably more than 50% of the trade.'[32]

It is generally acknowledged that the connection of the London Welsh with the milk trade was a natural progression from the long-established tradition of Welsh drovers taking cattle to the London livestock markets. A common element that linked the droving trade and the growth of dairying in London in the early nineteenth century was the presence of extensive pastures in areas, such as Islington, north of the city. Involvement in the city's dairy trade would not have been a difficult occupational move for migrants from rural mid and west Wales, with their pastoral background; and districts such as Islington would have been familiar to any connected with the droving trade because many of the drovers paused there to fatten their cattle before driving them through Clerkenwell to Smithfield.[33] For migrants from rural Wales, then, a permanent move to the Islington and Clerkenwell districts, whether to work in the dairying trade or in other forms of employment, was a natural progression from the links forged by the trade of the drovers. As we have seen, Welsh migrants did not show a tendency to residential clustering in London, but the 1881 census data suggest particularly strong migration links between Cardiganshire and Islington. Furthermore, this was the location of Jewin

[31] For a breakdown of these occupations see Cooper, 'Cardiganshire's rural exodus', 180.

[32] Jones, 'Early nineteenth century', p. 106.

[33] Jones, 'Victorian heyday', p. 110; Jones, 'Early nineteenth century', pp. 96, 102.

Crescent Chapel, the 'mother church of the Welsh Calvinistic Methodists', which would have acted as a powerful magnet for people whose day-to-day existence was rooted in chapel life. Indeed, this chapel came to be known as 'the mother church of Cardiganshire migrants in London'.[34]

As London expanded to cover the surrounding pasture-land, and the demand for fresh milk continued to grow, urban dairies with cows fed in stalls proliferated in the city.[35] Urban cow keeping, however, while guaranteeing fresh milk, was subject to the environmental difficulties of the provision of fodder and the disposal of manure.[36] As the railway network spread, more and more milk was being brought into the capital by rail. By the 1880s it was estimated that twenty million gallons arrived annually by churn at London's railway stations, particularly from the Home Counties, and milk sellers based in Islington were well placed to receive these deliveries.[37] Urban cow keeping was now very much in decline in London, and by 1900 a 'dairy' had mostly come to mean a shop that sold milk. Many dairies came to rely on the sale of groceries for the bulk of their turnover and so evolved the ubiquitous and indispensable Welsh corner shop.[38]

Many London Welsh in the milk trade were involved in family businesses. In 1881 there was a William Mason living in Islington; even at the age of 75 he was listed in the census as dairyman and cow keeper and household head. His was very much a family concern: William was a widower and his unmarried daughter, Mary (aged 24), acted as housekeeper, while her younger sister, Agnes (aged 15), was the general servant. William's unmarried son, William (aged 43), was the

---

[34] Griffiths, 'Lord's song', p. 166; Knowles, *Calvinists Incorporated*, p. 83.

[35] Jones, 'Early nineteenth century', p. 102; P. J. Atkins, 'The retail milk trade in London, *c*.1790–1914', *Economic History Review*, new series, 33 (1980), 524.

[36] One readily available urban source of fodder was spent grains from the city's breweries. In the 1850s, one enterprising Cardiganshire cow keeper, David James, began to supply fellow cow keepers in London with his surplus grains, and so a new company evolved. This has now developed into a worldwide industry: James and Son (Grain Merchants) Ltd, which supplies feed for ruminants sourced from the brewing and vegetable processing industries. *http://www.james-son.co.uk/index2.html*

[37] E. H. Whetham, 'The London milk trade, 1860–1900', *Economic History Review*, new series, 17 (1964), 372.

[38] Atkins, 'Retail milk trade', 525; Jones, 'Early nineteenth century', p. 101; Jones, 'Victorian heyday', p. 108.

cowman, and another unmarried son, James (aged 27), was a milk seller, while a further son, Morgan (aged 22), had no occupation. All had been born in Llanfihangel-y-Creuddyn (north Cardiganshire) except for Agnes who was born in London's Aldersgate, suggesting the timing of the family move to London. It is worth noting, from the point of view of cultural integration, that the family also had a London-born lodger: Hannah How (aged 20), an artificial flower maker.

There was also Richard Evans who left Llanilar in the late 1870s to work in a dairy in Praed Street, Paddington. His younger sister Sophia went with him to work as a dairymaid and later as Richard's housekeeper. In the early 1880s they were followed by their sister Margaret and her husband who was from Talybont and who later established a dairy business in Hackney. In 1884 the family presence in London was further swelled by the arrival of their brother, David Rowland Evans, his wife Mary and their five young children. David had been working as a maltster in Llanon, but the trade had gone into a decline there, and it is possible that the success of relatives and friends in the London dairy trade encouraged him to join them. He eventually established his own business in Hoxton that was later taken over by Express Dairies. David kept up a connection with 'home' even to the extent of having his suits made by Morgan's of Llanon: 'Mr Morgan would visit London to measure his client and then bring the suits up'. He was regarded as 'adventurous and successful' by his family in Cardiganshire.[39]

By no means all migrants had family or friends to provide employment and/or a home for them at their chosen destination. Many had to make their own way, and one such was Daniel Lloyd. Daniel was born in Tregaron in 1875 to Roderick and Catherine Lloyd and was the oldest of twelve children. Daniel married Hannah Jones of Llanddewi Brefi in 1898 and by 1901 they and their two young children had left the family farm in Tregaron and moved to London. Here they set up home in Loddiges Road, Hackney, and in the 1901 census Daniel is listed as a self-employed dairyman. It is not known how he financed himself but he gradually built up

[39] Interview with A.R., 27 April 2009.

Figure 6.2 D. Lloyd and Sons – a typical early twentieth-century London-Welsh dairy/shop with 'prams' ready for house-to-house milk delivery. Courtesy of Mrs H. J. Lloyd.

a thriving dairy/shop (see figure 6.2) and was subsequently able to make a substantial contribution to the purchase of the freehold of the family farm in Tregaron. Although he lived the rest of his life in London he kept in regular contact with 'home', his children returning for holidays on the family farm. On his death he was returned to Tregaron to be laid to rest in the family plot at Bwlch Gwynt Methodist Chapel.[40]

Great importance is, rightly, attributed to family connections in the migration process, but Daniel Lloyd and his siblings illustrate the experience of the countless Welsh migrants who possessed the independence and confidence to strike out alone. Of Daniel's nine siblings who survived to adulthood, eight moved away from home. They left because the family farm could not support them all, but also they wanted 'to get on'. Four went to the London area, two moved to Liverpool, one to Cyncoed, Cardiff, and one to Towcester in Northamptonshire. All apparently went independently of each other, finding their own accommodation and

---

[40] Interview with Shân Hayward, 27 February 2009.

employment. Nevertheless, for all of them Cardiganshire was still regarded as 'home'. Here they found their marriage partners, their children returned regularly for holidays on the family farm, and all are buried in the family plot in Tregaron.[41]

The lure of London was undeniable. As one descendent of a Cardiganshire migrant expressed it: 'That's where they all went . . . if they wanted to get on.'[42] The connection of Cardiganshire migrants with the dairy business in the late nineteenth and early twentieth centuries is still a source of pride and the subject of reminiscences for many families today.[43] Many established their own businesses, sometimes with the help of family money and labour, and often to the ultimate benefit of the family back home:

> He went to London in about 1900 to join his sister and brother-in-law who owned a dairy. . . He bought his own dairy with assistance from his brother-in-law. . . In 1920 he returned to Aberaeron because of failing health and invested the profits in the family business there.[44]

Sometimes the wider community gained from the success of its migrants. Alban Davies, born in Llanrhystud in coastal mid-Cardiganshire in 1873, went to London at the end of the nineteenth century, initially to work in his brother-in-law's dairy. After considerable commercial success running his own dairy business, he retired to Llanrhystud. One of his many philanthropic gestures was the purchase of land on the outskirts of Aberystwyth that he later donated to the university and that now houses the Penglais campus.[45]

As the Welsh droving trade is thought to have led to the involvement of many London Welsh in the milk trade, so Welsh hosiers may well have been the precursors of the numerous Welsh drapery stores in early nineteenth-century London. The hosiery and glove trade was of long standing in Wales and, as itinerant sellers gradually established

---

[41] Interview with Shân Hayward, 11 March 2009.
[42] Interview with E.J., 21 February 2009.
[43] For example J. Hughes, 'Evan the milk', *Dyfed Family History Journal*, 7 (2002), 341–2.
[44] Interview with E.D., 25 February 2009.
[45] *Dictionary of Welsh Biography* (London, 2001), pp. 3–4.

permanent bases in London, the drapery store became almost as much a Welsh phenomenon as the dairy. Towards the end of the century, William Booth commented that 'of those who come up to serve in London's drapery shops an abnormal population are from Wales' and he further noted that 'many of the employers are Welsh and give preference to their countrymen'.[46] Certainly, involvement in the drapery trade was the third most common occupation among the Cardiganshire males in the 1881 census study population (24 of 179 employed males).

As mass production increased, some of the drapery stores that originally specialized in traditional woollen goods, silks, linens and haberdashery diversified to meet the growing demands of London's expanding middle-class clientele, and so the department store evolved.[47] Larger concerns even provided hostel accommodation for their employees.[48]

Cardiganshire migrants arriving in London seeking work as drapers' assistants would have been familiar with the trade. In the 1851 census there were 156 male drapers (or their assistants) in Cardiganshire and by 1871 there were 260.[49] Trade directories can illuminate the picture further, though one needs to regard such directory evidence with caution because businesses were often omitted. Even so, in 1844 there were 42 linen and/or woollen drapery shops listed in Cardiganshire, while by 1880 there were 63 linen and/or woollen drapers, 17 combined drapery and grocery shops and 14 hosiers in the county.[50]

Given the traditional association of Cardiganshire people in London with the milk trade, it is surprising to find that by far the most common male occupation in the 1881 study population is that of carpenter/joiner, accounting for 49 out of 179 employed males, 42 of whom lived in Islington.

[46] Jones, 'Victorian heyday', p. 110.

[47] Some stores that have become household names are of Welsh origin, for example Peter Jones of Sloane Square, D. H. Evans of Oxford Street and Dickens and Jones of Regent Street. Jones, 'Victorian heyday', p. 110.

[48] Ibid., pp. 111, 112.

[49] These figures are for the registration county.

[50] *Pigot and Co's Royal National and Commercial Directory and Topography* (London, 1844), pp. 4, 7, 23, 42–3, 84; *Slater's Royal National Commercial Directory* (Manchester, 1880), south Wales section, pp. 12, 32, 34, 106, 161, 345.

What, then, might have accounted for the over-representation of Cardiganshire migrants in this occupational category in London? One result of industrialization was the mass production of standardized goods in urban centres, but, until these became widely available, local craftsmen were a vital element of the rural economy. Carpenters were in constant demand, not only for the construction of buildings, but for the making of essential farming equipment and domestic items and, in the case of Cardiganshire, for maintenance at the lead mines. The carpenter/joiner was equally in demand in urban areas, so it is hardly surprising that the heavily populated and industrialized counties of Glamorgan and Monmouth had the highest numbers of carpenters/joiners in Wales.[51] Somewhat more surprising, however, is the fact that by the mid-nineteenth century Cardiganshire had the third highest number although, in terms of population size, the county ranked only seventh out of thirteen in Wales. Indeed, carpenters and joiners were Cardiganshire's most numerous craftsmen during the nineteenth century, and it was the shipbuilding industry that provided a further significant dimension to the county's woodworking tradition.

The vessels, which carried the county's coastal trade from the late eighteenth century onwards, were mostly built in the county, as were some larger ocean-going vessels such as brigs and schooners.[52] Between 1800 and 1880 over 700 wooden ships were built in the county's main boatyards. This provided extensive employment opportunities, not only in the construction of the vessels but in the various ancillary trades and crafts.[53] However, as we have seen, commercial maritime activity in Cardiganshire began to wane from the 1860s, and the 1880s saw the construction of the last wooden sailing vessel in the county.[54] Thus, employment

---

[51] *1851 Census. Population Tables. Occupations.*

[52] D. Jenkins, 'Shipping and shipbuilding', in G. H. Jenkins and I. G. Jones (eds), *Cardiganshire County History*, vol. 3, p. 184; A. Eames, 'Ships and seamen of Wales in the age of Victoria: some Cardiganshire examples', *Ceredigion*, 8 (1978), 305.

[53] Jenkins, 'Shipping and shipbuilding', p. 185. In 1851 Cardiganshire ranked fourth for the numbers of boatbuilders per Welsh registration county. The top three were Glamorgan, Pembrokeshire and Caernarfonshire. *1851 Census. Population Tables. Occupations.*

[54] Jenkins, 'Shipping and shipbuilding', p. 190.

opportunities for Cardiganshire's carpenters and joiners were shrinking rapidly from the 1870s. In addition to the demise of shipbuilding, work at the lead mines was beginning to slump, and declining population levels in the county were causing the building industry to contract. Moreover, as we have seen, the increasing availability of mass-produced goods was threatening all the county's rural craftsmen, not just the carpenter/joiner. Table 6.1 illustrates the fortunes of Cardiganshire's carpenters and joiners from 1831 to 1911.

Table 6.1 Number of carpenters and joiners enumerated in Cardiganshire, 1831–1911

Year	No. of carpenters/joiners	% change
1831	523	
1851	1079	**106.3**
1871	1131	**4.8**
1891	852	−24.7
1911	601	−29.5

Source: Population censuses, 1831–1911.

Welsh artisans became involved in the rapid expansion of nineteenth-century London, especially from mid-century when the demand for labour in the building trade soared; and building firms owned by Welshmen in London's expanding areas such as Islington were a particular magnet for Welsh craftsmen.[55] Cardiganshire's strong woodworking tradition meant that there were many carpenters and joiners available to take advantage of this demand for their skills, especially at a time when employment opportunities at home were dwindling.

Even when the county's economy was fairly buoyant, however, there were those who left Cardiganshire for the brighter prospects of London. One such was Thomas Thomas who left Llandysul, south Cardiganshire, in the early 1850s aged about 20. He was a carpenter and had trained with his uncle, Daniel Thomas, a carpenter and timber merchant in Llandysul. Thomas joined his cousin, Evan Thomas, son of Daniel. Also a carpenter, Evan had left Llandysul earlier and

---

[55] Griffiths, 'Lord's song', pp. 165–6.

was lodging with a Welsh family in the St Luke's district of London where 'there were many from Cardiganshire at the time'. In 1854, Thomas married Henrietta Jarrard, an English girl from St Luke's, and the couple set up home in Islington where Thomas became a journeyman carpenter. The couple with their young family made several moves around the north London area but by 1870 Thomas had become a builder and they had settled at Green Lanes, Stoke Newington, where his wife also ran a 'Coffee and Eating House' in their home. Thomas spent the rest of his life in London, although he is thought to have returned to Llandysul for occasional visits.[56]

Another young man who left Cardiganshire in the 1850s was John Hopkins, from Llanfihangel-y-Creuddyn, where he had been working as a carpenter on Lord Lisburne's estate. John and his wife Elizabeth (Davies) from Penrhyncoch moved to Islington, but they apparently did not arrive there alone:

> They had no family here in London, but brought friends with them [from Cardiganshire] who shared their home . . . They were accompanied by one Richard Owens, also a carpenter, and David Williams, a missionary . . . A number of their contemporaries also went to the same part of Islington, and they named their street after the Rheidol Valley . . . John was related through his sister Sarah's marriage to some Lloyds and they also came to Islington.[57]

We saw evidence of this residential clustering by geographical origin and/or kinship ties in chapter V, especially among the boarders in the migrant population of the Glamorgan coalfield.[58] This tendency was certainly apparent in the Cardiganshire-born carpenters and joiners living in Islington in 1881. Of the 42 individuals, almost half (19) were boarders; 12 lived in households headed by a Cardiganshire native, 2 lived in households headed by natives of other Welsh counties, while only 5 lived in English-headed households. For example, there was Thomas Jenkins (aged 42), a

---

[56] Interviews with Mike Thomas, 12 July 2009, 4 November 2009.

[57] Interview with S.B., 20 July 2009. Rheidol Terrace and the adjoining Rheidol Mews, in Islington, N1, close to the Angel Underground station, tend to confirm a former connection of this area with Cardiganshire.

[58] See, for example, P. N. Jones, *Mines, Migrants and Residence in the South Wales Steamcoal Valleys: the Ogmore and Garw Valleys in 1881* (Hull, 1987), p. 59.

carpenter/joiner from Llanilar who was living in St James Street, Islington, in 1881 with his wife, Catherine (aged 41), from Lampeter. Thomas's unmarried brother John (aged 40), a carpenter/joiner from Llanilar, and James Hughes (aged 43), a joiner from Llanbadarn Fawr, also lived and possibly worked with Thomas; and also part of the household was Thomas's niece, Annie (aged 15), from Aberystwyth, who was still at school. We have already noted that Evan Thomas, from Llandysul, was living with a Welsh family in St Luke's in the 1850s and was joined by his cousin Thomas, and a trawl of the enumerator's schedules for 1871 and 1891 has revealed further examples of co-residing groups who originated from Cardiganshire.

The occupational data of our 1881 study population provides an indication of their social and economic status. The group was very much under-represented in both the professional and the unskilled classes and only 6 of the 440 individuals were in receipt of poor relief. These socio-economic features were typical of the London Welsh community at this time, for it has been remarked of them that they were 'fairly adept at improving their situation in a modest way, striving for respectability if not affluence'.[59]

London held a particular attraction for migrants from Cardiganshire, especially during the second half of the nineteenth century and despite the alternative pull of industrial south Wales.[60] Nevertheless, another area of England was exerting a significant counter-attraction during this time, namely the north-west of England, and in particular Merseyside.

[59] Jones, 'Early nineteenth century', p. 101.
[60] Knowles sees parallels between the migratory traditions linking Cardiganshire with London and those linking the French Auvergne with Paris. Knowles, *Calvinists Incorporated*, p. 82.

VII

THE MOVE TO LIVERPOOL AND THE NORTH-WEST

The area known as Merseyside embraces the land and conurbations on both the Lancashire and Cheshire banks of the Mersey estuary, forming a region that is linked economically and socially as well as physically. Employment on both sides of the estuary in the nineteenth century was dominated by the transporting, warehousing and processing of imports and exports, and by dock-related industry. The economy of Merseyside centred on Liverpool, one of the world's greatest seaports, and this port function made Victorian Liverpool a commercial and financial centre second only, in Britain, to London. Moreover, as the thriving city expanded, the development of its increasingly extensive suburbs provided significant employment opportunities for all those connected with the building trade.[1] For most of urban Lancashire and Cheshire in the nineteenth century, however, the major influence on the economy was the development of the textile industry, and in particular 'the manufacture of cotton, and the production of various fabrics from that article', although 'the woollen, linen and silk trades [were] not inconsiderable'. The centre of the textile industry was Manchester, and it was this that lifted the city 'to so high a pinnacle of consequence and wealth' in the nineteenth century.[2] The cotton yarn, textiles and goods produced in the north-west were not only for the domestic market; by the 1830s exports of these commodities accounted for just over half of Britain's overseas earnings and, as Manchester became the chief market for this trade, so Liverpool became the leading port.[3]

[1] R. M. Jones, 'The Liverpool Welsh', in R. M. Jones and D. B. Rees (eds), *The Liverpool Welsh and their Religion* (Liverpool, 1984), p. 22; J. A. Patmore and A. G. Hodgkiss (eds), *Merseyside in Maps* (Liverpool, 1970), pp. 17, 39, 41.

[2] *Pigot and Co's National Commercial Directory for 1828–9. Part 1. Cheshire to Northumberland* (London, 1829), pp. 340–1.

[3] D. Hey, *The Oxford Companion to Local and Family History* (3rd edn, Oxford, 2002), pp. 112–13.

Analysis at county level has revealed that geographical proximity combined with the size of the labour markets were the main factors controlling nineteenth-century migration except where more distant centres, such as London, Liverpool and Manchester, offered particular employment opportunities.[4] In 1851 the only English cities with communities of more than 10,000 Welsh-born individuals were Liverpool and London: Liverpool had 20,262 Welsh-born or 5.4 per cent of its population, while London had 17,575 Welsh natives or 0.7 per cent of its population. The next in rank was Manchester (with Salford) with 6,850 Welsh natives or 1.7 per cent of its population, followed by Bristol with 4,949 or 3.6 per cent of its population.[5] A similar picture emerges from the 1871 census, although now the Welsh-born population was beginning to filter into smaller towns and those more distant from Wales. The major centres of attraction outside Wales, however, were still London and Merseyside, and their popularity with Welsh migrants was growing.[6] Andrew Doyle reported to the Richmond Commission in 1882 that 'in such towns as Liverpool and Bristol the Welsh community is an appreciable proportion of the whole'.[7] Lord Mostyn commented in 1885: 'Year after year Liverpool becomes more than ever the metropolis of Wales.'[8] By the closing decade of the century there were over 82,000 Welsh natives living in the north-western counties of Lancashire and Cheshire.[9]

Although Welsh-born migrants were to be found throughout these two counties in the nineteenth century,

[4] C. G. Pooley, 'Welsh migration to England in the mid-nineteenth century', *Journal of Historical Geography*, 9 (1983), 291, 293; R. Lawton, 'Population changes in England and Wales in the later nineteenth century', *Transactions of the Institute of British Geographers*, 44 (1968), 68.

[5] C. G. Pooley, 'The residential segregation of migrant communities in mid-Victorian Liverpool', *Transactions of the Institute of British Geographers*, new series, 2 (1977), 366.

[6] The Welsh in London now exceeded those in Liverpool by about one thousand individuals. Pooley, 'Residential segregation', 366.

[7] *Royal Commission on Agriculture (Richmond Commission). Reports of the Assistant Commissioners. Mr Doyle's Reports* ([1882] 2nd edn, Shannon, 1969), p. 8.

[8] Lord Mostyn, 'Inaugural address', *Transactions of the Liverpool Welsh National Society*, 1 (1885), 3.

[9] *Census of England and Wales, 1891.Vol. II. Area, Houses and Population* ([1893], 2nd edn, Shannon, 1970), p. 384.

they were most numerous on Merseyside and to a much lesser extent around Manchester. Merseyside had long been a particularly important focus for Welsh migration, attracting individuals from all parts of the principality, although the majority came from the rural hinterland of north Wales. Because of its port function, Liverpool had a more cosmopolitan population than most Victorian cities but the three main immigrant groups identifiable culturally were the Irish, the Scots and the Welsh.[10]

It is usually assumed that relatively close residential proximity is necessary for a community to retain a degree of cultural cohesion. This is not necessarily so, as we saw of the Welsh community in London. Elsewhere in England, however, in urban centres where numbers permitted, communities clustered together to form a focus of Welsh cultural life. In the case of Merseyside, for instance, although the Welsh were to be found throughout the area, several locations were seen as particularly Welsh ones. On the Wirral peninsula there were sizeable Welsh communities, particularly in Birkenhead and Tranmere, while across the Mersey there were concentrations both in central Liverpool (remnants of the earliest Welsh community) and in the fast-growing suburbs of Kirkdale and Toxteth Park. The Welsh were most numerous, however, in Everton, an area typified by medium-density terraced housing and a respectable working-class population, and of which one contemporary commentator wrote in 1873: 'A large part of its population is from the Principality. Placards in the Welsh language may be seen on the walls and Welsh newspapers in the shop windows.'[11]

The Welsh community in Liverpool had gained a reputation for being honest and reliable, for 'on the whole they are an industrious, steady and sober race'.[12] Welsh rural migrants arriving in urban England were relatively poor but they were rarely ignorant. Most had benefited from a basic education and had acquired some skills that could be transferred to an urban labour market. The census confirms that

---

[10] Pooley, 'Residential segregation', 364.

[11] Pooley, 'Welsh migration', 299; J. A. Picton, *Memorials of Liverpool* (London, 1873), p. 353.

[12] Pooley, 'Welsh migration', 298; Picton, *Memorials*, p. 353.

by mid-century Welsh migrants were already well established in the employment structure of many English towns.[13] Although economically well integrated in the urban work-force, Welsh immigrant communities sought to preserve elements of their own distinctive rural Welsh culture: their language, beliefs and traditional values. It was this that bound together the Welsh (and also the Scots) on Merseyside, in contrast to the Irish community for whom socio-economic factors were the main cohesive force, and whose residential areas more closely resembled ghettos.[14]

Life in rural Wales encouraged a consciousness of, and identification with, locality so that the Welsh who moved to urban England became aware, perhaps for the first time, of their Welsh identity. The most obvious outward sign of this Welshness was their native language and it was a major force in binding the immigrant community together. Often rural Welsh migrants had little or no English on arrival, and the Welsh community on Merseyside actively promoted the continued use of their native language. Several Welsh-language newspapers were printed and circulated in Victorian Liverpool, and Welsh books and journals were published there.[15] There was also a network of local clubs, literary societies and eisteddfodau for the Welsh community; the Welsh National Eisteddfod was sometimes held in Liverpool, and in 1883 the Liverpool Welsh National Society was founded. Welsh continued to be spoken at home among some Liverpool-born families of Welsh extraction; and it is estimated that late Victorian Liverpool had a greater concentration of Welsh speakers than any other city with the possible exception of Cardiff.[16] The chapel, often a Welsh Calvinistic one, was at the heart of the Welsh immigrant community as one descendent of a Liverpool-Welsh family recalls:

[13] Pooley, 'Welsh migration', 298, 302.
[14] Pooley, 'Residential segregation', 364.
[15] The first Welsh-language newspaper, *Yr Amserau*, was founded in Liverpool. Jones, 'Liverpool Welsh', p. 38; M. Jones, 'Welsh immigrants in the cities of north-west England, 1890–1930: some oral testimony', *Oral History*, 9 (1981), 33.
[16] Pooley, 'Welsh migration', 299; Jones, 'Liverpool Welsh', pp. 22, 34, 42; D. B. Rees, 'The miracle and variety of two centuries of religion', in R. M. Jones and D. B. Rees (eds), *The Liverpool Welsh and their Religion* (Liverpool, 1984), p. 10.

> My grandfather was a Welsh speaker from Cardigan who spoke the
> language to other Welsh speakers in West Derby, Liverpool . . . He
> met my grandmother through the chapel . . . The family went round
> Liverpool visiting various chapels to hear the preachers. It was quite
> important for them to do this.[17]

By the later nineteenth century there was reputedly at least
one Welsh chapel in every town of any size throughout the
north of England. In Liverpool alone, there were twenty-
three Welsh chapels as well as a network of Sunday schools
and missions.[18] Here, worship and social activities were often
conducted in Welsh, thus encouraging a continued fluency
in the language.

For an immigrant community to maintain its cultural
identity in an alien environment it needs to be continually
reinforced by new arrivals from, and frequent contact with,
'home'.[19] The Welsh community on Merseyside maintained
family links with rural Wales, while kinship networks and
chapel contacts actively recruited from home, with offers
of help in finding both work and accommodation. Thus,
'home' continued to exercise a considerable influence in the
Welsh immigrant community, even to the extent that there
was often segregation by geographical origin as well as by
social class in chapel gatherings.[20]

The Welsh in Manchester have received little attention
from historians although the region attracted the greatest
volume of Welsh migrants in the later nineteenth century
after London and Liverpool. However, evidence suggests
that the close-knit community that the Welsh formed on
Merseyside and the contacts they maintained with home
were probably replicated in Manchester.[21] Indeed, much of
what is true of the Liverpool Welsh and the way in which they
organized themselves would probably have applied equally
well to Welsh communities in any of the rapidly growing
English Victorian towns.[22] Gradually, though, as the century
drew to a close and the volume of migration from Wales

---

[17] Interview with John Williams, 14 December 2009.
[18] Jones, 'Liverpool Welsh', pp. 21–2; Pooley, 'Welsh migration', 299.
[19] Pooley, 'Welsh migration', 301.
[20] Jones, 'Liverpool Welsh', p. 25; Jones, 'Welsh immigrants', 35.
[21] See, for example, Jones, 'Welsh immigrants', 33–41.
[22] Jones, 'Liverpool Welsh', p. 20.

slowed, the second and third generations became increasingly anglicized. They had no difficulty with the English language or with English ways, and once these had been mastered there was nothing to exclude them from English society.[23] Inevitably, this process eroded the strength of Welsh culture in urban England:

> those who left the chapel disappeared also from the [Welsh] community. The chapel was the organizer and the link with home . . . Those who eased themselves out of the chapel's embrace left their Welshness behind them.[24]

THE CARDIGANSHIRE WELSH IN THE NORTH-WEST

The census reveals that the north-west was consistently the second-ranked destination, after London, for those Cardiganshire migrants who left Wales in the second half of the nineteenth century. The high proportion of migrants from north Wales in the Welsh community of Lancashire and Cheshire is well known and is readily explained by geographical proximity. Not so immediately obvious is the reason for the movement of migrants from Cardiganshire to Liverpool and the north-west. As we saw in chapter VI, migration networks between Cardiganshire and London probably owed much to overland trading links and seasonal movements. It was maritime trade, however, that was the chief means of contact between Cardiganshire and the outside world until the advent of the railways, and the county had long-established commercial contacts with the other ports of the western seaboard of Britain, with London and with western Europe and North America. Of particular significance were the links with Liverpool.[25] This is confirmed by the list of sailings from Aberystwyth harbour in the mid-nineteenth century.[26] Although Cardiganshire's coastal trade declined

---

[23] Jones, 'Welsh immigrants', 38; Pooley, 'Welsh migration', 301–2; Jones, 'Liverpool Welsh', pp. 35–6.

[24] Jones, 'Liverpool Welsh', pp. 36, 38.

[25] M. I. Williams, 'Commercial relations', in G. H. Jenkins and I. G. Jones (eds), *Cardiganshire County History*, vol. 3, *Cardiganshire in Modern Times* (Cardiff, 1998), pp. 205–8.

[26] NLW, Aberystwyth Borough Records. F11, Port of Aberystwyth. (a) Vessels sailed 1842–51; (c) Vessels sailed 1851–1866. To view these records in tabular form,

rapidly from the 1860s, there was still some movement between Aberystwyth and Liverpool, of both cargoes and passengers, into the early twentieth century.[27] Thus, maritime trade undoubtedly played a significant role in forging migration links between Cardiganshire and Merseyside, while the awareness of the thriving nature of the urban economies of the north-west would have exerted a powerful attraction for would-be migrants as communications between Cardiganshire and the rest of Britain improved.

The movement from Cardiganshire to the north-west was already well underway by the time of the 1851 census and, of the 522 Cardiganshire natives resident in Lancashire and Cheshire at that time, over half were living in Liverpool. Numbers of migrants increased steadily over the next two decades, with almost a 40 per cent gain by 1871, but this was as nothing compared with the influx over the following two decades when numbers more than doubled. The decade of greatest increase was undoubtedly that between 1871 and 1881; it showed a massive gain of 76 per cent, although in terms of the Welsh population in the north-west the Cardiganshire element was very small, amounting to just 2 per cent of the Lancashire Welsh and just over 1 per cent of the Cheshire Welsh.[28] Numbers of Cardiganshire migrants in the north-west were almost static in the last decade of the nineteenth century, and thereafter began to decline. It is worth noting that the greatest increase in migration to the north-west did not coincide with the decade of Cardiganshire's greatest population loss (1881–91). This was also the case with the Cardiganshire migration to London, a fact that reaffirms the complex interaction of forces influencing both the decision to move and the choice of destination.

From 1861, statistics in the census birthplace tables are divided by male and female, and the data for Cardiganshire Welsh enumerated in the north-west reveal some interesting gender trends (see figure 7.1). In 1861 there were more

see K. J. Cooper, 'Cardiganshire's rural exodus' (unpublished Ph.D. thesis, Wales, Swansea, 1986), 243–5.

[27] Williams, 'Commercial relations', p. 207.

[28] *Census of England and Wales. 1881. Vol. III. Ages, Condition as to Marriage, Occupations and Birth-places* (London, 1883), p. 363.

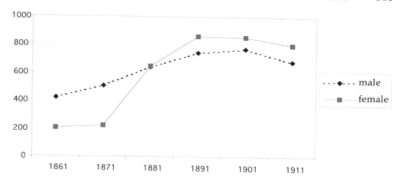

Figure 7.1 Cardiganshire migrants enumerated in the north-west, 1861–1911
Source: Population censuses, 1861–1911.

than twice as many males as females from Cardiganshire in Lancashire and Cheshire, yet within two decades females had come to outnumber the males slightly. Both groups, however, showed a marked growth in numbers over this period: by 1881 males had increased by over 50 per cent whereas females had more than trebled. Females then remained significantly in excess until 1911, so that the extremely high sex ratio (males per 100 females) of 209 in 1861 had plummeted to 85.5 by 1911.

CARDIGANSHIRE NATIVES IN THE NORTH-WEST IN 1881

The decade of greatest increase of Cardiganshire migration to the north-west occurred between 1871 and 1881. This increase coincided with Liverpool's greatest building boom of the nineteenth century (1876–80).[29] Could there have been a link between this housing boom and the dramatic increase in numbers of Cardiganshire's migrants? The 1881 enumerators' books for Lancashire and Cheshire have been searched for all Cardiganshire natives, and the data analysed in order to answer this question and to verify other key

---

[29] The other comparable period of rapid growth occurred between 1841 and 1845. J. P. Lewis, *Building Cycles and Britain's Growth* (London, 1965), appendix 8, p. 334.

aspects of the movement from Cardiganshire. Mention has already been made of the problems associated with the birthplace data in the Victorian censuses, and the data-gathering process revealed several anomalies in the birthplace data.[30] Those individuals patently not from Cardiganshire have been excluded from the study population.[31]

SOCIAL AND ECONOMIC INTEGRATION OF THE MIGRANTS

Indicators of cultural cohesion and change may be gained from many sources, all of which require careful interpretation.[32] In this instance, the data from the enumerators' books have been analysed to try to gauge the extent to which the Cardiganshire migrants were absorbed into the Welsh immigrant community, and their level of integration into the host society. The indicators used were areas of residence of the migrants, the nationalities of their spouses, the nationalities of their landlords and, for those apparently residing at their place of work, the nationalities of their employers.

The 1881 data revealed that although the migrants were to be found throughout the region, they were most numerous on Merseyside and to a much lesser extent around Manchester. In Lancashire 65 per cent of the migrants were living in Liverpool and its suburbs, with 20 per cent around Manchester. Although the migrant population in Cheshire was much more dispersed than that in Lancashire, almost 60 per cent were living on the Wirral, confirming the overwhelming popularity of Merseyside for Cardiganshire migrants.

The Welsh presence on Merseyside in the later nineteenth century was considerable, and although the Welsh were to

---

[30] For example, towns wrongly assigned to Cardiganshire, for example Swansea, and place-names misspelt, making identification impossible. A brief glance at the enumerators' books of other Welsh counties revealed similar geographical anomalies and errors. This has obvious implications for the accuracy of the statistics in the Victorian census birthplace tables.

[31] The search produced slightly fewer Cardiganshire natives than the number recorded in the census birthplace tables. The study population, however, was still large enough, at almost 90 per cent of the official volume, not to prejudice to any great extent the findings of the analysis.

[32] See, for example, Pooley, 'Residential segregation', 373–5.

be found throughout the area there were, as we have seen, certain localities that were identified as being particularly Welsh ones. The 1881 data were analysed to see how far Cardiganshire migrants on Merseyside tended to live in close proximity to one another, and also the extent to which they were drawn to Welsh residential areas. The data indicated a high level of residential clustering, and many favoured the distinctively Welsh areas. Central Liverpool alone accounted for almost one-fifth of the county's migrants in Lancashire, while a similar proportion of the migrants in Cheshire were living in Tranmere on the Wirral. Perhaps surprisingly, the top destinations in Lancashire and Cheshire for Welsh migrants – Everton and Birkenhead – ranked only second with the Cardiganshire migrants, confirming that particular county links existed within the Welsh immigrant community.[33]

The Cardiganshire Welsh community in the Manchester area in 1881 was far smaller and much more dispersed than that on Merseyside, but even so there is some evidence of residential clustering here too, notably at Chorlton on Medlock, Hulme and Broughton by Salford.[34]

The extent of residential clustering is not necessarily a definitive indicator of social segregation. The way in which the distribution of a migrant group is perceived by that group, and the ways in which it interacts are often as significant as the residential location of individuals, and a migrant community may remain culturally cohesive while being spatially integrated into the host community.[35] As we saw, this was demonstrably the case with the London Welsh community where we noted that it was chapel membership more than any other factor that bound the Welsh immigrant community together.

Another measure of the social segregation of a migrant group is the extent of intermarriage within that group. The

---

[33] Of the Welsh natives living in Cheshire in 1881, almost 30 per cent lived in Birkenhead urban sanitary district. *1881 Census. Vol. III.*, pp. 363–4.

[34] Incidentally, Chorlton on Medlock was the birthplace of the famous Welsh politican, David Lloyd George. For a breakdown of the residential distribution, see Cooper, 'Cardiganshire's rural exodus', 196–7, 203.

[35] Pooley, 'Welsh migration', 299; Pooley, 'Residential segregation', 374.

1881 data have been analysed to see what proportion of the Cardiganshire migrants, where both spouses were listed, had Welsh partners. It was immediately apparent that the marital trends differed between male and female as well as within the Lancashire and Cheshire groups. Overall, 65 per cent of male migrants had Welsh wives, while only 52 per cent of female migrants had Welsh husbands. Roughly a quarter of the migrants had Cardiganshire-born partners, and some migrants would have arrived in the north-west with partners whom they had met at a previous destination. In Cheshire 60 per cent of male migrants had Welsh wives while only 34 per cent of female migrants had Welsh husbands, and fewer of these migrants than those in Lancashire had Cardiganshire-born partners, but of course the Welsh community in Cheshire was much smaller than that in Lancashire, thus limiting the pool of available Welsh partners. Moreover, Welsh females in both counties in the later nineteenth century consistently outnumbered Welsh males, so that marriage outside the Welsh community was inevitable for a proportion of Welsh females despite any cultural preferences they may have had.[36] The 1881 data seem to confirm the preference of Cardiganshire male migrants in the north-west to marry within the Welsh community, although they obviously had a wider choice of Welsh partners. Even so, 35 per cent of them had non-Welsh wives, and this indicates a move towards social integration. As regards the female migrants, the fact that they were almost as likely to marry outside the Welsh community as within it inevitably led to a more rapid and far greater degree of assimilation within the host community.

The composition of households taking in lodgers can be an indication of the extent to which a migrant group is prepared to live with other nationalities. The 1881 census data revealed some surprising results. For a region with such a large Welsh population, it might be expected that the majority of Welsh migrants who took lodgings, and who were apparently keen to preserve their cultural identity, would have preferred to do so in Welsh households. This was not

[36] In 1881 the proportion was 58 per cent Welsh females to 42 per cent males in both counties taken together, and 60 per cent to 40 per cent in Cheshire alone. *1881 Census. Vol. III.*, p. 363.

the case with the study population, although availability of such lodgings would obviously have been a factor here. Cardiganshire migrants who boarded were almost evenly distributed between Welsh and non-Welsh households. This finding, however, agrees with a study that was made of the Welsh living in Liverpool in 1871, in which it was found that only half of Welsh-born lodgers in the sample were living in Welsh-headed households.[37]

Welsh migrants are generally acknowledged to have been well established in the employment structure of English towns by the Victorian era. As far as the 1881 study population is concerned, it was possible to test this theory only in those cases where the migrant resided with his or her employer. The number of males living with family firms that employed them was too small to be useful as an indicator, so the analysis covers only females in domestic service.[38] Here it was discovered that 86 per cent of domestic servants were employed in non-Welsh households and, as domestic service accounted for 77 per cent of all the employed females, this indicates a high degree of economic assimilation of unmarried females into the host community. It did not necessarily follow that Welsh-born employees in non-Welsh establishments had automatically abandoned their cultural identity, but inevitably their working lives ensured ever greater contact with English urban life, its traditions and society.

Studies of mid-Victorian Liverpool have demonstrated in the Welsh community a 'strong cultural coherence and a high degree of social segregation both from other migrants and, to a lesser extent, from the host population'. This lack of intermixing helped the Welsh community to preserve a strong sense of cultural identity during most of the nineteenth century.[39] The study population of Cardiganshire from the 1881 census certainly displayed a fair degree of

---

[37] This was an analysis of a 10 per cent sample of the enumerators' books. Pooley, 'Welsh migration', 301. For full details, see C. G. Pooley, 'Migration, mobility and residential areas in nineteenth-century Liverpool' (unpublished Ph.D. thesis, University of Liverpool, 1978).

[38] A few of these servants were not at their place of work on the night of the census and so are excluded from the calculation. Also excluded are females who apparently helped with domestic tasks in their own homes.

[39] Pooley, 'Residential segregation', 375–6, 379, 382.

residential and marital segregation. Yet there were signs of the move towards social absorption that was to culminate in the breakdown of the cultural cohesion of the Welsh community in the north-west by the early twentieth century.

AGE PROFILE OF THE MIGRANTS

Studies of the structure of Welsh households in Liverpool in 1871 have suggested that most of the migrants moved there either as single adults or as childless couples.[40] The ages of the Cardiganshire natives living in the north-west at the time of the 1881 census have been analysed to see if the profile revealed anything unusual (see figure 7.2). It was immediately apparent that the 15–44 age group was over-represented, accounting for almost 70 per cent of the migrant group at this date. Perhaps the most striking feature of the analysis, however, was the age distribution of the female migrants. In 1881 the sexes were almost evenly balanced at 638 males to 643 females, but the enumerators' manuscript data revealed that females were in the minority in all age groups except 0–14 years and 25–34 years. In this latter group they were significantly in excess. Reference to figure 7.1 confirms the massive increase in females in the Cardiganshire migrant population in the north-west that had taken place over the previous decade. It would seem that it was young adults who largely accounted for this dramatic rise. The employment opportunities drawing females to this region will be considered later. The fact that males had considerably outnumbered females until the 1870s probably accounts for the under-representation of females in the over-35 age groups in 1881. At the other end of the spectrum, the low proportion of children aged 14 or under is noticeable, and suggests that the majority of migrants were arriving either as single adults or as childless couples, which in turn confirms the findings of the 1871 study mentioned above.

[40] Pooley, 'Welsh migration', 296.

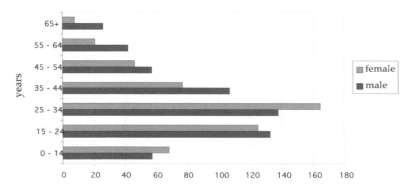

Figure 7.2 Age profile of the Cardiganshire migrants living in the north-west in 1881
Source: Population census, 1881.

MIGRATORY PATTERNS

The use of birthplace tables from the Victorian census to analyse migratory trends is seriously limited by the fact that they give only the position on a given day once a decade. However, as we have seen, vital clues to intervening moves may be gained from family birthplace data recorded in the enumerators' books, and these often reveal a range of migratory patterns. It appears that the shift of the Victorian population from countryside to town was more complex than many scholars had previously presumed and was achieved through a 'complex series of intermediate moves' that could include return migration and circulatory moves.[41] Some birthplace data reveal high rates of family mobility over long distances. For example, each member of the Jones family, living in Bolton Road, Westhoughton, in 1881, had a different birthplace, representing a minimum of six moves in the previous thirteen years. One of the moves, during which Evan was born, was a temporary, but apparently short-lived return to Cardiganshire. Perhaps John worked at the lead mines during this period.

[41] C. G. Pooley and J. Turnbull, 'Migration and urbanization in north-west England: a reassessment of the role of towns in the migration process', in D. J. Siddle (ed.), *Migration, Mobility and Modernization* (Liverpool, 2000), pp. 186–7.

The Jones family of Bolton Road, Westhoughton, Lancashire, 1881

Name	Age	Relationship	Occupation	Birthplace
John Jones	33	head	coal miner	**Aberystwyth, Cards**
Mary	35	wife		Wigan, Lancs
John	13	son	scholar	Llandovery, Carms
Evan	12	son	scholar	**Goginan, Cards**
Emma	10	daughter	scholar	Dent Head, Yorks
Alfred	7	son	scholar	Farnworth, Lancs
Alice	5	daughter	scholar	Westhoughton, Lancs
William	1	son		Mossley, Lancs

Source: Population census, 1881.
Note: Cardiganshire birthplaces are in bold script.

Traditional migration theory has assumed that rural-to-urban migration was a one-way, permanent movement, but it is now suggested that many migrants often engaged in return migration.[42] John Jones of Westhoughton is just one example from the 1881 census, and another is Josiah Rees, who was living in Newton in Makerfield in 1891.

The Rees family of Lawrence Street, Newton in Makerfield, Lancashire, 1891

Name	Age	Relationship	Occupation	Birthplace
Josiah Rees	39	head	wagon maker	**Llanon, Cards**
Elizabeth	43	wife		**New Quay, Cards**
Ann	15	daughter		Swansea, Glam
David	13	son		Earlstown, Lancs
Margaret	11	daughter		**Llanon, Cards**

Source: Population census, 1891.

Birthplace data further revealed individuals living in Lancashire in 1881 who were not Cardiganshire natives but who had at some point lived there. Although there is no way of knowing what was drawing these people to Cardiganshire in the 1860s and early 1870s, this was a time when the county's economy was reasonably buoyant, lead mining was flourishing and the railway network was beginning to make the county more readily accessible. Unfortunately, as we have seen, the crisis in the lead-mining industry from the later

[42] See, for example, Pooley, 'Welsh migration', 287–306; Pooley and Turnbull, 'Migration and urbanization', pp. 186–7.

1870s dealt a serious blow to the county's economy, and these families became just part of the dramatic exodus from the county. Sigificantly, many had made several long-distance moves by the time they reached Lancashire, confirming that geographical propinquity was by no means the only deciding factor in a migrant's choice of destination. One such was the Milward family, living in West Derby in 1881.

The Milward family of Agnes Street, West Derby, Liverpool, 1881

Name	Age	Relationship	Occupation	Birthplace
William Milward	42	head	engine fitter	Bristol, Glos
Amelia	42	wife		Monmouthshire
William J.	15	son	apprentice plumber	Battersea, Surrey
Alicia	13	daughter	scholar	Monmouthshire
John	8	son	scholar	**Aberystwyth, Cards**
Lilly	3	daughter		Pembroke Dock, Pembs

Source: Population census, 1881.

The enumerators' schedules also furnish evidence of return emigration. The character of emigration from Europe changed with the introduction, from the 1860s, of steamships on Atlantic crossings. Transit times and fares were drastically reduced, and with these innovations came the shift from mainly family emigration to individual emigration that also included many temporary migrants looking for short-term financial gain.[43] It was interesting, therefore, to find an example of short-term family emigration in this period.

The Nelson family of Lamb Street, Kirkdale, Liverpool, 1881

Name	Age	Relationship	Occupation	Birthplace
William Nelson	36	head	shipsmith	**Aberystwyth, Cards**
Mary	37	wife		Birmingham, Warks
Charlotte	12	daughter	scholar	**Aberystwyth, Cards**
Thomas	10	son	scholar	Luzerne County, USA[44]
Edith	5	daughter	scholar	Liverpool, Lancs
Albert	2 mths	son		Liverpool, Lancs

Source: Population census, 1881.

[43] D. Baines, *Migration in a Mature Economy* (Cambridge, 1985), pp. 128, 194–5.
[44] Pennsylvania.

FEMALE MIGRANT OCCUPATIONS

The rapid economic growth in north-western England from the late eighteenth century reflected the emergence of Lancashire's textile manufacturing area as 'one of the first specialist industrial regions of modern times'.[45] Demographers have concluded that the net inflow of migrants into the textile towns of Lancashire and Cheshire was predominantly of women, and the main attraction was employment in the textile mills.[46] It might be reasonable to assume, therefore, that the employment opportunities that were drawing such numbers of females to that area from Cardiganshire in the later nineteenth century would be those provided by the textile industry. Analysis of the 1881 study population revealed that this was not the case. Only 1.6 per cent of females in the group aged 15 or over worked in textile mills. Over half (55.4 per cent) were wives, widows or were of independent means, and had no listed occupation.[47] The major form of employment was domestic service, which accounted for 77 per cent of occupied females in the group, while the remainder were dressmakers, milliners, hospital nurses, shop assistants and a barmaid.

Throughout the nineteenth century, domestic service constituted the largest single occupational class for women in England and Wales; but in the final decades of the century employment opportunities were beginning to widen. The tasks associated with many of the newer jobs, such as factory, clerical and shop work, were often as monotonous as those of a domestic servant, but the women employed in them had more free time, they were not so socially isolated and so their marriage prospects were immeasurably greater than those of the domestic servants.[48]

---

[45] R. Lawton, 'Regional population trends in England and Wales, 1750–1971', in J. Hobcraft and P. Rees (eds), *Regional Demographic Development* (London, 1977), pp. 37–8.

[46] G. R. Boyer and T. J. Hatton, 'Migration and labour market integration in late nineteenth-century England and Wales', *Economic History Review*, new series, 50 (1997), 706.

[47] As noted above, female employment was notoriously under-recorded in the Victorian censuses. For more on this, see E. Higgs, *Making Sense of the Census: the Manuscript Returns for England and Wales, 1801–1901* (2nd edn, London, 1991), pp. 81–2.

[48] Ibid., p. 82; M. Ebery and B. Preston, *Domestic Service in Late Victorian and*

Entering domestic service as a young teenager had long been the usual expectation of girls from farming, artisan and labouring backgrounds, and the rapid commercial expansion of Victorian Britain and the growth of the middle classes were accompanied by a rise in demand for domestic servants. Rural women, such as the migrants from Cardiganshire, were generally regarded as the best servants. They were usually hard working and more willing to accept their position of social subordination than were their urban counterparts, who were less tolerant of the irksome restrictions and long working hours of service and had more knowledge of the improving opportunities for women in the urban labour market.[49]

Sometimes valued equally as status symbols as for their practical value, domestic servants have been described as part of the middle-class 'paraphernalia of gentility'. Studies have shown, however, that the employment of servants was not necessarily indicative of upper- or middle-class status. There were many working-class households that combined trade or commercial with living premises and where girls were employed to perform both domestic and trade tasks.[50] Undoubtedly, however, the middle-class one-servant household was by far the most widespread.[51] Certainly, within the 1881 study population, this category accounted for more than half of those in domestic service.

Lancashire was one of Victorian England's major growth regions.[52] We have already noted the effects of this growth in terms of house building in Liverpool, and the numerous adverts in contemporary newspapers such as the *Liverpool Daily Post* demonstrate the knock-on effect of this urban growth on the demand for domestic help.[53] More than this,

Edwardian England, 1871–1914 (Reading, 1976), pp. 102–3; G. P. Landow, 'The "mute and forgotten" occupation', *http://victorianweb.org/history/work/burnett3.html*

[49] E. Higgs, 'Domestic servants and households in Victorian England', *Social History*, 8 (1983), 208; Ebery and Preston, *Domestic Service*, p. 85; Hey, *Oxford Companion*, p. 137.

[50] Higgs, 'Domestic servants', 205.

[51] Hey, *Oxford Companion*, p. 137.

[52] Lawton, 'Regional population trends', 47.

[53] Recruitment of servants at this time was through adverts, recruitment agencies and by word of mouth. Ebery and Preston, *Domestic Service*, p. 85.

the adverts reveal some interesting attitudes among prospective employers. For instance, the preference of country girls
over town girls, and of English and Welsh girls over those of
other nationalities, is apparent. The following are typical of
such adverts:

> Wanted, a good General Servant. One from the country preferred.
> Wanted. General Servant, a clean tidy Young Girl of good character,
> aged about 16 or 18. English or Welsh.[54]

Religious affiliation was also sometimes specified:

> Wanted, an active trustworthy English Woman (a Roman Catholic)
> aged not more than 40, to live at a Grocery Establishment and do what
> is required in the house.
> Wanted, a respectable Girl (Protestant, and aged about 18) . . .
> Wanted immediately, a good Plain Cook in a gentleman's family . . .
> (English Churchwoman).[55]

Inevitably, the pool of potential domestic labour from the
country began to shrink as rural depopulation took its toll,
and certainly a decline in numbers of female migrants leaving
Cardiganshire for the north-west is apparent from 1891.
Moreover, life in domestic service was becoming increasingly
unpopular as employment prospects for women opened up
and personal expectations increased. As one commentator
remarked in the 1890s:

> it is quite evident that after a girl has had several years of intelligent
> schooling she will not be content to earn a livelihood by carting
> manure and hoeing turnips. She would rather be a domestic servant;
> though again, the domestic servant would rather be a dress-maker or
> a post-office clerk. Ambition has, as it were, fired the entire order of
> women compelled to work for a livelihood.[56]

MALE MIGRANT OCCUPATIONS

The occupations of Cardiganshire's male migrants in the
north-west in 1881 ranged from those of rag-gatherer to

---

[54] *Liverpool Daily Post*, 3 May 1871, 3, column 3.
[55] *Liverpool Daily Post*, 2 May 1871, 3, column 3; *Liverpool Daily Post*, 3 May 1871,
3, column 3.
[56] P. A. Graham, *The Rural Exodus* (London, 1892), p. 23.

surgeon. Despite this apparent diversity, the group was highly under-represented in both the professional and the unskilled classes and over-represented in the skilled manual group, especially in the building trade. These socio-economic characteristics were, in fact, typical of the Welsh community as a whole in the north-west at this time.[57] The majority of the employed males in the group were skilled or semi-skilled artisans or served in shops, while the professional classes were mostly represented by those in clerical positions. Integration of Cardiganshire's migrants into the employment structure was apparent: almost 95 per cent of all males aged 15 or over were employed, and only one individual was in receipt of poor relief.

It is particularly instructive to compare the occupational structure of this group with that of Cardiganshire's migrants in the London sample. Here again, the most common male occupation was that of carpenter/joiner, accounting for over one-fifth of the employed male migrants in the north-west. With the rapid expansion of urban Victorian England, the demand for craftsmen and labour in the building trade soared and, as we have seen, Cardiganshire's strong wood-working tradition meant that its carpenters and joiners were well placed to take advantage of the demand for their skills, particularly when employment opportunities at home were dwindling. On Merseyside, the Welsh dominated the house-building scene and tended to recruit both skilled and unskilled labour from home.[58] This was largely done through chapel networks and family contacts, as the following reminiscences, one from a Manchester family and the other from Liverpool, illustrate:

> It was like this . . . He had his own company, . . . and he knew of other builders and he could help if, say, a boy came from Wales, if he went to the chapel . . . there would be someone in that chapel who could help him to get on . . . to get work.[59]

---

[57] Pooley, 'Welsh migration', 296; C. G. Pooley and J. C. Doherty, 'The longitudinal study of migration: Welsh migration to English towns in the nineteenth century', in C. G. Pooley and I. D. Whyte (eds), *Migrants, Emigrants and Immigrants* (London, 1991), p. 152.

[58] Jones, 'Welsh immigrants', 35.

[59] Ibid., 37.

There were many builders in this town . . . [and] carpenters from Wales, . . . they gave them [newcomers from Wales] work . . . Someone would say, 'Oh my brother wants to come to Liverpool to improve himself', and so he would come.[60]

Welsh builders have made a significant contribution to the townscape of Victorian Merseyside. While English builders concentrated on commercial properties their Welsh counterparts dominated the house-building scene, evolving and specializing in the ubiquitous rows of terraced houses.[61]

Not infrequently, a carpenter or joiner subsequently became a builder in his own right. One such was Daniel Daniel who was born in Llangranog (southern coastal Cardiganshire) in 1834. Daniel moved to Birmingham in about 1854 where he worked as a joiner; by 1860 he was living and working in Liverpool, where 'by frugality and hard work he built a couple of houses in Upper Warwick Street; all the woodwork was done by him . . . at the rear of his house'. Daniel continued to build, in a modest way, in the Toxteth area, including houses in Amberley Street, where he is recorded living in the 1881. Here he is listed as a builder employing one boy.[62]

Another even more enterprising joiner from Cardiganshire was John Davies. He was born in New Quay in 1857 and his family moved to Kirkdale when he was a child. By the time of the 1881 census he was living in Park Hill Road, Toxteth, and he is listed as a joiner. Shortly after this, John emigrated to South Africa where he worked for about ten years as 'superintendent of joinery works in the gold mines'. Returning to Merseyside, possibly because of heightened political tensions that finally led to the Second Boer War, John lived and worked for the remainder of his life in Birkenhead.[63]

---

[60] Ibid., 35.
[61] J. R. Jones, *The Welsh Builder on Merseyside* (Liverpool, 1946), pp. 9–11. The Welsh house builders were first active in Bootle, Everton, Parliament Fields and Princes Road, and later in Litherland, Linacre, Crosby, Waterloo, Walton, Anfield, Fazakerley, Cabbage Hall, Wavertree, Smithdown Road, and finally their influence extended to Dingle, Aigburgh, Kensington, Childwall and Calderstones.
[62] Jones, *Welsh Builder*, p. 23; 1881 Census Enumerators' schedules.
[63] Jones, *Welsh Builder*, p. 26; 1881 Census Enumerators' schedules.

A further example of a carpenter turned builder was Evan Morgan. He left his native Llanarth in 1872 aged about 22, and he may have been recruited by a fellow Welshman. In the 1881 census he is listed as a house carpenter, lodging at Hamilton Road, West Derby, with Sylvanus Lloyd, also a house carpenter from Llanarth. This was an all-Welsh household; Sylvanus's wife, Margaret, was from Meifod (Montgom.), and there was another lodger, Owen Jones, born Carmarthenshire, also a house carpenter. It is possible that these two lodgers worked for the household head. Evan, however, had greater ambitions. He eventually became a builder, constructing both houses and shops in Anfield and Dingle.[64]

The second ranked occupation among the male migrants in 1881 was that of mariner, which accounted for almost 17 per cent of employed males. Unfortunately, this class of persons in the census is problematic from the point of view of migration studies. The first stage in the census process was the distribution of schedules for the recording by the household head of the details of all those in the household on the night of the census. Inevitably, there was a proportion of the population that was not present in 'normal' households on this night and so special arrangements for their enumeration had to be made.[65] With regard to the merchant marine, all crew members and passengers who were on board ship on census night were 'included among the general population of the Districts, Sub-districts and Parishes contiguous to the waters in which the vessels were lying' either in harbour on census night, or where they next docked.[66] Although the ships' crews and passengers who made up this 'floating population' could not be classed as normal residents of the places in which they were enumerated, they were very much a feature of ports and docklands and their exclusion from the statistics would have given a distorted picture of the population, society and economy of such places as London and Liverpool.[67] However, these 'special returns', which also

[64] Jones, *Welsh Builder*, p. 90; 1881 Census Enumerators' schedules.
[65] For more on this, see Higgs, *Making Sense*, pp. 37–46.
[66] *Census of England and Wales. 1881. Population. Vol. II* (London, 1883), p. 491.
[67] Higgs, *Making Sense*, p. 40.

covered inmates of institutions, the army and navy, and itin-erant and night workers, have implications for migration statistics based on birthplace data in the censuses.

Of the 79 Cardiganshire-born mariners in the 1881 migrant group, only 35 were living ashore on the night of the census. This obviously raises the issue of where the mariners on board ship actually belonged geographically. Did they live in the north-west or were they just on a trading visit? As the size of ships increased with the transition from sail to steam, and railway transportation began to erode coastal trade, activity at the numerous small ports along Cardigan Bay decreased, and the major ports of England and Wales became a magnet for displaced mariners. The strong commercial links between Cardiganshire and Merseyside made it an obvious choice for the county's mariners, and many seafaring families are known to have moved there. Nevertheless, it is impossible to tell from the census where the Cardiganshire-born mari-ners who were enumerated on board ship and included in the Lancashire and Cheshire returns in 1881 actually lived, and this obviously has ramifications for the statistics of Cardiganshire migrants in the north-west.

Retail outlets employing the Cardiganshire migrants included grocery, chemist and drapery shops. Those in the latter employment formed by far the largest group in this category, accounting for almost 8 per cent of the employed males, and thus were the third most common male occupa-tion in the study population in the north-west as well as in the census sample in London. In the north-west migrant group 26 of the 37 drapers or draper's assistants lived in Liverpool, and again many of them lived in hostels. Coincidentally, Liverpool was where Owen Owen, linen-draper and founder of the department store group, made his fortune. Owen Owen came from farming stock and was born in 1847 in the Llyfnant Valley on the border between Cardiganshire and Montgomeryshire.[68] His rise to financial success began in 1868 with the opening, on Liverpool's London Road, of his first shop. By the early twentieth century Owen Owen had become a limited company and Liverpool's London Road

[68] D. W. Davies, *Owen Owen: Victorian Draper* (Aberystwyth, 1984), p. 3.

store was one of the largest department stores in the north of England.[69] With a reputation gained by Welsh employers in urban England for giving preference to their countrymen, it is tempting to surmise that some of the Cardiganshire-born drapers would have been employed in Owen Owen's London Road store.

During most of the nineteenth century, migration to urban England did not entail a culture change for the Welsh. Like other migrant groups, they formed supportive communities that recruited from home with offers of work and housing. The traditions of Welsh rural society were sustained in an urban context through the network of chapels, Sunday schools and other organizations that provided a focus for the Welsh community; and their cultural identity was preserved by regular contact with their rural origins. Chapel, both at home and in the emigrant community, and the maintenance of family ties were vital elements in the migration networks. As the century drew to a close, however, the movement from Wales to the north-west was slowing down, and without the reinforcement of frequent new arrivals the Welsh emigrant community began to lose its cultural coherence.[70] Analysis of the census data confirms that the move towards social integration into the host society was already discernible in the Cardiganshire migrant community by 1881.

Rural Welsh migrants to England in the nineteenth century appear to have had little trouble adjusting to an urban labour market, and analysis of the 1881 census data supports previous findings that Welsh migrants to the north-west were well integrated into the employment structure of the region. A major factor in the rapid urbanization of Victorian Britain and the large-scale rural exodus was the move towards industrialization and mass production. In the second half of the century, however, the building, transport and service sectors were growing more rapidly than the manufacturing industries.[71] This economic trend is reflected in the Cardiganshire migration to the north-west both in the

---

[69] Ibid., pp. 93, 95.
[70] Pooley, 'Welsh migration', 301–2; Jones, 'Liverpool Welsh', pp. 35–6.
[71] Lawton, 'Regional population trends', 46–7.

sharp increase in their numbers and in their employment in the building trade, retail outlets and domestic service rather than in the textile mills that dominated north-western England at this time.

VIII

EMIGRATION

No study of nineteenth-century rural out-migration would be complete without some mention of emigration. As we have seen, many of Cardiganshire's migrants left not only their county of birth but also their homeland, settling in significant numbers in urban England, particularly in London and on Merseyside. Yet others ventured even further afield. This chapter will examine emigration from Cardiganshire during the nineteenth century, and it will concentrate on the first half of the century because for Cardiganshire, as for Britain as a whole, more information is currently available for that period.[1]

SOURCES AND PROBLEMS

There are no accurate statistics about the numbers who emigrated from Cardiganshire, or indeed from Wales, during the nineteenth century. However, at least ten million people are thought to have left Britain for overseas destinations during the hundred years following the end of the Napoleonic Wars in 1815.[2] By mid-century it was noted that emigration had 'proceeded since 1750 to such an extent, as to people large states in America'.[3]

Unfortunately, there is no data that show the county of birth of these emigrants, and British statistics did not distinguish Welsh from English emigrants until 1908, although emigrants from Scotland and Ireland were recorded separately.[4] The only exception to this is the complete emigration

---

[1] D. Baines, *Migration in a Mature Economy* (Cambridge, 1985), p. 3.
[2] Ibid., p. 9.
[3] *Census of Great Britain, 1851. Population Tables. 1. Numbers of the Inhabitants, Vol. I* ([1852] 2nd edn, Shannon, 1970), p. lxxxii.
[4] D. Williams, 'Some figures relating to emigration from Wales', *Bulletin of the*

return, by county, for England and Wales for the first half of 1841.[5] Nineteenth-century port records of emigration from England and Wales add little to our current knowledge as many are lost, and those that survive are often incomplete and scattered among a variety of archives, or give only very generalized information.[6] Nor can the American ship lists clarify the situation about precise geographical origins of immigrants. Although some captains recorded the immigrant's last city or country of residence, which was not necessarily their place of birth, most did not.[7] In the absence of quantitative data, therefore, a method has been evolved for estimating the county of birth of all Welsh and English emigrants by using the registrar general's reports of births and deaths together with the county-of-birth statistics from the census; however, as the birthplace data were recorded in the census only from 1851 onwards, the calculations can be made only for the second half of the century.[8]

Thus, studies of available passenger lists together with the post-1851 censuses can reveal much about the scale, demography and occupational structure of later nineteenth-century English and Welsh emigration, but only in a general way.[9] Compared with the official records on emigration for many European countries, those for England and Wales reveal little detail about the migrants' backgrounds or motivations.[10] Some insight into the motives of individual emigrants can

---

Board of Celtic Studies, 7 (1935), 397–8. For more on problems concerning the accuracy of the data after 1908, see ibid., 398–400.

[5] This was part of the census taken in June 1841.

[6] A. K.Knowles, *Calvinists Incorporated* (London, 1997), p. 5; Baines, *Migration*, p. 3; R. Kershaw, *Emigrants and Expats: A Guide to Sources on U.K. Emigration and Residence Overseas* (Richmond, 2002), p. 9.

[7] W. van Vugt, 'Welsh emigration to the U.S.A. during the mid-nineteenth century', *Welsh History Review*, 15 (1990–1), 546. For more on American ship lists see C. Erickson, 'Emigration from the British Isles to the U.S.A. in 1831', *Population Studies*, 35 (1981), 175–97. The most comprehensive printed source for North American immigration data is to be found in P. Filby and M. Meyer, *Passenger and Immigration Lists Index*, 3 vols with annual supplements to 2000 (Detroit, 1981). Unfortunately for the purposes of this study, the index does not give the immigrant's point of departure, although, of course, this was not necessarily their birthplace or their place of residence immediately prior to emigration.

[8] Baines, *Migration*, p. 5.

[9] Knowles, *Calvinists Incorporated*, p. 13

[10] van Vugt, 'Welsh emigration', 546.

be gained through the letters that passed between them and their original homes, but the number of surviving letters is very small in comparison with the volume of emigration; and without a clearer picture of the groups who were emigrating and the communities from which they left, conclusions about the 'long- and short-term causes of the movement must remain largely conjectural'.[11]

Some indication of the movement overseas from Wales during the earlier part of the nineteenth century, and of the socio-economic structure and motivations of the emigrants, can be gained from contemporary letters, newspapers and periodicals, and from the literature produced for intending emigrants.[12] A further source that has been the subject of a recent study is the collection of obituaries of Welsh immigrants into the United States. By the late 1830s there were sufficient numbers of Welsh settlers in that country to support a Welsh-language press based in New York. Early publications took the form of Nonconformist monthly periodicals, and a fifteen-year run of obituaries, from 1838 to 1853, has been analysed and the information that these contain effectively spans the period of Welsh emigration to the United States from the beginnings of its modern phase in the 1790s to the middle of the nineteenth century.[13] As with any historical source, information from these obituaries is subject to inaccuracies and omissions. In addition, they represent only emigration from Welsh-speaking regions of Wales to communities in the United States that had retained their cultural identity and religious affiliations.[14] Fortunately for the purposes of this book, rural Cardiganshire was one of those Welsh-speaking, Nonconformist sending areas whose emigrants tended to cluster together in particular settlements, and the obituaries can, therefore, provide details of the social and geographical origins of a fair proportion of the county's emigrants, and shed some light on the context in which they made the decision to move.

---

[11] D. Baines, *Emigration from Europe, 1815–1930* (London, 1991), p. 15; Erickson, 'Emigration', 175.

[12] Williams, 'Some figures', 397; B. Owen, 'Ymfudo o Sir Aberteifi (Emigration from Cardiganshire), 1654–1860, III. 1795–1860', *Ceredigion*, 2 (1952–5), 169.

[13] For more on this see Knowles, *Calvinists Incorporated*, pp.10–13.

[14] Ibid., p. 25.

BACKGROUND TO NINETEENTH-CENTURY EMIGRATION

The great age of passenger travel at sea came during the later nineteenth and early twentieth centuries when the combination of goods and mail transportation, emigration and tourism fuelled the rise of the famous shipping lines such as Cunard, P & O and the White Star Line. In the days of sailing ships, the typical transatlantic crossing time from Britain was between four and seven weeks, although this could be longer in adverse weather conditions.[15] From the 1860s, steamships began to replace sail on transatlantic routes, and this reduced the crossing time to as little as eight days.[16] This drastic reduction paved the way for a change in the character of emigration from Europe: the transition from mainly family emigration, where the intention was to settle permanently, to individual emigration that included many temporary migrants who were looking for short-term financial gain.[17] Indeed, it is thought that, for the half-century ending with the First World War, inward passenger movement to Britain contained about 40 per cent of outward emigrants returning home.[18]

Between forty-four and fifty-two million emigrants are recorded as having left Europe for overseas destinations during the period from 1815 to 1914.[19] Although there were large fluctuations in the timing and volume of the exodus from the various regions, the rate of emigration was greater in the 1880s from every northern and western European country with a history of emigration.[20] This emigration peak also applied to England and Wales.[21] This timing has, in the

---

[15] van Vugt, 'Welsh emigration', 556.

[16] Steamships also cut the passage to Australia from between ten and seventeen weeks to about four to six weeks. Kershaw, *Emigrants*, p. 8.

[17] *Third Report from the Select Committee on Emigration from the United Kingdom: 1827* ([1827], 2nd edn, Shannon, 1968), p. 226; Baines, *Migration*, p. 195; Erickson, 'Emigration', 176.

[18] Baines, *Migration*, p. 128. Alien inward passengers were first distinguished from British passengers after 1876.

[19] Ibid., p. 1.

[20] Ibid., pp. 9, 179.

[21] Ibid., p. 180; W. A. Armstrong, 'The flight from the land', in G. E. Mingay (ed.), *The Victorian Countryside* (London, 1981), p. 130. However, as noted in chapter IV, emigration from Cardiganshire may well have peaked by 1850.

past, been linked to the agricultural depression.[22] However, the majority of these emigrants have now been shown to have come from urban areas, and it has been suggested that the major economic impetus was the rapid expansion experienced during this decade by the United States and, to a lesser extent, by Australia and Argentina.[23]

The most striking characteristic of nineteenth-century European emigration was its diversity. There were emigrants from every European country, and they included people from virtually all occupations and social classes. However, not only did the intensity of emigration vary greatly from place to place, but it varied within the same region, and this variation suggests that the decision to emigrate was not dependent solely on social and economic factors.[24] Emigration is a personal choice, and it is thought that the most important single influence on both the decision to move and the choice of destination was the 'flow of information'.[25] Emigration involved many uncertainties, so that it is reasonable to suppose that information, both from letters, as in figure 8.1, and from returned emigrants, and the maintenance of a bond between the immigrant settlement and the home community could increase the tendency for emigration from a particular locality, thereby accounting for the variation in emigration patterns within regions of broadly similar social and economic conditions.[26] This process, as will be demonstrated below, can be seen at work in rural Cardiganshire.

Funding and promotion

Nineteenth-century emigration was actively promoted by governments, shipping lines, railways, land companies,

---

[22] Baines, *Migration*, p. 178.

[23] Erickson, 'Emigration', 176; Baines, *Migration*, pp. 178–9, 205–6; Armstrong, 'Flight from the land', p. 130.

[24] Baines, *Migration*, pp. 9, 141; Knowles, *Calvinists Incorporated*, p. 13; W. D. Jones, *Wales in America: Scranton and the Welsh, 1860–1920* (Cardiff, 1991), p. xix.

[25] Baines, *Migration*, p. 23; J. D. Gould, 'European inter-continental emigration, 1815–1914: patterns and causes', *Journal of European Economic History*, 8 (1979), 660.

[26] Figure 8.1 shows a letter from my great-grandfather's brother who emigrated to Illinois from Pembrokeshire in 1864. A copy can be seen at NLW, Williams and Williams 26222, letter from George Drinkwater.

Chicago Oct 9 1879
Illinois

My Dear Nephew
              I feel obliged to you
for sending me a cateloge of what
is to be sold from my poor Brothers
farm. I perceive he has farmed very
different from what he used to do.
He used to keep about ten horses
and sow more grain. I suppose he
found raising stock paid him better.
I am of your opinion that the rent
the new parties are going to pay
they will not make much out of it.
There is a great deal of poor land on the
farm unless it is greatly improved
since I left. I see by the papers
that the crops are much damaged in
England and Wales. It is so much the
better for this country. The crops
hear are exceedly good. We have had
beautiful weather for saving them.
Business in general is much improved.
Can scarcely get Vessels and cars [railway wagons] to
take the grain from hear. We have
only got till about the middle of
November when navigation will close.
After that it will be dangerous to
ship on the lakes. Our lakes are
large hear. We live at the head of Lake
Michigan. It extends North of us
five hundred miles. In the winter
the railroads have all their own way
when they charge higher rates.
My Family all join in love
to you and yours. I remain
your affectionate

           Uncle G Drinkwater

Figure 8.1 Transcript of George Drinkwater's letter of 9 October 1879
Note: The original contains no punctuation; this has been added here, but the original format and spelling have been preserved.

emigration societies, trade unions, friendly societies and private individuals. Nevertheless, the great majority of emigrants paid their own fares, although they were sometimes assisted by friends or relatives. In the early decades of the century, emigration was perceived by some countries, including Britain, as a useful way of relieving poverty and removing undesirables. Government funding in Britain, however, was mostly directed towards populating the colonies, although assisted passages to Australia and New Zealand were offered only when the economy was buoyant. By mid-century the volume of emigration from most western European countries made government emigration schemes no longer necessary.[27]

EMIGRATION FROM CARDIGANSHIRE

Pre-1815
The fragmentary nature of the statistical evidence for nine-teenth-century emigration from Britain inevitably applies to Cardiganshire. However, some indication of the scale of emigration from Cardiganshire in the first half of the century can be gained from other sources. One commentator has estimated that more than 5,000 emigrants left Cardiganshire for North America between 1794 and 1860.[28] Unfortunately, his sources are not identified beyond the generalized comment, 'based on information derived from original letters, documents, newspapers, and periodicals'; the estimate is, therefore, unverifiable.[29] Cardiganshire's local newspapers can throw no light on early emigration from the county as publication did not begin until the later nineteenth century.[30] However, the relative abundance of

[27] Baines, *Emigration*, pp. 53, 71–2.

[28] This was the main destination for Cardiganshire's emigrants. Only a handful of Cardiganshire people joined the Welsh settlers in Patagonia whose aim was to establish an independent, Welsh-speaking, Nonconformist community.

[29] Owen, 'Ymfudo (emigration)', 166–9. The author stresses that these are only crude estimates. Owen's vast collections of notes, newspaper cuttings etc. on emigration from Cardiganshire are now deposited in several unsorted boxes in the National Library of Wales, but they are mostly of little use because of the lack of a provenance for most of his material. On this, see also P. Thomas, *Strangers from a Secret Land* (Llandysul, 1986), p. 10.

[30] The holdings at the National Library of Wales, Aberystwyth, for the county's

other source material for the first half of the century means that it is possible to gain some idea of geographic and social origins, although the motivations of the emigrants remain elusive.

The 1790s are known to have marked the beginning of the modern emigration movement from Wales.[31] For British ships trading with North America at this time passengers were a costly extra; emigrants generally travelled cabin class because steerage passage was unavailable. Moreover, transatlantic sailings from Welsh ports were rare, and Cardiganshire's emigrants would usually have travelled to Liverpool or Bristol and taken lodgings there while negotiating for, and awaiting, a passage. There was thus an inbuilt check on the flow of emigration, and it has been suggested that the typical Welsh emigrant of this era was a farmer or artisan of some means and education and with a knowledge of English.[32] These criteria placed emigration out of the reach of the majority of the rural population of west Wales. Contemporary travellers, such as Walter Davies and Benjamin Malkin, noted that Welsh was used 'almost without exception' in Cardiganshire at this time, and in Malkin's opinion there were many who were

> discontented with their dreary quarters and hard fare, and disposed to emigrate in quest of high wages, and . . . the comforts of life. But while they are isolated by a tongue of their own, they are tied down by a peculiar necessity to the place that gave them birth.[33]

Later eighteenth-century Wales had witnessed the beginnings of an awareness of a distinct cultural identity and an attendant revitalization of the Welsh language. This change, which has been mainly attributed to the Methodist revival, expressed itself in various ways such as a new output of literature, the founding of the *eisteddfod* in its modern form and the rise of a 'school of mighty pulpit orators' as

nineteenth-century newspapers are as follows: the *Aberystwyth Observer* from July 1869, the *Cambrian News* (Aberystwyth edition) from 1878, and the *Cardigan and Tivyside Advertiser* from 1884.

[31] Williams, 'Some figures', 396.

[32] Thomas, *Strangers*, pp. 42–3.

[33] Ibid., p. 34; B. H. Malkin, *The Scenery, Antiquities, and Biography of South Wales*, 2 vols (London, 1807), vol. 2, p. 28. Neighbouring Carmarthenshire and Pembrokeshire were also predominantly Welsh-speaking areas.

Nonconformism took a strong hold in Wales.[34] For the inhabitants of late eighteenth- and early nineteenth-century Nonconformist Wales, life in the New World seemed to promise not only an improvement in their economic and social conditions but also a chance for their religion, language and culture to flourish unhindered. In his assessment of the cultural isolation of monoglot Welsh communities, Malkin had greatly underestimated the potential of the channels of communication that were being established between dissenting Wales and the dissenting Welsh communities in North America.[35] It was most likely to have been lack of funds that kept many would-be emigrants at home at this time. A Welsh emigrant on a return visit to Newcastle Emlyn, on the Cardiganshire–Carmarthenshire border, wrote to a contact back in Philadelphia in 1801:

> I cannot describe to you the condition of our poor country, thousands of the poor move about the country begging for bread . . . Myriads would emigrate if they had money . . . I wish a method was devised to take them over, and let them work at the money after they got over.[36]

Unfortunately, we have no way of assessing the volume of the movement overseas from Cardiganshire at this time. In 1801 one of Cardiganshire's major landowners wrote: 'Vast emigrations are going to America from this county; we can but ill spare them.'[37] However, it seems likely that he exaggerated the scale of this exodus from what was, after all, a very sparsely populated county.

1815–1830

Transatlantic crossings in small sailing ships were made even more perilous at the beginning of the nineteenth century

---

[34] The London Welsh community was instrumental in the eisteddfod movement. E. Jones, 'The age of societies', in E. Jones (ed.), *The Welsh in London, 1500–2000* (Cardiff, 2001), p. 76. W. S. Shepperson, *British Emigration to North America* (Oxford, 1957), pp. 32–3; A. H. Dodd, *The Character of Early Welsh Emigration to the United States* (Cardiff, 1957), p. 20.

[35] For more on this, see G. A. Williams, *The Search for Beulah Land: The Welsh and the Atlantic Revolution* (London, 1980), pp. 126–33; Dodd, *Character of Early Welsh Emigration*, pp. 19–24.

[36] Williams, *Search for Beulah Land*, pp. 129–30.

[37] R. J. Moore-Colyer (ed.), *A Land of Pure Delight: Selections from the Letters of Thomas Johnes of Hafod, Cardiganshire (1748–1816)* (Llandysul, 1992), p. 155.

because of the wars with France and the sensitive relations between the United States and Britain. By 1815, however, the Atlantic was again reasonably safe for shipping, and this encouraged British merchants to consider exploiting the timber resources of British North America as an alternative to Baltic timber, which was subject to punitive duties. Moreover, the timber ships sailing to North America mostly carried slate ballast on the outward journey as there was little demand for imported goods in the sparsely populated Canadian colonies; thus the 'capacity for steerage passengers was enormous'.[38]

Not only were the cultural factors that impelled the Welsh emigrants from the 1790s still in place after Waterloo, but the calamitous social and economic conditions of the immediate post-war years provided further incentives. This was a time of 'unprecedented difficulty and distress' due to disastrous harvests, continuing enclosure of the commons and land hunger, all compounded by a population that was nevertheless rising steeply.[39] With the transatlantic timber trade operating out of many of the ports that dotted the Welsh coastline from Bangor to Carmarthen came a dramatic improvement in the opportunity for Welsh people to emigrate. Alongside the timber trade the commercial selling of emigration began on a large scale. Possibly the first advertisement for passage to North America from north Wales appeared in May 1816.[40] That from south Wales appeared in August 1817.[41] The first documented post-war departure of Cardiganshire emigrants seems to have been in April 1818 when the brig *Fanny* sailed from Carmarthen for Halifax, Nova Scotia, with 112 passengers from Carmarthenshire and Cardiganshire.[42] An advertisement for this voyage is reproduced in figure 8.2.

April 1819 saw the first post-war emigrant voyage leaving directly from Cardiganshire itself when the brig *Albion* sailed from Cardigan to St John, New Brunswick, with over

---

[38] Thomas, *Strangers*, pp. 66, 77.

[39] *Cambrian*, 25 June 1816, 2; the population of Cardiganshire rose by 17 per cent between 1801 and 1811 and by 15 per cent between 1811 and 1821.

[40] Bangor to Boston. Thomas, *Strangers*, p. 79.

[41] Carmarthen to Miramichi, New Brunswick, Canada. *Carmarthen Journal*, 8 August 1817, 3; Thomas, *Strangers*, p. 107.

[42] Thomas, *Strangers*, p. 108.

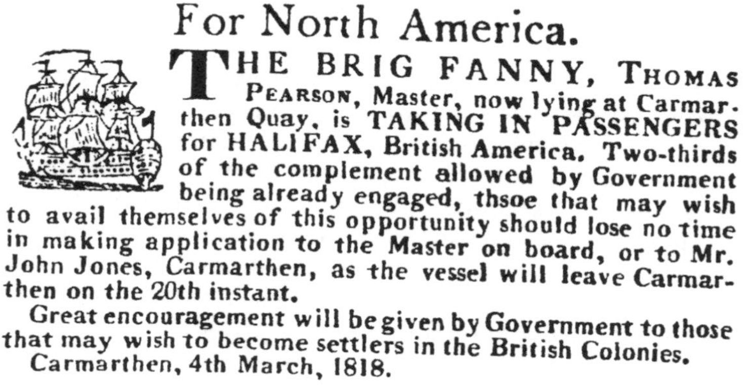

For North America.

THE BRIG FANNY, THOMAS PEARSON, Master, now lying at Carmar. then Quay, is TAKING IN PASSENGERS for HALIFAX, British America. Two-thirds of the complement allowed by Government being already engaged, thsoe that may wish to avail themselves of this opportunity should lose no time in making application to the Master on board, or to Mr. John Jones, Carmarthen, as the vessel will leave Carmarthen on the 20th instant.

Great encouragement will be given by Government to those that may wish to become settlers in the British Colonies. Carmarthen, 4th March, 1818.

Figure 8.2 Advertisement for emigration on the brig *Fanny*, 1818
Source: Carmarthen Journal, 6 March 1818, 3.

200 emigrants.[43] So began the long and prosperous timber trade between Cardiganshire and Canada in which the occasional conveying of emigrants, along with the ballast on the outward voyage, was an incidental but remunerative extra.[44] Documented emigrant sailings from Cardiganshire at this time include *The Fair Cambrian*, which arrived in St John barely two months after the *Albion*, in August 1819, with eighty-one emigrants, and the *Active*, which sailed for St John in April 1822, with seventy-two emigrants from Cardiganshire and Pembrokeshire on board. After this, the demand for emigrant berths from west Wales seems to have fallen off for about a decade.[45]

Early nineteenth-century Cardiganshire's timber ships traded out of Cardigan, in the south of the county, and it seems reasonable to suppose that this departure point would have favoured emigrants from the lower Teifi Valley.[46] This

[43] Ibid., p. 127.

[44] D. Jenkins, 'Shipping and shipbuilding', in G. H. Jenkins and I. G. Jones (eds), *Cardiganshire County History*, vol. 3, *Cardiganshire in Modern Times* (Cardiff, 1998), p. 188.

[45] Thomas, *Strangers*, pp. 23, 164 and 184.

[46] The timber trade from Aberystwyth started later in the century as Aberystwyth gradually eclipsed Cardigan as the county's major port, and the trade flourished well into the second half of the century. See NLW, Aberystwyth Borough Records, F11,

supposition is substantiated by those geographical origins that have been identified for emigrants on the 1819 voyage of the *Albion*: that is, Cardigan, Llangoedmore and Llanrhystud (Cardiganshire); St Dogmaels, Clydey, Cilrhedyn and Newport (Pembrokeshire); and Newcastle Emlyn, Trelech a'r Betws and Blaenywaun (Carmarthenshire).[47] Although the available evidence suggests that emigration from Cardiganshire in the early nineteenth century was mainly from the south of the county, it would certainly have been feasible for would-be emigrants from other areas of the county to connect with different emigration routes via the small ports and landing places that dotted the length of the county's coastline.

In the early nineteenth century, emigration was viewed with concern by those who saw their communities being deprived of valuable skilled artisans and their families.[48] At this time, as noted above, government incentives were available, and the following are typical of the inducements carried by advertisements for passengers on ships bound for North America:

> Good encouragement will be given to Farmers, Masons, Carpenters, Blacksmiths, Tailors etc. who may embrace the present opportunity.[49]

> Great encouragement will be given by Government to those that may wish to become settlers in the British Colonies.[50]

> . . . and a total exemption from taxes and poor-rates are enducements [*sic*] which it holds out to persons disposed to emigrate . . . to the United States, or any of his Majesty's Colonies.[51]

As post-war Poor Law rates continued to rise, however, there was growing local sentiment in favour of emigration as a radical means of relieving paupers.[52] However, the number

Port of Aberystwyth, (b) Vessels Arrived, 1842–54, and (d) Arrivals and Departures, 1860–74.

[47] Thomas, *Strangers*, pp. 119 and 126. Llanrhystud, situated in central coastal Cardiganshire about 30 miles north of Cardigan, is the slight anomaly in this group of geographical origins.

[48] See, for example, ibid., p. 118; Moore-Colyer, *Land of Pure Delight*, p. 155.

[49] *Carmarthen Journal*, 8 August 1817.

[50] Ibid., 6 March 1818. See figure 8.2 for an image of this advertisement.

[51] *Cambrian*, 25 January 1820.

[52] Poor Law payments reached their peak in Cardiganshire in 1819. Thomas, *Strangers*, p. 107.

of paupers removed overseas from England and Wales in the nineteenth century is thought to have been 'quantitatively unimportant'.[53] Some instances of removals from Cardiganshire include the following:

> March 18, 1818: was agreed then to give Evan Evans . . . the sum of Twenty pounds towards assisting him and his family to emigrate to Halifax North America . . .[54]

> March 9, 1819: agreed that the Overseers be authorized to agree with the Capt. of a vessel about to sail to America, for taking charge of Mary Roberts, a pauper, and conveying her to Baltimoor [sic] in America and to advance to the said Capt. for the said purpose a sum not exceeding fifteen pounds.[55]

> April 16, 1819: was agreed to make payments 'Towards going to America' of £40 to Evan Thomas, his wife and eight children; £35 to Thomas Thomas, his wife and eight children; £20 to Evan Zacharias, his wife and children together with the bastard child of John Francis.[56]

1831–1850

In 1832 the *Welshman* reported that 'the mania for emigration rages just now'.[57] Certainly, available evidence suggests that the number of Welsh emigrants greatly increased in the 1830s, starting with those from Cardiganshire and Montgomeryshire.[58]

The relative ease of access to British North America via the timber ships had ensured that Cardiganshire natives were established in several communities in Canada. Canadian statistics of nineteenth-century immigration are, however, inflated: many immigrants were merely using the St Lawrence route to enter the United States because fares were cheaper on British ships bound for British colonies.[59] The typically collaborative nature of nineteenth-century Welsh

[53] Baines, *Migration*, p. 71.

[54] Owen, 'Ymfudo (emigration)', 225, quoting the Bettws Ifan vestry book, 18 March 1818.

[55] Thomas, *Strangers*, p. 118, quoting the Llanrhystud vestry book, 9 March 1819.

[56] Thomas, *Strangers*, p. 118, quoting the Llanfihangel ar Arth vestry book, 16 April 1819. Vestry books can be consulted at NLW, Aberystwyth.

[57] *Welshman*, 20 April 1832, 2.

[58] Shepperson, *British Emigration*, pp. 33–4.

[59] Thomas, *Strangers*, p. 108; Shepperson, *British Emigration*, p. 34; *Third Report*

migration meant that the majority, though by no means all, of the emigrants tended to cluster together residentially, with those from the different Welsh counties favouring particular settlements, bound not only by ties of religion, customs and language but also by a shared background of geographical and family origins. A prime example of this is the growth of a Welsh settlement in Waukesha County, Wisconsin, that was founded in 1840 by a pioneer family from Cardiganshire. Over the next decade the community was swiftly augmented by settlers from just a few specific parts of Wales, such as the neighbourhood of Pontrhydfendigaid, a village in east-central Cardiganshire.[60]

The favoured destination in the United States for the majority of Cardiganshire emigrants in the early to mid-nineteenth century was Ohio. The Revd Benjamin Chidlaw, writing in the late 1830s, commented that 'In latter years hundreds have emigrated here from Cardiganshire'.[61] Chidlaw, originally from Bala in north Wales, was a bilingual preacher based in Ohio.[62] He was one of the more prominent private promoters of Welsh emigration at this time, and visited Wales twice in the 1830s to encourage emigration, particularly to Ohio.[63] In Ohio, it was mainly the Jackson and Gallia counties that were attracting Cardiganshire's emigrants. Moreover, not only was the bulk of this overseas movement concentrated in less than two decades, but the emigrants were drawn mainly from an area in central Cardiganshire known as *Mynydd Bach*.[64] This episode in Welsh immigration to the United States was still remembered half a century later:

> The emigration from 1830 to 1850 was so great that parts of Cardiganshire were left almost desolate; a large number settled in Jackson and Gallia. In 1850, about the time emigration ceased, there

from the Select Committee on Emigration from the United Kingdom: 1827 ([1827] 2nd edn, Shannon, 1968), pp. 226–7.

[60] Knowles, *Calvinists Incorporated*, p. 117. For more on this, see D. J. Williams, *The Welsh Community of Waukesha County* (Columbus, OH, 1926).

[61] Knowles, *Calvinists Incorporated*, p. 157.

[62] Ibid., p. 20.

[63] Shepperson, *British Emigration*, p. 28; Dodd, *Early Welsh Emigration*, p. 32; M. L. Hansen, *The Atlantic Migration, 1607–1860* (Cambridge, MA, 1945), p. 143.

[64] Knowles, *Calvinists Incorporated*, p. 116.

were about 3,000 Welsh settlers in these two counties, two-thirds of them from Cardiganshire.[65]

The effects of this dramatic overseas exodus on the society and economy of the home communities were no doubt significant, but census statistics indicate that the 'desolation' alluded to in this article probably owed more to exaggerated memory and journalese than to historical fact. Nevertheless, population declines occurred in a surprising number of parishes and townships throughout Cardiganshire between 1831 and 1851, as table 8.1 demonstrates, although by no means all the movement out of these communities was due to emigration.[66] Despite this outward movement, the population of Cardiganshire increased by over 9 per cent (from 64,700 to 70,796) during this period, which demonstrates the way that the complex pattern of population movements at local level may be masked by county statistics.

Table 8.1 Numbers of Cardiganshire parishes and townships showing a decrease in population between 1831 and 1851[67]

Registration district	Total number of parishes or townships	Number of parishes or townships showing a loss between 1831–51	% population gain by registration district, 1831–51
Cardigan*	9	3	3.6
Newcastle Emlyn*	12	8	0.3
Lampeter*	10	4	5.9
Aberayron	13	7	6.9
Aberystwyth	31	10	15.7
Tregaron	27	9	1.2

Source: Census of Great Britain, 1851. Population Tables. I. Numbers of the Inhabitants. Vol. II ([1852], 2nd edn, Shannon, 1970), pp. 446–53.
*Only parishes within the administrative county of Cardigan are included here.

As noted above, the only complete Victorian emigration return, by county, for England and Wales was included

[65] Owen, 'Ymfudo (emigration)', 230.
[66] See, for example, 1851 Census. Population Tables. I. Vol. II, footnotes to pp. 446–53.
[67] At this time the enumeration unit in the Cardigan, Newcastle Emlyn, Lampeter and Aberayron districts was the parish, and that in the Aberystwyth and Tregaron districts was the township.

in the census for 1841.[68] This return shows that, although Cardiganshire had the greatest percentage loss by emigration (273 individuals or 0.4 per cent of the population) in that half-year, of any county in Wales and Monmouthshire, the actual losses were numerically insignificant, and even for Wales as a whole the loss amounted only to 1,149 or 0.1 per cent of the population.[69] Also recorded in the 1841 census are the total numbers reputedly lost through emigration by each parish or township since the previous census.[70] This evidence confirms the picture that is emerging of the county's emigration pattern: a low but sustained volume of movement overseas from the south of the county, and a dramatic but short-lived one from central Cardiganshire. By contrast, the north and east of the county showed little loss by emigration.

Official statistics need to be approached with caution, however, as comparison of these with other contemporary sources often reveal anomalies. For example, according to the notes in the 1841 census tables of parish/township populations, 348 emigrants had left Cardiganshire during the previous decade, but other sources indicate that this number was seriously underestimated.[71] Evidence from a combination of sources suggests that more than 650 people left the county for overseas destinations between 1831 and 1841, and this may not be the full total.[72] These data also highlight other instances of possible inaccuracies in government emigration statistics. For example, the return for 1841 of emigrants leaving from the ports of Britain records a sailing from Cardigan, presumably the *Thomas and William*, but none from Aberystwyth, although the *Messenger* had sailed from there in May.[73] The emigration return for 1842 has no record of any

---

[68] The census was taken on 7 June 1841 and the emigration return included only those who had emigrated since 31 December 1840.

[69] Williams, 'Some figures', 401; *Census of Great Britain, 1841. Abstract of the Answers and Returns. Enumeration Abstract. Part 1. England and Wales* ([1843] 2nd edn, Shannon, 1971), p. 78.

[70] Ibid., pp. 519–21.

[71] Ibid.

[72] For details, see K. J. Cooper, 'Cardiganshire's rural exodus' (unpublished Ph.D. thesis, University of Leicester, 2008), 243.

[73] *Returns Relating to Emigration from the United Kingdom in 1841* ([1842] 2nd edn,

sailings from Cardigan although the *Triton* sailed from there
in April.[74] While the return records 142 emigrants leaving
from Aberystwyth harbour, the port book of Aberystwyth
lists a total of 248 emigrants.[75] Emigration statistics for 1847
are even more confusing. The official return lists two ships
and 300 emigrants leaving Aberystwyth.[76] The Aberystwyth
port book lists two ships, but does not record the number
of emigrants, while contemporary newspapers give the total
numbers of emigrants as in excess of eighty on the *Ann Jenkins*,
and 462 passengers and crew on the *Tamerlane*.[77] The confusion does not stop here, however. Records of ships' arrivals
in Canada state the numbers of arrivals on the *Tamerlane* vari-
ously as 243 passengers, 189 passengers, and 231 passengers
with one death.[78] The figure of 462 is invariably cited as the
actual number of emigrants on the *Tamerlane*, although in the
Welshman article this figure included the crew. In any case, it
seems almost certainly to have been either an exaggeration
or a misprint. Although the official statistics of Britain and
Canada do not agree as to the exact number of passengers,
they agree on a figure of about two hundred, which is considered to be the optimum number of passengers on a sailing
ship of 700 tons burthen.[79]

The volume of the exodus overseas from Cardiganshire
continued to grow as the 1840s progressed. In 1842 the
Welshman reported:

> The emigration from Cardiganshire has been greater this season from
> the port of Aberystwyth than for several years past. The *Pilot* has taken
> upwards of 50 emigrants to Liverpool – their ultimate destination
> being the United States. The brigs *Credo* and *Rhydiol* take upwards of
> 200 for Quebec.[80]

Shannon, 1970), p. 10. These would be dependent on the accuracy of the figures
supplied by the individual port authorities.

[74] *Return of the Number of Emigrants Embarked from British Ports during 1842* ([1843]
2nd edn, Shannon, 1971), p. 10.

[75] NLW, Aberystwyth Borough Records, F11, Port of Aberystwyth. (a) Vessels
sailed, 1842–51.

[76] *Returns Exhibiting the Emigration from the United Kingdom Between the Years 1846
and 1850 Inclusive* ([1851] 2nd edn, Shannon, 1971), p. 419.

[77] *Carnarvon and Denbigh Herald*, 8 May1847, 3; *Welshman*, 4 June 1847, 3.

[78] *http://www.theshipslist.com/1847/BPP-1847.html*; *http://www.theshipslistcom/1847/
shipsjuly1847b.html.*

[79] Personal communication from David Jenkins, 20 February 2005.

[80] *Welshman*, 15 April 1842, 3. See also NLW, Aberystwyth Borough Records, F11,

However, it was in 1847 that the overseas exodus from central Cardiganshire appears to have peaked, once again catching the attention of the Welsh press:

> A greater proportion than the usual annual average of the agricultural population of the upper part of Cardiganshire, seemed determined this year to improve their fortune by emigrating to America. Last week [20 April] the new barque, the *Anne Jenkins*, of 400 tons . . . sailed from Aberystwyth for New York with upwards of 80 emigrants; and in the beginning of June, the *Tamerlane*, of 700 tons . . . capable of accommodating 200 passengers, is expected to sail for Canada.[81]

The sailing of the *Tamerlane* was reported at some length in the *Welshman*:

> On Monday morning the ship *Tamerlane*, of 700 tons burthen, left the port of Aberystwyth for Quebec, with the greatest number of emigrants that ever sailed from that port in one vessel. The number on board, including infants and the ship's crew, amounted to 462.[82]

According to the *Welshman* article, these emigrants 'came chiefly from the . . . neighbourhood of Lledrod, *Mynydd Bach* and Taihirion-y-rhos'. So what, in fact, precipitated this dramatic movement overseas from central Cardiganshire at this juncture? Knowles maintained that it could be explained neither by 'enclosure, ideology, nor declining rural industry', and concluded that it was an illustration of 'the classic development of chain migration in an isolated region'.[83]

A catalyst in this overseas movement was undoubtedly the Revd Edward Jones of Ohio. Originally from near Aberystwyth, he had made it his mission to persuade the rural Welsh to emigrate in search of a better life. In 1837 he spent several months in Cardiganshire, preparing the first comprehensive guide for Welsh emigrants to the United States, in which he promised they would

> have sufficient room for themselves and their children, and that the parishes may be saved from paying for those who cannot work,

---

Port of Aberystwyth. (a) Vessels sailed 1842–51; *http://www.theshipslist.com/ships/ Arrivals/1842a.htm*

[81] *Carnarvon and Denbigh Herald*, 8 May 1847, 3.

[82] *Welshman*, 4 June 1847, 3. Note the difference in passenger numbers on the *Tamerlane* in these two articles.

[83] Knowles, *Calvinists Incorporated*, p. 22. On chain migration, see ibid., p. 28; Baines, *Emigration*, p. 33.

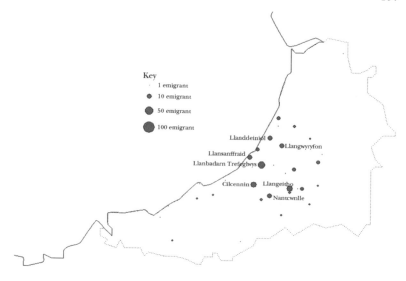

Figure 8.3 Origins, where identified, of Cardiganshire's nineteenth-century emigrants to Jackson and Gallia counties, Ohio

through acquainting them with places where many of their kind have had a comfortable living without support.[84]

Jones promoted Ohio as a destination, and especially the Welsh settlements in Jackson and Gallia counties, where families from central Cardiganshire had settled in the early years of the century.[85] Jones's influence seems to have encouraged further outward movement that then quickly gathered its own momentum. Analysis of the known geographical origins of Cardiganshire settlers in the Jackson and Gallia communities shows how localized the influence of this sending area was (see figure 8.3).

As far as the socio-economic status of the emigrants from *Mynydd Bach* to Ohio is concerned, the party that left in 1842 was made up of 'all small farmers and the better order of

---

[84] Knowles, *Calvinists Incorporated*, pp. 114–15; E. Jones, *The American Traveler: Or Advice to Emigrants from Wales to America* (Aberystwyth, 1837), p. 2. For more on this, see Knowles, *Calvinists Incorporated*, pp. 114–16.

[85] The Cilcennin and Llanbadarn Trefeglwys areas. Knowles, *Calvinists Incorporated*, p. 116; *CN*, 19 November 1993, 1; *Welsh Gazette*, 24 February 1955, 1.

peasantry, parting with their father-land apparently in very
good humour. We could see no sign of poverty amongst
them.'[86] Similarly, those who left in 1847 consisted 'chiefly
of small freeholders, farmers, and the more respectable of
the rural labouring class'.[87] These descriptions agree with
Knowles's findings from her researches into the social and
geographical backgrounds of the Ohio immigrants, namely,
that the families that emigrated from the *Mynydd Bach* region
came predominantly from the 'upper-middle stratum of agricultural society'.[88] It does seem logical, given the expense
involved, that emigrant families would need to be above
subsistence level. A family with four children could expect to
pay £30–£40 to reach Ohio from Wales even by the cheapest
route. Where poorer families managed to emigrate, they
were dependent on loans from family or friends for their
passage.[89]

The report in the *Welshman* of the sailing of the *Tamerlane*
from Aberystwyth in 1847 provides some useful demographic
background. Information about the occupational structure
of the emigrants was supplied to the paper by the ship's
owner, Mr John Evans, who

> had a view of the list of passengers . . . [and] found that 73 consisted
> of the class of farmers and their families, 65 of labourers ditto, 13 of
> carpenters ditto, 17 of tailors ditto, 6 of blacksmiths ditto, 5 of hatters
> ditto, and 10 miners, and the rest were of miscellaneous occupations.[90]

The total number of these passengers, excluding those in
the category of 'miscellaneous occupations', comes to 189.[91]
What is immediately apparent from this passenger list is that
emigration from Cardiganshire towards the middle of the
nineteenth century was still predominantly family based.
The *Welshman* also gives us an indication of the age profile
of the group. Only eighteen emigrants fell into the 52–63
age group, and 'the rest were chiefly young – some infants'.

[86] *Welshman*, 15 April 1842, 3.
[87] *Carnarvon and Denbigh Herald*, 8 May 1847, 3.
[88] Knowles, *Calvinists Incorporated*, p. 119.
[89] Ibid., pp. 120, 122.
[90] *Welshman*, 4 June 1847, 3.
[91] This list of emigrants is invariably misquoted as: 73 farmers, 65 labourers etc.
See, for example, Knowles, *Calvinists Incorporated*, p. 132.

Figure 8.4 Painting, by D.J. Lewis, of the brig *Credo* near the entrance to Aberystwyth harbour (no date, probably 1840s)
Ceredigion County Library, Aberystwyth. Slide Collection

Furthermore, the article identifies the ethnic origins of the group, and allows an insight into the close-knit and mutually supportive nature of emigration: 'it was remarked that there was not an English family amongst the whole; and from their coming from the same neighbourhood, they appeared as if they were all of the same family'.[92]

The movement overseas from Cardiganshire appears to have slackened off again by 1850, certainly as far as emigration to the two major destinations of Ohio and Wisconsin is concerned.[93] The last documented emigrant sailings from Aberystwyth harbour were in 1849 when the *Credo* (see figure 8.4) and the *Ann Davies* took emigrants to Quebec, and the *Energy* took emigrants to Liverpool for onward sailing.

Although there was a noticeable increase in passenger shipping using Aberystwyth harbour during the 1850s, the traffic was predominantly to local ports. Of the longer distance passenger destinations, Liverpool predominated, but it is not

[92] *Welshman*, 4 June 1847, 3.
[93] Knowles, *Calvinists Incorporated*, p. 19; Williams, *Waukesha County*, p. 107.

possible to tell from the extant Aberystwyth port books the extent to which these passengers were emigrants, migrants to the north of England, or those just visiting Liverpool.[94] This activity was relatively short lived: coastal traffic, both of freight and passengers, went into decline following the arrival of the railway network in Aberystwyth in 1864.[95]

1851–1900

We have already noted that emigration from England and Wales reached a peak in the 1880s.[96] Assisted passages, such as those provided by newly formed trade unions and friendly societies, were becoming available.[97] In 1882, Cardiganshire's local newspaper reported that

> extraordinary facilities offered to emigrants by competing lines of ocean steamers are such that no man or woman need now stay at home . . . all are invited who have either capital to spend or muscle wherewith to work.[98]

Shipping lines advertised regularly in the *Cambrian News* in the 1880s, and typically offered assisted passages to North America for 'Farmers, Agricultural Labourers, General Labourers and mechanics . . . @ £5, and Female Domestic Servants @ £4'.[99] As population mobility increased, and the general level of literacy improved, information even in quite remote areas became much more generally available to the extent that even 'remote railway stations flaunt placards' tempting people to emigrate.[100] Reports of the buoyant economies in North America and the advantages of emigration were widespread:

> young men who can work with their hands see at the other side of the Atlantic immediate opportunities of substantial well-being, which they cannot hope to reach here in less than a lifetime of toil and hardship

---

[94] During the nineteenth century Liverpool was the major port of emigration from Britain to North America. Kershaw, *Emigrants*, p. 12.
[95] For a list of passenger sailings from Aberystwyth harbour between 1832 and 1862, see Cooper, 'Cardiganshire's rural exodus', 243–5.
[96] Baines, *Migration*, p. 180.
[97] *CN*, 21 April 1882, 4; Armstrong, 'Flight from the land', p. 129.
[98] *CN*, 11 August 1882, 2.
[99] See, for example, *CN*, 14 April 1882, 2.
[100] *CN*, 11 August 1882, 2.

Table 8.2 Estimates of emigration from Cardiganshire as a percentage of the total native population, 1861–1900

	1861–70	1871–80	1881–90	1891–1900
% of native population	3.0–3.9	1.0–1.9	3.0–3.9	2.0–2.9

Source: Baines, *Migration*, pp. 188–91.

> . . . [and] the vast resources of Canada and the United States offer not only good wages for men and women, but bright prospects for children.[101]

The result was 'the vast crowds of emigrants who flock in ever increasing numbers from Liverpool and other ports to seek their fortunes in the West'.[102]

At this time the *Cambrian News* carried regular advertisements for passage, not just to North America but to the Cape and Australia as well.[103] Emigration direct from Cardiganshire, however, was no longer on offer, and Liverpool had become the main port of exit for all Britain's emigrants. Unfortunately, as we have seen, lack of detail in official records means that we know little about who these emigrants were, the backgrounds from which they came, or their ultimate destinations. Dudley Baines's estimates of emigration from Cardiganshire during the second half of the nineteenth century can be seen at table 8.2. If one takes into account the population decline from the 1870s, his calculations suggest that the overseas movement was at its highest in 1861–70. Despite all the inducements of the 1880s, however, the documentary evidence suggests that emigration from Cardiganshire had probably reached its peak in the 1840s.

Lack of detail about the emigrants' backgrounds and motivations in the official records of nineteenth-century emigration from England and Wales means that historians must look elsewhere for this information. As noted above, one valuable source is emigrants' letters, and the National Library of Wales in Aberystwyth contains several such collections, some of which are now available through

---

[101] *CN*, 21 April 1882, 4.
[102] *CN*, 11 August 1882, 2.
[103] See, for example, *CN*, 14 April 1882, 2.

the Wales–Ohio project.[104] Among these letters is a series written in the 1880s by a Cardiganshire-born emigrant in Ohio, Jack Edwards, to his family in Aberystwyth.[105] These letters allow an insight into the attitudes and experiences of a late nineteenth-century Cardiganshire emigrant. They also illustrate the importance within the immigrant Welsh community in North America of a common religion, culture and language, and shared geographical and family origins, as well as providing interesting information about the emigration process.

Jack Edwards emigrated from Aberystwyth to Ohio via Liverpool, where he stayed overnight at 'The American Eagle' in Union Street as part of his passage. He sailed to New York on the *England* on 15 April 1880, and the crossing took thirteen days.[106] At this time Liverpool was not only the major port of emigration from Britain to North America, it was also the departure point for many emigrants from mainland Europe.[107] These latter heavily outnumbered emigrants from England and Wales on Jack's outward voyage:

> We were about 1,450 on board including crew. Not above 70 or 80 Welsh and English together, all the rest being devided [sic] between Irish, German & Swedes . . .[108]

Jack's letters do not make it clear what his motives for emigrating were but it was clearly not a step in the dark; he was going to join his brother Edward in Cincinnati. There is a hint that Edward, however, may have emigrated for health reasons. Jack, on his arrival at Edward's home, wrote back to his family: 'Ned . . . doesn't cough at all now.'[109] Respiratory diseases, including various forms of tuberculosis, were rife in nineteenth-century Britain, and were often fatal until well into the twentieth century. Although generally associated with overcrowded living conditions in industrial towns, pulmonary disease was also prevalent in damp regions such

---

[104] This project was set up to digitize a selection of Welsh Americana relating to the state of Ohio. See *http://ohio.llgc.org.uk/*

[105] NLW, MS 20995 E. Letters from Jack Edwards from America, 1880–87.

[106] Jack Edwards's letter, 14 April 1880.

[107] Kershaw, *Emigrants*, p. 12.

[108] Jack Edwards's letter, 30 April 1880.

[109] Jack Edwards's letter, 8 May 1880.

as rural Cardiganshire.[110] In the case of Jack, however, there is no hint that he emigrated for health reasons. Moreover, he was leaving a secure, well-paid job, working at the post office in Aberystwyth:

> Of course my situation there [in the post office] was all that could be desired . . . but . . . if I could get its equal, even, I would prefer staying in this country for many reasons.[111]

Why, then, did he emigrate? There does not seem to have been an economic motive; perhaps it was just the urge for a change. Unfortunately, nor do we learn from his letters what the 'many reasons' for staying in Ohio were.

Jack Edwards's letters furnish us with glimpses of family values in later nineteenth- century Cardiganshire. He wrote home frequently, showing the need to maintain close contact with his family, and, although a young adult, he was still anxious to have their approval of his decision to stay in Ohio:

> Before making up my mind to stay in this country [I] should like to get your combined opinion upon the subject... If I may stay, please telegraph 'Yes' otherwise 'No'.[112]

Jack's letters highlight linguistic differences in what was obviously a close-knit Welsh family, and illustrate the increasing anglicization that was taking place in Cardiganshire, and particularly in Aberystwyth, as the nineteenth century progressed.[113] Whereas Jack's letters addressed only to his father were written in Welsh, those to his sisters were written in English, suggesting that the younger generation was more comfortable with that language.

As crossing times reduced and fares became more affordable, temporary emigration and return visits by emigrants became increasingly common. Indeed, Jack's initial trip may well have been made simply in order to decide whether or

---

[110] In England and Wales, Cardiganshire consistently had one of the highest mortality rates. R. Woods and N. Shelton, *An Atlas of Victorian Mortality* (Liverpool, 1997), pp. 100, 102. See also, above, chapter II.

[111] Jack Edwards's letter, 8 May 1880.

[112] Ibid.

[113] See, for example, J. W. Aitchison and H. Carter, 'The Welsh language in Cardiganshire, 1891–1991', in G. H. Jenkins and I. G. Jones (eds), *Cardiganshire County History*, vol. 3, *Cardiganshire in Modern Times* (Cardiff, 1998) , p. 573; D. Jones, *Statistical Evidence relating to the Welsh Language, 1801–1911* (Cardiff, 1998), p. 330.

not he wanted to settle in Ohio. On his initial journey to the United States he had met an ex-Cardiganshire man:

> There is a farmer from Lampeter here, going in the same boat, he has been back [to Lampeter] before, a jolly old fellow he is too.[114]

During his stay in Ohio, Jack himself made regular return visits to Aberystwyth. Trips home to Wales had obviously become a common occurrence among Welsh emigrants, and on Jack's voyage back to America after one of these journeys he wrote:

> a large number of my fellow passengers on the homeward trip are returning on this boat making me feel more at home.[115]

It is worthy of note that although he had by this time lived in Ohio for more than four years, he still regarded Aberystwyth as 'home'.

It was on this journey back to New York in August 1884 that Jack encountered a hazard that, from his description of it, was a fairly commonplace one at this time. His ship, the *Alaska*, engaged in a transatlantic race with the *Oregon*:

> which caused us to stop several times . . . to let the engines cool down and to crown it all broke down Saturday morning, having by over-driving split the cylinder head . . . to the great disappointment of those who had staked money on the race . . . they should not be allowed to risk the safety and comfort of the passengers for such purposes.[116]

It seems that chapel life was at the heart of the nine-teenth-century Welsh emigrant community whether in the Glamorgan coalfield, urban England or the New World. Jack Edwards quickly became established in a community in Ohio that had chapel life at its centre, although, through his interest in music, he became connected with various Nonconformist groups:

> Every other Sunday evening . . . I have attended the Welsh Church . . . Old Mr Chidlaw taking part in the service.[117]

---

[114] Jack Edwards's letter, 14 April 1880.
[115] Jack Edwards's letter, 17 August 1884.
[116] Ibid.
[117] Jack Edwards's letter, 12 October 1886. Benjamin Chidlaw, mentioned earlier, was one of the more prominent private promoters of Welsh emigration in the 1830s and 1840s, and was still obviously remembered in Cardiganshire several decades later.

Next Sunday I fill the place of bass at a Methodist Episcopal Church
. . . At some of these places I'm paid and at some I don't, it makes very
little difference which, I go all the time.[118]

Music making was obviously a very important part of Jack's
life. He became a member of the Young Men's Mission Band
of the First Presbyterian Church, and of the Cincinnati Welsh
Choral Society based at the Welsh Calvinistic Methodist
Chapel.

Welsh emigrants to North America tended to cluster
together, bound not only by ties of religion, customs and
language but also by a shared background of geographical and family origins. Evidently, Jack's new community
contained not only people with a common religious and
cultural background but also those with close birthplace ties:

Richards the chap from Llanbadarn [Fawr] that Brought my clothes
over is down here looking for work . . .[119]

Met J. C. Jones . . . that young fellow from Capel Dewi . . .[120]

Despite all the benefits of living in a mutually supportive
Welsh emigrant community in the New World, Jack Edwards
did not remain in Ohio. His letters do not indicate why, but
after some years he returned home again to Aberystwyth
where he took over the running of his father's bookshop.[121]

Although not first-hand evidence, family histories, as
mentioned earlier, can make a valuable contribution to
the study of migration. We have seen the effect of the
demise of the lead-mining industry on the populations
of Cardiganshire's lead-mining townships, and on that of
Trefeirig in particular. The evidence indicated that many
of the displaced lead miners moved to the Glamorgan coalfield; inevitably, given the choice of destinations on offer,

[118] Jack Edwards's letter, 20 July 1883.
[119] Jack Edwards's letter, 9 August 1883.
[120] Jack Edwards's letter, 12 October 1886. Capel Dewi is a tiny hamlet about 2
miles east of Aberystwyth.
[121] In the 1881 census, Jack's father, Edward, was listed as a master bookbinder
employing two men. He apparently lived and worked at 26 Great Darkgate Street.
This is the site of the present-day clothes shop Bon Marché; the Victorian building
has been replaced fairly recently. The *Welsh Gazette* of 20 May 1954 carried a notice
of the closure of Jack Edwards's Welsh Bookshop.

there were exceptions, and family stories can confirm this. Lewis Morris, for example, left Penrhiwnewydd, Trefeirig, in the 1870s. He was more than 40 years old at the time, but the crisis in lead mining probably left him little choice, and he and his growing family moved not to Glamorgan but to Lancashire. His three nephews, however, being younger, were far more adventurous. Morgan Edward Lewis (born 1863), exchanged lead mining in Trefeirig for gold mining in Australia, possibly in the 1880s.[122] He settled at Charters Towers, northern Queensland, where gold had been discovered in 1870. Morgan worked there during the boom years, achieving considerable occupational and personal success:

> He became manager at Clarke Mine [Charters Towers]; was known to be a hard taskmaster with very high standards but always fair to the men if they worked hard. He remained on the management of the gold mine, was also a member of a hospital board for a number of years, was president of the board of 2 colleges, and an elder at the Presbyterian church.[123]

As the fortunes of lead mining waned at home the brighter prospects in metal mining abroad apparently appealed to the Lewis family; Morgan's two younger brothers, John Daniel and David Llewelyn, left the lead mines of Trefeirig in the 1890s, initially for the coal mines of Glamorgan but shortly afterwards for the gold and silver mines of Colorado. John (born 1867) emigrated first, arriving in New York in 1895. His destination was the Silver Lake Mine, near Silverton in San Juan County, where he was

> believed to have become an inspector or supervisor, and also held the (possibly unpaid) post of secretary/treasurer of the Western Federation of Miners (of Colorado and Utah) with 10,000 members.

His younger brother, David (born 1878), arrived in New York in 1899 on his way to join his brother in Silverton. We have noted the tendency of immigrant groups to cluster together residentially, and this was apparently particularly noticeable among the frontier mining communities in Colorado:

---

[122] He appears as a lead miner in the 1881 census for Trefeirig.
[123] Interview with L. Mair Jones, Dewi Thomas Jones and Russell Jackson, 5 November 2009.

Figure 8.5 The *Er Cof* ring made for Jane Lewis
Courtesy of Dewi Thomas Jones

they tended to stay in their national colleagues' groups and did not mix with migrants from other countries.[124]

Sadly, the brothers were not together for long. John's promising career was cut short when he died in an avalanche in 1900, when he was out with a team of colleagues inspecting mining equipment. He was just 33 years old.

Despite the long distances separating them, some emigrants did manage to maintain contact with the families they had left behind. Of the three brothers, John was the only one who did this. On the death of his sister in Penrhiwnewydd, he composed a short poem, which was added to her headstone at Salem [Penrhyncoch] chapel. He also sent a small amount of gold back from Colorado for a ring for his mother, Jane Lewis. Unfortunately, before the ring could be made John had died in the mining accident, so 'it was decided to fashion the ring to be in memory of him – hence the inscription *Er Cof* [in memoriam] on the front' (see figure 8.5).[125]

During the nineteenth century emigration from western Europe tended to be a localized phenomenon, and it is thought that potential emigrants were influenced as much

---

[124] Ibid.

[125] Interviews with L. Mair Jones, Dewi Thomas Jones and Russell Jackson, 5 November 2009, 13 November 2009.

by available information as by the prevailing economic and social conditions at home.[126] This raises the question of the appropriate geographical unit for the study of emigration, since a county may have areas of both high and low emigration and different timescales. Available evidence has demonstrated that this was certainly true for Cardiganshire, which experienced a dramatic overseas exodus from a fairly localized central region in the two decades up to 1850. Despite its place on the western seaboard of Britain and its long-established seafaring tradition, however, emigration was only a minor facet of the county's rural exodus. Nevertheless, the influences behind the decision to emigrate, the regional nature and the local impact of the movement are significant aspects of the county's social and economic history.

[126] Knowles, *Calvinists Incorporated*, p. 13.

IX

CONCLUSION

An early trend towards urbanization characterized Britain's history, although the chronology and influences have varied from region to region. Rural out-migration, one of the relevant factors, has been, and still is, a subject of wide European importance, and in much of Europe a rural exodus is still being experienced today. The issue of so-called 'marginal' regions is one of major public and economic concern. Cardiganshire may be considered as one of these regions, and its rural exodus preceded that of almost all such regions on the Continent.

It has been claimed that migration in Britain from rural central and west Wales formed the most consistent depopulation trend, with the exception of the movement out of the Scottish Highlands.[1] Certainly, the census evidence demonstrates that, among the counties of England and Wales, Cardiganshire had one of the most dramatic percentage decreases of population in the later nineteenth century. Numbers in the county mirrored the national upward trend from 1801 until 1871, after which they fell away rapidly in the final decades of the century. This was despite a natural increase and indicates that considerable out-migration was taking place. The rural exodus affected Cardiganshire in a variety of ways, one of which was that by 1911 the county's population, when compared with that in 1851, was an ageing one, a situation that was exacerbated by the very low sex ratio due to high male out-migration. At the start of the nineteenth century the county had a deficit of males, the sex ratio (males per 100 females) being 90.5; by 1911 this ratio had fallen to 81.7, at a time when that for England and Wales as a whole was 93.6.[2] Cardiganshire was, in fact, one of the

[1] D. Friedlander and J. Roshier, 'A study of internal migration in England and Wales: part 1', *Population Studies*, 19 (1966), 263–4.
[2] J. Saville, *Rural Depopulation in England and Wales 1851–1951* (London, 1957), p. 90.

few counties in England and Wales from which males were consistently more migratory than females. The increasing excess of women in Cardiganshire meant that a significant proportion of them would not marry, and this, in turn, progressively lowered the rate of natural increase that would contribute further to the population decline.

Although the number of people enumerated in Cardiganshire was rising up to 1871, census birthplace data reveal that out-migration was already well established by this date. Indeed, there were Cardiganshire natives living in every county of England and Wales by mid-century. County-based statistics, however, can conceal significant local variations, and it is clear from analysis of the data at parish level that the timing and volume of the outward movement from Cardiganshire varied considerably from district to district, as did the popularity of destinations.

The broad chronology of the outward movement from Cardiganshire, based on county-level statistics, diverged significantly from national patterns. From 1841 to 1881, rural to urban migration rates were high in England and Wales and emigration rates were low. For Cardiganshire, emigration was possibly at its highest in the 1840s, while migration rates to other parts of Britain were low until after 1871. The greatest volume of outward movement from Cardiganshire to other parts of Britain occurred between 1881 and 1891, while, conversely, for Britain as a whole rural–urban migration declined in the 1880s, although emigration increased sharply.[3] Surprisingly, perhaps, considering its place on Britain's western seaboard, the rate of emigration from Cardiganshire was consistently well below the national average during the second half of the century.[4] As regards destinations, however, the county's migrants conformed more closely to national patterns. In England the top migrant destinations between 1841 and 1881 were London followed by Manchester and Liverpool; while, of the nine colliery districts of England and Wales, Glamorgan attracted the most

---

[3] L. L. Price, 'The census of 1891 and rural depopulation', *Journal of the Royal Agricultural Society of England*, 3rd series, 5 (1894), 43.

[4] D. Baines, *Migration in a Mature Economy* (Cambridge, 1985), p. 202.

migrants in the period 1841 to 1911.[5] Glamorgan was consistently by far the most popular destination for Cardiganshire migrants throughout the century, followed at some distance by Carmarthenshire, while the move from Cardiganshire to industrial Monmouthshire dwindled from mid-century. In England, the most favoured locations were London and Merseyside. The overall picture of Cardiganshire's outward movement in the second half of the century was one of considerable short-distance migration but with longer-distance moves centred on major industrial and commercial centres, a pattern that coincides with conventional Victorian migration theory.[6]

Studies of migration flows and patterns in Victorian England and Wales have revealed the 'immensely complex drift between counties'.[7] There is, however, dissension in the literature about the main destinations of nineteenth-century migrants from rural Wales. The census data for Cardiganshire does not totally support the viewpoints of either the Brinley Thomas school of thought or that of Dudley Baines.[8] It revealed that the county's migrants were at least three times more likely to stay in Wales from 1851 to the end of the century, after which time the trend had slowed to just over two and a half times.[9]

Historical geographers have long recognized the value of studying a region by comparing it with others. How, then,

---

[5] G. R. Boyer and T. J. Hatton, 'Migration and labour market integration in late nineteenth-century England and Wales', *Economic History Review*, new series, 50 (1997), 706.

[6] See, for example, C. G. Pooley and J. Turnbull, *Migration and Mobility in Britain since the Eighteenth Century* (London, 1998), pp. 11–13.

[7] C. T. Smith, 'The movement of population in England and Wales in 1851 and 1861', *Geographical Journal*, 117 (1951), 210. For a detailed analysis of population streams between 1851 and 1951, see Friedlander and Roshier, 'Study of internal migration'.

[8] Brinley Thomas's view was that up to 1880 most went either to England or overseas, while between 1880 and 1914 most of the Welsh rural exodus stayed in Wales, being principally absorbed by the industrial south. J. Williams, 'Move from the land', in T. Herbert and G. E. Jones (eds), *Wales, 1880–1914* (Cardiff, 1988), pp. 21, 25 and 38. Baines calculated that Welsh rural migrants throughout the second half of the nineteenth century, taken together, were about twice as likely to go to England as to Glamorgan. Baines, *Migration*, pp. 276–8.

[9] In 1851 there were 2,935 Cardiganshire migrants living in England and 10,419 living in Wales. In 1911 there were 9,134 Cardiganshire migrants living in England and 24,757 living in Wales.

does the migration flow from Victorian Cardiganshire compare with that of, say, Cornwall? Superficially, these counties had many socio-economic factors in common. Both were relatively remote regions in the 'Celtic' west of Britain where Nonconformity predominated. Agriculture and metal mining were the significant elements of both economies, while their long coastlines had led to strong maritime traditions of sea fishing and coastal trade. There are also superficial parallels between the fortunes of the rural industries of metal mining in both counties. Cornwall's copper and tin mining had long made significant contributions to the economy of Britain as well as to that of the county itself, but both industries went into decline from the 1860s. Inevitably, many copper and tin miners were driven to seek work elsewhere. John Rowe has estimated that about a quarter of them found work in the expanding china-clay works that were destined to survive metal mining and become Cornwall's most important industry, and there was also some movement to other parts of Britain, particularly to the Welsh and Lanarkshire coalfields, but the majority of the displaced miners emigrated to work in the metal mines of North and South America, South Africa and Australia.[10] Yet, by no means all nineteenth-century Cornish emigration was connected with the decline of copper and tin mining. According to Dudley Baines, Cornwall had the highest male and the second highest female emigration rates of natives of all the counties of England and Wales throughout the period from 1861 to 1900. By contrast, Cardiganshire had one of the lowest.[11] The significant point of convergence between Cardiganshire and Cornwall in terms of the rural exodus was that they were two of only six counties of England and Wales whose populations in 1911 were lower than in 1841.[12]

This raises important questions: what factors operating within Victorian Cardiganshire informed the decision to move and the choice of destination, and to what extent was

---

[10] J. Rowe, *Cornwall in the Age of the Industrial Revolution* (Liverpool, 1953), pp. 48, 305, 324–6; Baines, *Migration*, p. 159.

[11] Baines, *Migration*, pp. 150, 159.

[12] The others were Huntingdon, Rutland, Montgomery and Radnor. D. Hey, *The Oxford Companion to Local and Family History* (2nd edn, Oxford, 2002), p. 401.

migration influenced by socio-economic features unique to the county? It has long been recognized that some factors responsible for the nineteenth-century rural exodus were general to all the rural areas of England and Wales.[13] Moreover, potential English and Welsh rural migrants had an exceptional range of destination choices. For those who opted not to emigrate, Britain had many major growth areas such as London, Lancashire, south Wales, the west Midlands, Teeside, Humberside and the West Riding of Yorkshire, while many of the hitherto predominantly rural counties had developing urban and industrial centres.[14] The question arises as to how and why migrants made their choices. The decision to move is essentially a personal one, but scarcity of information from the migrants themselves means that our interpretation of nineteenth-century migration is somewhat speculative. By considering sending areas in detail, however, we can confirm factors that were operating generally in the decision-making process and reveal those specific to a particular region. Indeed, Victorian commentators recognized the complexity of the process:

> there can be no doubt that many causes contribute their quota, and it may well be that in each locality some one of these contributory causes . . . may, owing to the special circumstances of the country or district, become so important as even to be predominant. Further, . . . the many contributing causes act and re-act upon one another [in a way] which is far from easy to unravel.[15]

A brief survey of the socio-economic background of nineteenth-century Cardiganshire revealed a fairly remote county, and at the start of the century 90 per cent of the people were rural dwellers. The rural population continued to increase until the 1860s after which numbers began to fall, the greatest decline occurring between 1881 and 1891. By contrast, the urban sector increased slowly but steadily throughout the century so that by 1901 it accounted for one-quarter of the county's inhabitants. Nevertheless, the towns remained few in number and modest in size with a fairly

[13] See, for example, Saville, *Rural Depopulation*, p. 201.
[14] Baines, *Migration*, p. 215.
[15] G. G. Longstaff, 'Rural depopulation', *Journal of the Royal Statistical Society*, 56 (1893), 413.

narrow commercial base and no significant manufacturing or heavy industry. Thus, it was rural Cardiganshire that was the main loser by out-migration and the county's urban areas were unable to absorb much of this loss.

Analysis of the data in the Victorian censuses has identified which sectors of the rural population were leaving Cardiganshire in the later decades of the nineteenth century. Research has indicated that this period witnessed a steep decline throughout Wales of those employed in agriculture, but that much of this decline was in the number of farm workers rather than in the number of farmers.[16] Certainly, this was the case in Cardiganshire. In 1891 there were 28 per cent fewer male farm workers (agricultural labourers and farm servants) than in 1851, while females in this category showed a massive 78 per cent decrease over the same period. On the other hand, the increase in numbers of female farmers effectively counterbalanced the decline in numbers of male farmers in the period so that overall there were over 3 per cent more farmers in the county in 1891 than in 1851. The reduction in the number of those working in agriculture in Cardiganshire, and indeed throughout Wales, did not lead to an abandonment of the land: the Welsh Land Commission reported in 1896 that unoccupied farms were 'unknown in Wales'.[17] This was in sharp contrast to the situation in parts of England where: 'As a rule, wherever the depopulation is most marked, either many of the farms are vacant or let at a greatly reduced rent.'[18] Despite the all too evident harshness of farming life in Cardiganshire, many people displayed a marked reluctance to abandon this way of life, confirmation of the deep attachment to the land that characterized rural west Wales.[19]

The nineteenth-century rural exodus was more than just a move from the land; it embraced the rural community as a whole, not solely those engaged in agriculture. In Cardiganshire, all the rural trades and crafts, with the excep-

---

[16] Williams, 'Move from the land', p. 18.
[17] D. L. Thomas, *The Welsh Land Commission: A Digest of its Report* (London, 1896), p. 137.
[18] P. A. Graham, *The Rural Exodus* (London, 1892), p. 16.
[19] See, for example, Thomas, *Digest*, p. 139.

tion of those connected with the woollen industry, showed varying degrees of loss between 1851 and 1891; but numbers employed in the county's two major occupational categories after agriculture showed the greatest losses. In 1891 there were 60 per cent fewer male general labourers than in 1851 and 87 per cent fewer female labourers, while similar percentage decreases are to be found among those employed in lead mining during the same period.

Why, then, were so many people leaving Cardiganshire in the later nineteenth century? Scholars have concluded that migration in Victorian Britain was driven by economic incentives.[20] It seems clear that economic motives did play a significant part in the decision to move from Cardiganshire. Contemporary evidence for the county confirms that, due to the predominantly pastoral nature of farming, neither the agricultural depression nor the introduction of mechanization in farming were major forces in the move from the land as they were in English arable counties. However, in Cardiganshire, as in the rest of Britain, farm work provided little scope for personal advancement. The relentless competition for farm tenancies, a facet of the 'land hunger' characteristic of nineteenth-century Cardiganshire, meant that farmers' sons and farm labourers were often unable to realize their ambition to have holdings of their own.[21] Inevitably, the higher wages and shorter working hours available for unskilled and semi-skilled labour in Britain's urban/ industrial centres were attracting labour from all parts of the country, and, similarly, industrial south Wales was drawing Cardiganshire's farm workers and general labourers alike. As mass-produced goods became more widely available and country dwellers increasingly more mobile, the demand

---

[20] See, for example, J. S. Nicholson, *The Relations of Rents, Wages and Profits in Agriculture, and their Bearing on Rural Depopulation* (London, 1906), p. 161; R. Lawton, 'Regional population trends in England and Wales, 1750–1971', in J. Hobcraft and P. Rees (eds), *Regional Demographic Development* (London, 1977), p. 66; Boyer and Hatton, 'Migration and labour market integration', 731; Pooley and Turnbull, *Migration and Mobility*, p. 12; C. G. Pooley and J. Turnbull, 'Migration and urbanization in north-west England: a reassessment of the role of towns in the migration process', in D. J. Siddle (ed.), *Migration, Mobility and Modernization* (Liverpool, 2000), p. 201.

[21] See, for example, *CN*, 31 March 1882, 5.

for rural crafts and services dwindled countrywide; and declining rural population levels only exacerbated the downward spiral in the demand for these traders and craftsmen. In some areas of England, shrinking communities meant that 'building is at an entire standstill . . . and cottages fall into disrepair'.[22] Significant as all these factors no doubt were for the decision to move, the census evidence suggests that it was the rapid demise of the lead-mining industry and the knock-on effect on the ancillary communities, that affected the livelihoods of so many people, that provided the major economic impetus for the rural exodus from Cardiganshire in the closing decades of the nineteenth century.

Even today, the visible remains of the impact of metal mining on the landscape of northern Cardiganshire are reminders of the important role the industry has played in the social and economic development of the county, while the chronology of its final, Victorian, phase was closely linked to both the increase and the decline of the county's population levels. As the demand for lead soared in the middle decades of the century, so the influx of labour into the mining regions boosted existing settlements and created new ones. Nevertheless, census analysis reveals that Cardiganshire saw only a modest net gain by in-migration from outside the county. In 1871, the county's population high point, over 90 per cent of Cardiganshire's inhabitants were native to the county.[23] The census further reveals that much of the gain in numbers in the northern, lead-mining townships was caused by in-migration from neighbouring non-lead-mining ones. During this period, lead mining provided employment in the county on a scale second only to agriculture. However, work in the mines was often seasonal or part time, and for some families lead mining was simply the means of earning enough to enable them to retain possession of their farms and smallholdings. The chief attraction of lead mining was that it offered unskilled work at about twice the pay for agricultural

---

[22] Graham, *Rural Exodus*, p. 18.
[23] *Census of England and Wales, 1871. Population Abstracts. Ages, Civil Condition, Occupations and Birth-places of the People. Vol. III* ([1873] 2nd edn, Shannon, 1970), p. 609.

labour locally.[24] Thus the industry in its buoyant phases offered an alternative for local labourers who might otherwise consider seeking work further afield in, for example, industrial south Wales. Moreover, the presence of the mines and mining communities generated a significant demand for local trades and services, so that when the industry went into steep decline from the late 1870s the effect on the economy at local and county level was devastating. During the next decade the population of Cardiganshire fell by almost 11 per cent as numbers in the mining areas plummeted and many whose livelihoods depended on the mines were driven to seek employment elsewhere.

Inextricably woven with the economic incentives for migration was the desire for a better standard of living. Contemporary government reports and newspaper articles revealed the poverty and privations widespread in much of nineteenth-century rural Cardiganshire. Areas with poor housing, crowded living conditions and lack of sanitation were to be found throughout rural Victorian Britain and are widely regarded as major factors in the rural exodus, despite the privations of life in Britain's poorer urban districts. Improved levels of literacy and communications were encouraging the spread of ideas and information, although the scattered nature of Cardiganshire's rural population, the poor road system and the comparatively late extension of the railway network to the county meant that the rural population experienced significant isolation and self-sufficiency for longer than did those in less remote areas of Britain. Inevitably, there was a gradual widening of horizons, a raising of personal expectations and an increasing knowledge of options and opportunities elsewhere; and encouraged by cheaper and easier travel, people were becoming more inclined to seek the reportedly better living conditions, higher pay and superior social attractions of urban life, seemingly undeterred by the fact that there were 'many signs that people in towns are equally dissatisfied with the life there'.[25]

---

[24] A. K. Knowles, 'The structure of rural society in north Cardiganshire, 1800–1850', in G. H. Jenkins and I. G. Jones (eds), *Cardiganshire County History*, vol. 3, *Cardiganshire in Modern Times* (Cardiff, 1998), p. 85.

[25] Graham, *Rural Exodus*, p. 29.

Rural poverty and lack of employment prospects, however, were by no means the only motivations for moving. For younger people there was the urge for a change or simply the need to escape the isolation and boredom of rural life. As one second-generation member of the Liverpool Welsh community expressed it when asked why his father had left Wales, 'I think his attitude was that they were too inward looking, too small a community'; another migrant remembered: 'You had nothing in Morfa Bychan only chapel all day Sunday . . . and Prayer meeting . . . and the singing festival once a year . . . and that was our lot.'[26] Personal reminiscences and family traditions can also give valuable insights into the migrants' feelings about their new lives: 'I like to go home . . . but I like to come back . . . I like living in Liverpool . . . I've been very happy in Liverpool.'[27] It is worth noting that many apparently happily settled migrants still regarded Wales as 'home'; but it is also clear that many felt that they had improved on the lives they had left behind. This led in some cases to feelings of superiority both towards those back home and to newly arrived migrants: 'We felt that we had that certain urban slickness . . . By Jove, we were class!'[28] 'You were someone of consequence, you know.'[29] For their part, families in rural Wales often felt proud of their more adventurous relatives and friends.[30] Others were a little in awe of them, as the reminiscences of one Llangeitho woman illustrate:

> Uncle Wil was not well-known to me when I was a child, as he lived in London . . . where they kept a flourishing shop and dairy business . . . I can remember him paying us a visit when he came on holiday, always smartly dressed and with a London aura about him. So, we children were a little shy of him.[31]

Studies of many parts of the world have shown that the 'bulk of migrants moved along paths that had already been

---

[26] M. Jones, 'Welsh immigrants in the cities of north-west England, 1890–1930: some oral testimony', *Oral History*, 9 (1981), 34.

[27] Ibid., 34.

[28] Ibid., 40.

[29] Ibid., 35.

[30] Interview with E.D, 25 February 2009.

[31] G. B. Thomas, 'The Williams family of Dolau Aeron', *Cardiganshire Family History Society Journal*, 3 (2002–3), 106–7.

taken by friends and relations'.[32] How had the pathways from Cardiganshire evolved? In many cases, migrant destinations would have resulted from commercial links and seasonal migrations as temporary contact gave way to permanent moves and communities of mutual help and support evolved. In the case of Cardiganshire, until the arrival of the railway network the main means of contact with the outside world had been through maritime trade, especially with other ports on the western seaboard of Britain, with London and with western Europe and North America. Of particular significance were the nineteenth-century maritime links with Merseyside, and the presence of a thriving Cardiganshire Welsh community in the north-west lends support to the relevance of such links for migration. Even longer established were overland contacts that would have been forged between Cardiganshire and south-eastern England both through the cattle droving trade and the seasonal movement of women to London and Kent to work in the market gardens and hop fields. Thus, it is no surprise that London held a particular attraction for migrants from Cardiganshire despite the alternative lure of closer destinations in urban-industrial England and, more particularly, in south Wales. The presence of strong Welsh communities in both London and on Merseyside to welcome and support new arrivals from rural Wales would have strengthened the appeal of these two destinations for Cardiganshire's would-be migrants.

Demographers have concluded that the most important single influence on the migrant's choice of destination was the flow of information. This was particularly so in the case of emigration, a process that involved many uncertainties, and it accounts for the variation in emigration patterns throughout nineteenth-century Europe in regions of broadly similar social and economic conditions.[33] Studies have shown that in countries with high immigration the distribution of most foreign-born populations was highly clustered.[34] In the United States, for instance, Welsh migrants from different

[32] Baines, *Migration*, p. 26.
[33] Ibid., p. 23; J. D. Gould, 'European inter-continental emigration, 1815–1914: patterns and causes', *Journal of European Economic History*, 8 (1979), 660.
[34] Baines, *Migration*, p. 27.

counties favoured particular settlements, bound together not only by religious beliefs, customs and a common language but also by family and birthplace ties.[35] In the case of Cardiganshire, the destination of choice was Ohio, and more specifically the counties of Gallia and Jackson. Indeed, the colonization of areas of Ohio by people from Cardiganshire was a classic example of the operation of 'chain migration'. Not only was much of the movement to these settlements concentrated in the decades between 1830 and 1850, but the emigrants were drawn mainly from a particular area in central Cardiganshire known as the *Mynydd Bach*.[36] This situation left many unoccupied houses in the district and caught the attention of the census takers.[37] Communication and support were thus vital components of the migration process; and kinship networks and chapel contacts in Welsh migrant communities, both in Britain and overseas, actively recruited from home with offers of help in finding work and accommodation.

Migration to these various destinations was not necessarily achieved by a direct, one-way move. A major drawback in the use of birthplace tables in the Victorian censuses is that they give only the position on a given day once a decade, and this has led to a distorted and oversimplified view in conventional migration theory of the move from rural to urban Victorian Britain. We now have access to all the Victorian census enumerators' books, and it is becoming apparent from the family birthplace data that the shift of the population from countryside to town was often more complex than scholars have hitherto presumed. It seems clear that for many migrants this process was achieved through a series of intermediate moves that could include return migration.[38] Analysis of the data from the census enumerators' schedules for the Cardiganshire migrants, as well as family traditions, certainly supports this view. Mention has been

---

[35] See, for example, P. Thomas, *Strangers from a Secret Land* (Llandysul, 1986), p. 83; A. K. Knowles, *Calvinists Incorporated* (London, 1997), p. 117; D. J. Williams, *The Welsh Community of Waukesha County* (Columbus, OH, 1926).

[36] Knowles, *Calvinists Incorporated*, p. 116.

[37] *1851 Census. Population Tables. 1. Vol. II*, p. 39.

[38] Pooley and Turnbull, 'Migration and urbanization', pp. 186–7.

made of Edward Llewellyn Lloyd who left the family home, Brynhope Farm, Tregaron, in 1882 aged 19. He first settled in Cardiff and worked as a draper, but by the mid-1880s he had followed his married sister and brother to London where they all remained for the rest of their lives.[39] Another illustration of this stage migration is provided by John Hopkins and Elizabeth Davies. John, a carpenter, left Llanfihangel-y-Creuddyn in about 1855 for Salisbury 'where apparently there was on-going work for carpenters on the Cathedral'. John married Elizabeth Davies from Penrhyncoch in Salisbury, by licence in 1855, although whether or not the couple met before they left Cardiganshire is unclear. Shortly afterwards, they moved on to live in Islington.[40]

Various social and economic factors influenced the choice of residential location of newly arrived migrants in urban Victorian Britain. However, it has been demonstrated that a strong sense of cultural coherence, such as that of nineteenth-century Welsh migrants, was sufficient to override the other socio-economic forces that contributed to patterns of urban residence and resulted in significant residential segregation by geographical origin by these migrant groups.[41] Analysis of the 1881 census enumerators' returns confirm this conclusion, revealing a marked tendency to residential clustering by Cardiganshire's migrants in the industrial hinterland of Glamorgan and in northern rural Carmarthenshire, on Merseyside and, to a lesser extent, in the Manchester area. The notable exception to this pattern is the scattered residential distribution of the Welsh in Victorian London; no one district in the capital could be regarded as either predominantly or even distinctively Welsh.[42] Here again, Cardiganshire natives conformed to Welsh migrant residential patterns in that they were to be found living throughout London. They were, however, at all times most numerous

[39] Interview with Joan Paparo, 3 July 2009.

[40] Interview with S.B., 20 July 2009.

[41] C. G. Pooley, 'The residential segregation of migrant communities in mid-Victorian Liverpool', *Transactions of the Institute of British Geographers*, new series, 2 (1977), 368; P. N. Jones, *Mines, Migrants and Residence in the South Wales Steamcoal Valleys: the Ogmore and Garw Valleys in 1881* (Hull, 1987), p. 72.

[42] E. Jones, 'The early nineteenth century', in E. Jones (ed.), *The Welsh in London, 1500–2000* (Cardiff, 2001), p. 89.

in Islington, demonstrating the particularly strong links between that district and Cardiganshire that had evolved as a result of cattle droving.

Analysis of the enumerators' returns also gave an indication of the socio-economic characteristics of the migrant groups, and it was immediately apparent that there were some striking contrasts between the individuals who moved to south Wales and those who moved to England. The occupational profiles of the migrants in the north-west of England and in the sample population in London were broadly similar: most males were skilled or semi-skilled artisans, or shop workers, while domestic service was the predominant female occupation. It seems that some skills found in rural nineteenth-century Cardiganshire were readily transferable to expanding urban Victorian England, and although the migrants were decidedly under-represented in the professions, there were also very few in the unskilled classes or who were paupers. Given the traditional link of the Cardiganshire Welsh with the dairy trade, it was perhaps surprising that the occupation of cow keeper/dairyman was only the second ranked male occupation in the 1881 London census sample. However, we noted the very strong woodworking tradition in nineteenth-century Cardiganshire that owed much to the county's boatbuilding industry, and the skill of the carpenter/joiner was in great demand in the rapid urban expansion. Although their contribution is now sometimes overlooked, the carpenter/joiner was by far the most common male occupation among the county's migrants in 1881 both in the London sample and in the north-west. Further evidence of the county's maritime heritage is apparent in the considerable number of Cardiganshire-born mariners enumerated on Merseyside in 1881. The third most common form of male employment, both in the London sample and in the north-west, was provided by drapery outlets. The occupational data thus confirm that the socio-economic status of the Cardiganshire migrants was generally typical of the Welsh community as a whole in London and the north-west at this time.[43]

---

[43] See, for example, Jones, 'Early nineteenth century', p. 101; C. G. Pooley, 'Welsh migration to England in the mid-nineteenth century', *Journal of Historical Geography*,

In his report to the Royal Commission on Agriculture of 1882, Andrew Doyle observed: 'The younger members of Welsh families of the agricultural class never hesitate to seek employment away from home; they emigrate and migrate freely and without hesitation.'[44] Certainly, studies of the structure of Welsh households in Liverpool in 1871 suggest that most of the migrants moved there either as single young adults or as childless couples.[45] The census data for the Cardiganshire migrants in the north-west in 1881 supports this conclusion. It reveals that 70 per cent of the migrants were aged between 15 and 44 years. The individuals in the London census sample were also found to be over-represented in the young-adult age group.[46]

The Cardiganshire migrants in the south Wales census sample displayed very different socio-economic characteristics from those in London and north-west England. Among rural Welsh counties, Cardiganshire was reputedly a major contributor of labour to the Glamorgan coalfield in the second half of the century. The data from the 1881 Glamorgan census study supports this conclusion; 45 per cent of employed males worked in the coal mines. Indeed, most of the migrants were to be found in the industrial hinterland, and the group was heavily over-represented in the unskilled categories and under-represented in all other groups. The coalfield element of the sample demonstrated the main characteristics that have been shown to exist in all Britain's nineteenth-century mining communities.[47] As well as being occupationally very specialized, it was predominantly youthful, had a very unbalanced male/

9 (1983), 296; C. G. Pooley and J. C. Doherty, 'The longitudinal study of migration: Welsh migration to English towns in the nineteenth century', in C. G. Pooley and I. D. Whyte (eds), *Migrants, Emigrants and Immigrants* (London, 1991), p. 152.

[44] *Royal Commission on Agriculture (Richmond Commission). Reports of the Assistant Commissioners. Mr Doyle's Reports* ([1882] 2nd edn, Shannon, 1969), p. 8.

[45] Pooley, 'Welsh migration', 296.

[46] This has been shown to be a characteristic of the migrant population in urban Victorian England. See, for example, R. Lawton, 'Population changes in England and Wales in the later nineteenth century', *Transactions of the Institute of British Geographers*, 44 (1968), 56; D. Friedlander, 'Occupational structure, wages, and migration in late nineteenth-century England and Wales', *Economic Development and Cultural Change*, 40 (1992), 304.

[47] Jones, *Mines, Migrants and Residence*, p. 22.

female sex ratio in the teenage and young adult age groups and had a prominent male boarder component. The towns of coastal Glamorgan provided a modest counter-attraction for Cardiganshire migrants, but this group conformed more closely to the socio-economic characteristics of the county's migrants in London and the north-west.

By contrast with all the other migrant groups studied here, the move to Carmarthenshire was predominantly a rural-to-rural one. Only a small percentage of the migrants were urban based, and agriculture dominated the employment structure of the remainder, accounting for about half of employed male and female migrants in the sample. The native agricultural population was forsaking rural Carmarthenshire for industrial south-east Wales.[48] The census evidence indicates that farmers and farm labourers from neighbouring Cardiganshire were moving in to take their places, in some cases because of land hunger and competition for farms at home. Research has revealed that a west-to-east movement of the agricultural labour force across south Wales towards the industrial districts of east Carmarthenshire, Glamorgan and Monmouthshire had been going on at least since mid-century.[49] The census evidence suggests that farmers and farm workers from Cardiganshire were part of this stage-migration.

Nineteenth-century commentators feared that migration was destructive of family ties, but it is now clear that the theory that 'industrialization disrupted the family' is no longer entirely tenable. Twentieth-century research has suggested that, at least in the first generation, family contacts were actively pursued.[50] Family traditions in Cardiganshire certainly support this view. Studies of the migrant population of the Glamorgan coalfield and of the Welsh communities in urban England demonstrate the importance of both kinship

---

[48] The number of males engaged in agriculture in Carmarthenshire fell from nearly 13,000 in 1851 to just over 9,000 in 1881. Williams, 'Move from the land', p. 31.

[49] S. Thomas, 'The agricultural labour force in some south-west Carmarthenshire parishes in the mid-nineteenth century', Welsh History Review, 3 (1966–7), 72.

[50] M. Anderson, 'Recent work on the analysis of nineteenth-century census returns', Family History, 11 (1980) , 154; W. A. Armstrong, 'The flight from the land', in G. E. Mingay (ed.), The Victorian Countryside (London, 1981), p. 128.

and geographical origins in the migration process.[51] Analysis of the Cardiganshire migrant data from the census confirms these findings, demonstrating the existence not only of small communities with close birthplace ties, but also of co-residing groups with close kinship ties and geographical origins.

Research has suggested that Welsh migrants to mid-Victorian England fitted easily into the urban labour market while managing to maintain their cultural identity.[52] This latter was achieved partly through membership of Welsh societies and clubs, and was sustained by regular contact with 'home' and also through the continuous flow to urban England of people from rural Wales with shared traditions, religious beliefs and a common language. However, it was the Nonconformist chapel, and in particular that of the Welsh Calvinistic Methodists, that bound the Welsh emigrant community together.[53] It catered for the spiritual needs as well as supplying a full social life for its members; it provided opportunities for young migrants to find Welsh marriage partners; and it brought potential employers and available labour together. Analysis of the census data, while confirming a marked degree of social and cultural segregation among the Cardiganshire migrants, using such indicators as nationality of marriage partners, employers and heads of households providing lodgings, has produced evidence of the beginnings of the trend towards social assimilation into the host society.

Preserving a Welsh identity in urban England posed problems, especially for the next generation, and was often a cause of friction, as one second-generation Liverpool Welshman recalled:

> I don't think it's good for . . . one's maturing . . . because you learn to be one thing here and another thing there . . . I think immigrants should . . . become absorbed – they've no right to play with the

---

[51] See, for example, Jones, *Mines, Migrants and Residence*; Pooley, 'Welsh migration'.

[52] Pooley, 'Welsh migration', 287.

[53] In Cardiganshire both old and new Dissent were well represented, but Calvinistic Methodism predominated. Calvinistic Methodism was found almost exclusively in Wales; its incidence in England (with the exception of the Countess of Huntingdon's Connexion) coinciding with areas notable for Welsh migration. K. D. M. Snell and P. S. Ell, *Rival Jerusalems* (Cambridge, 2000), p. 167.

kids' lives. They should . . . come into this country and become this country.[54]

Cultural assimilation was, perhaps, inevitable and was certainly well under way in the Manchester area by the early years of the twentieth century:

> There were degrees of Welsh people in Manchester. There were what I would call the wholly Welsh . . . as I was, who spoke Welsh at home and everything . . . Then there were the people who would call themselves Welsh . . . but they wouldn't *speak* Welsh [outside the home] . . . And then there were the ones who, as so many of my contemporaries, had Welsh parents but . . . they didn't speak Welsh at home and the children really couldn't get away quickly enough. They became English and they were Welsh only with a Welsh name.[55]

In London, too, integration and anglicization were generally seen as the way forward, but for migrants who were monoglot Welsh this process could be challenging:

> my grandmother, who moved to London when she was eight, could not speak English so she had to learn rapidly when they arrived. She acted as translator for her mother who never spoke English properly.[56]

Moving away from home can be stressful and even traumatic. Some migrants took time to adjust to their new surroundings: 'he regularly cycled home from London during the first few years'.[57] Others, despite being among family and friends, remained homesick:

> Mary never settled in London and was often unwell as was her youngest child. They made extended visits 'home' on doctor's orders.[58]

The vast majority adapted to their new situations, with varying degrees of success. For some migrants and their descendents, though, despite being happily settled, Cardiganshire was always 'home'. Organizations such as the London Cardiganshire Society and the Liverpool Welsh Society may be regarded on one level as expressions of *hiraeth* – the longing for home – demonstrating the value that

---

[54] Jones, 'Welsh immigrants', 39–40.
[55] Ibid., 39.
[56] Interview with A.R., 27 April 2009.
[57] Interview with E.D., 25 February 2009.
[58] Interview with A.R., 27 April 2009.

later generations continued to attach to their families' Welsh origins.

Sometimes family traditions confirm what has been deduced about aspects of migration, such as the role of the flow of information, residential clustering, help with finding work, social segregation and marrying within the immigrant community, as the following account illustrates:

> It was to Wallasey that my maternal *Taid* [Grandfather] walked from Cross Inn near Llanarth, a stroll of some 150 miles! He was then a young single man aged 22 and was 'taken in' by one of the local Welsh families. He soon got a job as a cabinet-maker with one of the Wallasey firms that supplied the ships that rose on the stocks near Birkenhead. He joined the community of Martin's Lane Welsh Congregational Chapel and it was there that he met, and married Jane, his beloved Siân . . . from Mostyn in North Wales.[59]

In the closing decades of the nineteenth century Britain's rural exodus was the subject of much discussion: 'Few topics in connection with English agriculture have occupied a larger space in the public mind during recent years than the influx of rural labour to the towns.'[60] Some commentators considered that the volume of rural out-migration had been 'multiplied by imaginative rumour into wholesale abandonment of the country for the attractions of the town', and that this exaggeration had happened because of the increased attention focused on issues such as the competition of newcomers in the housing and labour markets.[61] Statisticians argued about the actual extent of the movement and whether or not Britain was experiencing rural depopulation; and the definition of rural areas became crucial to this question.[62] Calculations based on the census categories of urban and rural sanitary districts demonstrated that the rural population, *'taken as a whole* is still increasing, though it be but slowly'.[63] Many statisticians, however, felt that the official definition of rural and urban was too broad and did not take

[59] D. S. Evans, 'A long walk to work', *Cardiganshire Family History Society Journal*, 3 (2002–3), 65.
[60] Price, 'Census of 1891', 40.
[61] Ibid.
[62] See, for example, Longstaff, 'Rural depopulation', 380.
[63] Ibid., 381 [his italics].

into account variations at local level; and more detailed analysis by them revealed that 'a *local* depopulation . . . is actually occurring in many localities'.[64]

In 1911, despite a modest stream of in-migration, Cardiganshire's population level was more than 15 per cent lower than it had been in 1851, but it had actually fallen by a weighty 18 per cent from the high point of 1871. This was despite the rising life expectancy over this period. By the close of the nineteenth century, contemporary commentators had concluded that although a rural depopulation in England and Wales was 'very general in its extent . . . its intensity has been greatly exaggerated; in the few spots where it is at its worst, it only amounts to a thinning of the people'.[65] Local opinion in Cardiganshire took a less sanguine view of the situation in their county. The following prescient remark appeared in the *Cambrian News* in 1882 and, although it was written just before the county's rural exodus began to assume dramatic proportions, it foreshadowed a population decline that would continue until the second half of the twentieth century:

> the youth of the country is being rapidly drafted away . . . The population of Cardiganshire is rapidly decreasing, not only in the mining districts, but in purely agricultural localities, and there is every reason to suppose that the exodus of the people will continue.[66]

A major problem in studying nineteenth-century migration from Cardiganshire, and indeed Britain as a whole, is the scarcity of first-hand personal histories. Consequently, any primary evidence, such as the letters that emigrant Jack Edwards wrote to his family while he was in Ohio, is of considerable importance in deepening our understanding of the thoughts and attitudes of the migrants.[67] One further such

---

[64] Ibid., [his italics]. See, also, Price, 'Census of 1891', 59; A. L. Bowley, 'Rural population in England and Wales', *Journal of the Royal Statistical Society*, 77 (1914), 597–609; Nicholson, *Relations of Rents*, pp. 132, 137.

[65] Longstaff, 'Rural depopulation', 412; Nicholson, *Relations of Rents*, p. 143.

[66] *CN*, 31 March 1882, 5. The downward trend continued until the 1950s; by 1951 numbers had fallen by 27.4 per cent from the high point of 1871. B. R. Mitchell, *Abstract of British Historical Statistics* (Cambridge, 1962), pp. 20, 22.

[67] NLW, MS 20995 E. Letters from Jack Edwards from America, 1880–7. See above, chapter VIII. For more letters from Welsh emigrants, see The Wales–Ohio Project at the NLW, *http://ohio.llgc.org.uk/dig-lib.php?type=manuscript*.

piece of useful primary evidence is a questionnaire circulated to elementary school head teachers in Cardiganshire in 1920.[68] These documents offer a first-hand insight into prevailing attitudes of the early decades of the twentieth century as the county's rural exodus continued. As well as the specifically school-related topics, the questionnaire also covered employment opportunities for school leavers and levels of migration from the district. The detail in many of the head teachers' responses to these latter queries indicates the importance of these issues for the local community; and because the questionnaire was distributed throughout the county, the replies afford us an idea of both the similarities and differences that characterized the various districts.

We have seen how agriculture still dominated the county's occupational structure at the beginning of the twentieth century despite considerable movement of labour out of the industry; and we noted the fairly narrow range of employment opportunities in nineteenth-century Cardiganshire. We also saw how the collapse of lead mining forced many people to seek employment outside the county. What effect, then, did the rural exodus of the later nineteenth century have on the county's employment situation by the early twentieth century? The evidence from the head teachers' questionnaire suggests that there was no shortage of employment for school leavers in 1920. However, the lack of range in employment opportunities we noted in previous decades had been exacerbated by the decline of sea fishing, the coastal trade and shipbuilding and their ancillary trades and industries; and also by the reduction in small-scale rural industries such as lime burning, slate quarrying and the woollen industry, as well as many of the rural trades and crafts. Indeed, the head teachers' responses indicated that the range of occupations for school leavers in 1920 was extremely narrow: 'There is little or no choice. Agriculture is the only industry of importance.'[69] Yet there was no actual shortage of work – in fact quite the opposite: 'These lads and lasses experience

---

[68] Ceredigion Archives, CDC/ED/28, questionnaire completed by head teachers of elementary schools in Cardiganshire, May 1920.
[69] Head teachers' questionnaire from Pontrhydfendigaid.

no difficulty whatever to get employment on the farms – labour being very scarce.'[70] In particular, the children of farming families were 'kept on the farm or seek employment on neighbouring farms'.[71] Other widespread employment opportunities for school leavers included shop messengers, the mercantile marine and apprenticeships to carpenters, blacksmiths and tailors.

Although some of the head teachers reported very little movement of people into or out of their districts, the theme of the majority of the head teachers' responses was very similar, and the following are a few examples:

> After leaving school at 14 years of age most of the pupils become farm servants. Then in about 4 or 5 years most of the boys leave the county for Glamorgan ... Agricultural workers with large families cannot possibly afford, financially, to give their children either a good secondary education or train them up in different trades.[72]

> Several young people leave this district for the South Wales coalfield and a few others for the dairy business in London.[73]

> Many of the young people leave to find work in the large towns and cities, being better paid and the conditions of life being more go-ahead.[74]

> Boys and girls choosing any other employment [than agriculture] leave this district – generally to colliery districts and other industrial centres, also to the dairy business in London. These seldom return and settle down there.[75]

> Emigration to south Wales has been constant. The higher wages offered, together with hopes of a higher standard of living – better houses, better opportunities of placing children, better food – being the chief incentives.[76]

It is abundantly clear that the urge to move away from Cardiganshire was still strong throughout the county in 1920, and that industrial south Wales and London still exercised

---

[70] Head teachers' questionnaire from Mydroilyn.
[71] Head teachers' questionnaire from Tregaron.
[72] Head teachers' questionnaire from Mydroilyn.
[73] Head teachers' questionnaire from Blaenpennal.
[74] Head teachers' questionnaire from Cardigan.
[75] Head teachers' questionnaire from Pontrhydfendigaid.
[76] Head teachers' questionnaire from Llanarth.

the strongest pull. Moreover, apart from the main economic impetus to out-migration caused by the rapid demise of the lead-mining industry in the 1880s, similar underlying influences informing the decision to move and the choice of destination were still operating in Cardiganshire almost half a century later.

BIBLIOGRAPHY

1. PRIMARY SOURCES

i. Manuscript

Census of England and Wales, 1881, Enumerators' Schedules for Carmarthenshire, Cheshire, Glamorgan, Lancashire and London.

Ceredigion Archives, Ed. Bk. 88.

Ceredigion Archives, CDC/ED/28, questionnaire completed by head teachers of elementary schools in Cardiganshire, May 1920.

National Library of Wales, Aberystwyth Borough Records, F11, Port of Aberystwyth, (a) Vessels sailed 1842–51; (c) Vessels sailed 1851–66, and June–October 1886.

National Library of Wales, 1759B1 Agriculture, material relating to agriculture in South Wales collected by Walter Davies during journeys undertaken for the Board of Agriculture in the early nineteenth century.

National Library of Wales, RA 33 Gogerddan Estate Rental, 1797–8.

National Library of Wales, Gogerddan Estate, Box 44, lead mining letters, R. Owens to Col. Williams, 21 July 1892.

National Library of Wales, MS 20995 E, letters from Jack Edwards from America, 1880–7.

National Library of Wales, Williams and Williams 26222, letter from George Drinkwater, 9 October 1879.

ii. Typescript

Ceredigion County Library, Aberystwyth, Local History Section, Transcripts of the Census.

Enumerators' Schedules for the North Cardiganshire Rural Districts, Trefeirig, 1851–91.

Ceredigion County Library, Aberystwyth, Local History Section, *Monumental Inscriptions with Indexes* (typescript, 1994– ongoing).

K. J. Cooper, 'Cardiganshire's rural exodus' (unpublished Ph.D. thesis, University of Leicester, 2008).

A. M. E. Davies, 'Poverty and its treatment in Cardiganshire' (unpublished MA thesis, University of Wales, 1968).

M. J. Davies, 'Population mobility 1835–1885: rural and urban perspectives' (unpublished Ph.D. thesis, University of Wales, Swansea, 1986).

C. G. Pooley, 'Migration, mobility and residential areas in nineteenth-century Liverpool' (unpublished Ph.D. thesis, University of Liverpool, 1978).

iii. Newspapers

Cambrian, 1816, 1820.

Cambrian News, 1878, 1880, 1882, 1901, 1993.

Carmarthen Journal, 1817, 1818.

Carnarvon and Denbigh Herald, 1847.

Liverpool Daily Post, 1871.

Mining Journal, 12 May 1877.

Welshman, 1832, 1842, 1847.

Welsh Gazette, 1955.

iv. Official papers

Census of Great Britain, 1841, Abstract of the Answers and Returns, Enumeration Abstract, Part 1, England and Wales ([1843] 2nd edn, Shannon, 1971).

Census of Great Britain, 1851, Population Tables, 1, Numbers of the Inhabitants, Vol. 1 ([1852] 2nd edn, Shannon, 1970).

Census of Great Britain, 1851, Population Tables, 1, Numbers of the Inhabitants, Vol. II ([1852] 2nd edn, Shannon, 1970).

Census of Great Britain, 1851, Population Tables, II, Ages, Civil Condition, Occupations, and Birth-Places of the People, Vol. 1 ([1854] 2nd edn, Shannon, 1970).

Census of England and Wales, 1861, Vol III, General Report ([1863] 2nd edn, Shannon, 1970).

Census of England and Wales, 1871, Vol. IV, General Report ([1873] 2nd edn, Shannon, 1970).

Census of England and Wales, 1871, Population Tables, Vol. II ([1872] 2nd edn, Shannon, 1970).

Census of England and Wales, 1871, Population Abstracts, Ages, Civil Condition, Occupations and Birth-places of the People, Vol. III ([1873] 2nd edn, Shannon, 1970).

Census of England and Wales, 1871, Vol. IV, General Report ([1873] 2nd edn, Shannon, 1970).

Census of England and Wales, 1881, Population, Vol. II (London, 1883).

Census of England and Wales, 1881, Vol. III, Ages, Condition as to Marriage, Occupations and Birth-places (London, 1883).

Census of England and Wales, 1881, Vol. IV, General Report ([1883] 2nd edn, Shannon, 1970).

Census of England and Wales, 1891. Vol. II. Area, Houses and Population (1893, 2nd edn, Shannon, 1970).

Census of England and Wales, 1891, Vol. III, Ages, Condition as to Marriage, Occupations, Birth-places and Infirmities ([1893] 2nd edn, Shannon, 1970).

Census of England and Wales, 1891, Vol IV, General Report ([1893] 2nd edn, Shannon, 1970).

Census of England and Wales, 1901. County of London, Area, Houses and Population (London, 1902).

Census of England and Wales, 1911, Vol. IX, Birthplaces (London, 1913).

Census of England and Wales, 1911, Vol. X, Occupations and Industries, Part I (London, 1914).

England and Wales, Return of Owners of Land, House of Commons Papers lxxii (1874).

Minutes of Evidence taken before The Commissioners Appointed to Inquire into the Condition of all Mines in Great Britain (Kinnaird Report) ([1864] 2nd edn, Shannon, 1969).

Report on the Decline in the Agricultural Population of Great Britain, 1881–1906 (London, 1906).

Return of the Number of Emigrants Embarked from British Ports during 1842 ([1843] 2nd edn, Shannon, 1971).

Returns Relating to Emigration from the United Kingdom in 1841 ([1842] 2nd edn, Shannon, 1970).

Returns Exhibiting the Emigration from the United Kingdom Between the Years 1846 and 1850 Inclusive ([1851] 2nd edn, Shannon, 1971).

Royal Commission on Agriculture (Richmond Commission), Reports of the Assistant Commissioners, Mr Doyle's Reports ([1882] 2nd edn, Shannon, 1969).

Royal Commission on Agriculture, Minutes of Evidence, Vol. IV ([1896] 2nd edn, Shannon, 1969).

Royal Commission on Agriculture, Final Report (London, 1898).

Royal Commission on Labour, Fifth and Final Report, Part I, The Report ([1894] 2nd edn, Shannon 1970).

Third Report from the Select Committee on Emigration from the United Kingdom: 1827 ([1827] 2nd edn, Shannon, 1968).

v. Books and journal articles

Barclay, J., *Barclay's Complete and Universal English Dictionary* (London, 1842).

Bateman, J., *The Great Landowners of Great Britain and Ireland* ([1876] Leicester, 1971).

Bear, W. E., 'Advantages in agricultural production', *Journal of the Royal Agricultural Society of England*, 3rd series, 5 (1894), 250–84.

Bowley, A. L., 'Rural population in England and Wales', *Journal of the Royal Statistical Society*, 77 (1914), 597–652.

Britannia Depicta; or Ogilby Improv'd (London, 1720).

Cannan, E., 'The decline of urban immigration', *National Review*, new series (1894), 624–34.

A Chronological Summary of the Chief Events in the History of the Castle of Aberystwyth (Aberystwyth, 1872).

Davies, J. H., 'Cardiganshire freeholders in 1760', *West Wales Historical Records*, 3 (1912–13), 73–116.

Graham, P. A., *The Rural Exodus* (London, 1892).

Jones, E., *The American Traveler: Or Advice to Emigrants from Wales to America* (Aberystwyth, 1837).

Kebbel, T. E., *The Agricultural Labourer* ([1870] 2nd edn, London, 1887).

Kelly's Directory of Monmouthshire and the Principal Towns and Places in South Wales (London, 1884).

Lewis, S., *A Topographical Dictionary of Wales* (London, 1833).

——, *A Topographical Dictionary of Wales*, 2 vols (2nd edn, London, 1850).

Longstaff, G. G., 'Rural depopulation', *Journal of the Royal Statistical Society*, 56 (1893), 380–442.

Malkin, B. H., *The Scenery, Antiquities, and Biography of South Wales*, 2 vols (London, 1807).

Mostyn, Lord, 'Inaugural address', *Transactions of the Liverpool Welsh National Society*, 1 (1885), 3–15.

Nicholson, J. S., *The Relations of Rents, Wages and Profits in Agriculture, and their Bearing on Rural Depopulation* (London, 1906).

Picton, J. A., *Memorials of Liverpool* (London, 1873).

Pigot and Co.'s National Commercial Directory for 1828–9, part 1, *Cheshire to Northumberland* (London, 1829).

Pigot and Co.'s National Commercial Directory ([1835] Norwich, 1996 facsimile edn).

Pigot and Co.'s Royal National and Commercial Directory and Topography (London, 1844).

Price, L. L., 'The census of 1891 and rural depopulation', *Journal of the Royal Agricultural Society of England*, 3rd series, 5 (1894), 39–59.

Purdy, F., 'On the decrease of the agricultural population of England and Wales, 1851–61', *Journal of the Statistical Society of London*, 27 (1864), 388–400.

Slater's Royal National Commercial Directory (Manchester, 1880).

Stirton, T., 'Small holdings', *Journal of the Royal Agricultural Society of England*, 3rd series, 5 (1894), 84–93.

Thomas, D. Ll., *Bibliographical, Statistical and other Miscellaneous Memoranda, being Appendices to the Report of the Royal Commission on Land in Wales and Monmouthshire* (London, 1896).

——, *The Welsh Land Commission: A Digest of its Report* (London, 1896).

Worrall's Directory of South Wales (Oldham, 1875).

vi. Online

Census of England and Wales, 1831, Enumeration Abstract, Part 2 (London, 1832), *http://www. histpop.org/ohpr/servlet/*

Census of England and Wales, 1861, Population Tables, II, Ages, Civil Condition, Occupations, and Birthplaces of the People (London, 1863), *http://www. histpop.org/ohpr/servlet/*

Census of England and Wales, 1881, Population, Vol. II (London, 1883), *http:// www.histpop.org/ohpr/servlet/*

Census of England and Wales, 1881, Vol. III, Ages, Condition as to Marriage, Occupations and Birth-places (London, 1883), *http://www.histpop.org/ ohpr/servlet/*

Census of England and Wales, 1901, County of Chester, Area, Houses and Population (London, 1902), *http://www.histpop.org/ohpr/servlet/*

Census of England and Wales, 1901, County of Lancaster, Area, Houses and Population (London, 1902), *http://www.histpop.org/ohpr/servlet/*

Pigot and Co's National Commercial Directory for 1828–9, part 1, *Cheshire to Northumberland* (London, 1829), *http://www.historicaldirectories.org*

Wales–Ohio Project, *http://ohio.llgc.org.uk/*

2. SECONDARY SOURCES

i. Printed

Aitchison, J. W. and H. Carter, 'The population of Cardiganshire', in G. H. Jenkins and I. G. Jones (eds), *Cardiganshire County History*, vol. 3. *Cardiganshire in Modern Times* (Cardiff, 1998), pp. 1–18.

——, 'The Welsh language in Cardiganshire, 1891–1991', in G. H. Jenkins and I. G. Jones (eds), *Cardiganshire County History*, vol. 3, *Cardiganshire in Modern Times* (Cardiff, 1998), pp. 570–87.

Anderson, M., *Family Structure in Nineteenth-Century Lancashire* (London, 1971).

——, 'Recent work on the analysis of nineteenth-century census returns', *Family History*, 11 (1980), 151–72.

——, 'The social implications of demographic change', in F. M. L. Thompson (ed.), *The Cambridge Social History of Britain 1750–*

1950, vol. 2, *People and their Environment* (2nd edn, Cambridge, 1993), pp. 1–70.

Armstrong, W. A., 'The flight from the land', in G. E. Mingay (ed.), *The Victorian Countryside* (London, 1981), pp. 118–35.

Atkins, P. J., 'The retail milk trade in London, c.1790–1914', *Economic History Review*, new series, 33 (1980), 522–37.

Baines, D., *Migration in a Mature Economy* (Cambridge, 1985).

——, *Emigration from Europe 1815–1930* (London, 1991).

Bartholomew, K., 'Women migrants in mind', in C. G. Pooley and I. D. Whyte (eds), *Migrants, Emigrants and Immigrants* (London, 1991), pp. 174–87.

Bick, D. E., *The Old Metal Mines of Mid-Wales*, part 1, *Cardiganshire – South of Devil's Bridge* (Newent, 1974).

——, *The Old Metal Mines of Mid-Wales*, part 2, *Cardiganshire – The Rheidol to Goginan* (Newent, 1975).

——, *The Old Metal Mines of Mid-Wales*, part 3, *Cardiganshire – North of Goginan* (Newent, 1976).

Boon, G. C., *Cardiganshire Silver and the Aberystwyth Mint in Peace and War* (Cardiff, 1981).

Bowen, E. G., 'A clinical study of miners' phthisis in relation to the geographical and racial features of the Cardiganshire lead mining area', in I. C. Peate (ed.), *Studies in Regional Consciousness and Environment: Essays presented to H. J. Fleure* (London, 1930), pp. 189–202.

Boyer, G. R. and T. J. Hatton, 'Migration and labour market integration in late nineteenth-century England and Wales', *Economic History Review*, new series, 50 (1997), 697–734.

Carter, H. and S. Wheatley, *Merthyr Tydfil in 1851* (Cardiff, 1982).

Colyer, R. J., *The Welsh Cattle Drovers* (Cardiff, 1976).

——, 'The gentry and the county in nineteenth-century Cardiganshire', *Welsh History Review*, 10 (1980–1), 497–535.

——, 'Some aspects of land occupation in nineteenth-century Cardiganshire', *Transactions of the Honourable Society of Cymmrodorion* (1981), 79–97.

Cooper, K. J., 'Rhydhir Uchaf: the history of a Cardiganshire farm', *Ceredigion*, 9 (1982–3), 245–56.

——, 'Trefeurig, 1851–1891: a case study of a lead mining township', *Ceredigion*, 16 (2009), 81–116.

Cummins, S. Lyle, 'Tuberculosis as a social disease', *Journal of State Medicine*, 36 (1928), 1–4.

Davies, D.W., *Owen Owen: Victorian Draper* (Aberystwyth, 1984).

Davies, J., 'The end of the great estates and the rise of freehold farming in Wales', *Welsh History Review*, 7 (1974–5), 186–212.

Davies, J. L., 'The livestock trade in west Wales in the nineteenth century', *Aberystwyth Studies*, 13 (1934), 85–105.

Davies, J. W., 'Merched y gerddi: a seasonal migration of female labour from rural Wales', *Folk Life*, 15 (1977), 12–23.

Davies, R., *Secret Sins: Sex, Violence and Society in Carmarthenshire, 1870–1920* (Cardiff, 1996).

Dictionary of Welsh Biography (London, 2001).

Dodd, A. H., *The Character of Early Welsh Emigration to the United States* (Cardiff, 1957).

Eames, A., 'Ships and seamen of Wales in the age of Victoria: some Cardiganshire examples', *Ceredigion*, 8 (1978), 304–9.

Ebery, M. and B. Preston, *Domestic Service in Late Victorian and Edwardian England, 1871–1914* (Reading, 1976).

Eckley, S. and E. Jenkins, *Rhondda* (Bath, 1994).

Erickson, C., 'Emigration from the British Isles to the U.S.A. in 1831', *Population Studies*, 35 (1981), 175–97.

Evans, D. S., 'A long walk to work', *Cardiganshire Family History Society Journal*, 3 (2002–3), 65–7.

Evans, W. G., 'Education in Cardiganshire, 1700–1974', in G. H. Jenkins and I. G. Jones (eds), *Cardiganshire County History*, vol. 3, *Cardiganshire in Modern Times* (Cardiff, 1998), pp. 540–69.

Filby, P. and M. Meyer, *Passenger and Immigration Lists Index*, 3 vols with annual supplements to 2000 (Detroit, 1981).

Fox, H., 'Landscape history: the countryside', in D. Hey, *The Oxford Companion to Local and Family History* (2nd edn, Oxford, 2002), pp. 266–73.

Friedlander, D., 'Occupational structure, wages, and migration in late nineteenth-century England and Wales', *Economic Development and Cultural Change*, 40 (1992), 295–318.

—— and J. Roshier, 'A study of internal migration in England and Wales: part 1', *Population Studies*, 19 (1966), 239–79.

Gould, J. D., 'European inter-continental emigration, 1815–1914: patterns and causes', *Journal of European Economic History*, 8 (1979), 593–679.

Griffiths, R., 'The Lord's song in a strange land', in E. Jones (ed.), *The Welsh in London, 1500–2000* (Cardiff, 2001), pp. 161–83.

Hansen, M. L., *The Atlantic Migration, 1607–1860* (Cambridge, MA, 1945).

Hey, D., *The Oxford Companion to Local and Family History* (3rd edn, Oxford, 2002).

Higgs, E., 'Domestic servants and households in Victorian England', *Social History*, 8 (1983), 201–10.

——, *Making Sense of the Census: the Manuscript Returns for England and Wales, 1801–1901* (2nd edn, London, 1991).

Hill, B., 'Rural-urban migration of women and their employment in towns' *Rural History*, 5 (1994), 185–94.

Hodges, T. M., 'The peopling of the hinterland and the port of Cardiff', *Economic History Review*, 17 (1947), 62–72.

Howell, D. W., 'The agricultural labourer in nineteenth-century Wales', *Welsh History Review*, 6 (1972–3), 262–87.

Hughes, J., 'Evan the milk', *Dyfed Family History Journal*, 7 (2002), 340–5.

Hughes, P. G., *Wales and the Drovers* ([1943] new edn, Carmarthen, 1988).

Hughes, S. J. S., *The Cwmystwyth Mines* (Sheffield, 1981).

Jenkins, D., 'Shipping and shipbuilding', in G. H. Jenkins and I. G. Jones (eds), *Cardiganshire County History*, vol. 3, *Cardiganshire in Modern Times* (Cardiff, 1998), pp. 182–97.

Jenkins, J. G., *The Welsh Woollen Industry* (Cardiff, 1969).

——, 'Rural industry in Cardiganshire', *Ceredigion*, 6 (1968–71), 90–127.

——, 'Rural industries in Cardiganshire', in G. H. Jenkins and I. G. Jones (eds), *Cardiganshire County History*, vol. 3, *Cardiganshire in Modern Times* (Cardiff, 1998), pp. 135–59.

——, *Welsh Ships and Sailing Men* (Llanrwst, 2006).

Jones, D., 'Pauperism in the Aberystwyth Poor Law Union, 1870–1914', *Ceredigion*, 9 (1980), 78–101.

——, 'Counting the cost of coal: women's lives in the Rhondda, 1881–1911', in A. V. John (ed.), *Our Mothers' Land: Chapters in Welsh Women's History, 1830–1939* (Cardiff, 1991), pp. 109–33.

——, *Statistical Evidence relating to the Welsh Language, 1801–1911* (Cardiff, 1998).

Jones, E., 'The age of societies', in E. Jones (ed.), *The Welsh in London, 1500–2000* (Cardiff, 2001), pp. 54–87.

——, 'The early nineteenth century', in E. Jones (ed.), *The Welsh in London, 1500–2000* (Cardiff, 2001), pp. 88–109.

——, 'Victorian heyday', in E. Jones (ed.), *The Welsh in London, 1500–2000* (Cardiff, 2001), pp. 110–26.

Jones, I. G., *Explorations and Explanations: Essays in the Social History of Victorian Wales* (Llandysul, 1983).

Jones, I. W., *Money Galore: The Story of the Welsh Pound* (Ashbourne, 2004).

Jones, J. R., *The Welsh Builder on Merseyside* (Liverpool, 1946).

Jones, M., 'Welsh immigrants in the cities of north-west England, 1890–1930: some oral testimony', *Oral History*, 9 (1981), 33–41.

Jones, P. N., 'Some aspects of immigration into the Glamorgan coalfield between 1881 and 1911', *Transactions of the Honourable Society of Cymmrodorion* (1969), 82–98.

——, *Mines, Migrants and Residence in the South Wales Steamcoal Valleys: the Ogmore and Garw Valleys in 1881* (Hull, 1987).

——, 'Population migration into Glamorgan 1861–1911: a reassessment', in P. Morgan (ed.), *Glamorgan County History*, vol. 6, *Glamorgan Society, 1780–1980* (Cardiff, 1988), pp. 173–202.

Jones, R. C., *Arian: The Story of Money and Banking in Wales* (Swansea, 1978).

Jones, R. M., 'The Liverpool Welsh', in R. M. Jones and D. B. Rees (eds), *The Liverpool Welsh and their Religion* (Liverpool, 1984), pp. 20–43.

Jones, W. D., *Wales in America: Scranton and the Welsh 1860–1920* (Cardiff, 1991).

Joyce, P., 'Work', in F. M. L. Thompson (ed.), *The Cambridge Social History of Britain 1750–1950*, vol. 2, *People and their Environment* (Cambridge, 1990), pp. 131–94.

Kershaw, R., *Emigrants and Expats: A Guide to Sources on U.K. Emigration and Residence Overseas* (Richmond, 2002).

Knowles, A. K., *Calvinists Incorporated* (London, 1997).

——, 'The structure of rural society in north Cardiganshire, 1800–1850', in G. H. Jenkins and I. G. Jones (eds), *Cardiganshire County History*, vol. 3, *Cardiganshire in Modern Times* (Cardiff, 1998), pp. 76–93.

Lawton, R., 'Rural depopulation in nineteenth-century England', in R. W. Steel and R. Lawton (eds), *Liverpool Essays in Geography* (London, 1967), pp. 227–55.

——, 'Population changes in England and Wales in the later nineteenth century', *Transactions of the Institute of British Geographers*, 44 (1968), 55–74.

——, 'Regional population trends in England and Wales, 1750–1971', in J. Hobcraft and P. Rees (eds), *Regional Demographic Development* (London, 1977), pp. 29–70.

Lewis, C. R. and S. E. Wheatley, 'The towns of Cardiganshire, 1800–1995', in G. H. Jenkins and I. G. Jones (eds), *Cardiganshire County History*, vol. 3, *Cardiganshire in Modern Times* (Cardiff, 1998), pp. 212–32.

Lewis, E. D., *The Rhondda Valleys* (London, 1959).

Lewis, G., 'Mobility, locality and demographic change: the case of north Cardiganshire, 1851–71', *Welsh History Review*, 9 (1978–9), 347–61.

Lewis, J. P., *Building Cycles and Britain's Growth* (London, 1965).

Lewis, W. J., 'The condition of labour in mid-Cardiganshire in the early nineteenth century', *Ceredigion*, 4 (1963), 321–35.

——, *Lead Mining in Wales* (Cardiff, 1967).

——, 'Lead mining in Cardiganshire', in G. H. Jenkins and I. G. Jones (eds), *Cardiganshire County History*, vol. 3, *Cardiganshire in Modern Times* (Cardiff, 1998), pp. 160–81.

May, J., *Rhondda 1203–2003: The Story of the Two Valleys* (Cardiff, 2003).

Mills, D. and J. Mills, 'Rural mobility in the Victorian censuses', *Local Historian*, 18 (1988), 69–75.

Mitchell, B. R., *Abstract of British Historical Statistics* (Cambridge, 1962).

Moore-Colyer, R. J., 'Farmers and fields in nineteenth-century Wales: the case of Llanrhystud, Cardiganshire', *National Library of Wales Journal*, 26 (1989–90), 32–57.

——, 'Coastal limekilns in south-west Wales', *Folklife*, 28 (1989–90), 19–30.

——, 'Agriculture and land occupation in eighteenth- and nineteenth-century Cardiganshire', in G. H. Jenkins and I. G. Jones (eds),

Cardiganshire County History, vol. 3, *Cardiganshire in Modern Times* (Cardiff, 1998), pp. 19–50.

——, 'The landed gentry of Cardiganshire', in G. H. Jenkins and I. G. Jones (eds), *Cardiganshire County History*, vol. 3, *Cardiganshire in Modern Times* (Cardiff, 1998), pp. 51–75.

——, *Welsh Cattle Drovers* (Ashbourne, 2002).

—— (ed.), *A Land of Pure Delight: Selections from the Letters of Thomas Johnes of Hafod, Cardiganshire (1748–1816)* (Llandysul, 1992).

Morgan, G., *A Welsh House and its Family: The Vaughans of Trawsgoed* (Llandysul, 1997).

Nair, G. and D. Poyner, 'The flight from the land? Rural migration in south-east Shropshire in the late nineteenth-century', *Rural History*, 17 (2006), 167–86.

Newson, A. J., *Some Aspects of the Rainfall of Plynlimon, Mid-Wales* (Wallingford, 1976).

Owen, B., 'Ymfudo o Sir Aberteifi (emigration from Cardiganshire), 1654–1860. III. 1795–1860', *Ceredigion*, 2 (1952–5), 225–40.

Palmer, H., 'Documentary evidence on the lives of the poor in the later nineteenth century in Cardiganshire', *Ceredigion*, 13 (1998), 11–30.

Parkinson, A. J., 'Wheat, peat and lead: settlement patterns in west Wales, 1500–1800', *Ceredigion*, 10 (1985), 111–30.

Patmore, J. A. and A. G. Hodgkiss (eds), *Merseyside in Maps* (Liverpool, 1970).

Pooley, C. G., 'The residential segregation of migrant communities in mid-Victorian Liverpool', *Transactions of the Institute of British Geographers*, new series, 2 (1977), 364–82.

——, 'Welsh migration to England in the mid-nineteenth century', *Journal of Historical Geography*, 9 (1983), 287–305.

—— and J. C. Doherty, 'The longitudinal study of migration: Welsh migration to English towns in the nineteenth century', in C. G. Pooley and I. D. Whyte (eds), *Migrants, Emigrants and Immigrants* (London, 1991), pp. 143–73.

—— and J. Turnbull, *Migration and Mobility in Britain since the Eighteenth Century* (London, 1998).

——, 'Migration and urbanization in north-west England: a reassessment of the role of towns in the migration process', in D. J. Siddle (ed.), *Migration, Mobility and Modernization* (Liverpool, 2000), pp. 186–214.

Price, D. T. W., *A History of Saint David's University College Lampeter*, 2 vols (Cardiff, 1977).

Rees, D. B., 'The miracle and variety of two centuries of religion', in R. M. Jones and D. B. Rees (eds), *The Liverpool Welsh and their Religion* (Liverpool, 1984), pp. 7–19.

Rowe, J., *Cornwall in the Age of the Industrial Revolution* (Liverpool, 1953).

Saville, J., *Rural Depopulation in England and Wales 1851–1951* (London, 1957).

Shepperson, W. S., *British Emigration to North America* (Oxford, 1957).

Skeel, C., 'The cattle trade between Wales and England from the fifteenth to the nineteenth centuries', *Transactions of the Royal Historical Society*, 4th series, 9 (1926), 135–58.

Smith, C. T., 'The movement of population in England and Wales in 1851 and 1861', *Geographical Journal*, 117 (1951), 200–10.

Smith, P., *Houses of the Welsh Countryside* (London, 1975).

——, 'The domestic architecture of the county. I. The rural domestic architecture', in G. H. Jenkins and I. G. Jones (eds), *Cardiganshire County History*, vol. 3, *Cardiganshire in Modern Times* (Cardiff, 1998), pp. 233–98.

Snell, K. D. M. and P. S. Ell, *Rival Jerusalems* (Cambridge, 2000).

Thomas, B., 'The migration of labour into the Glamorganshire coalfield (1861–1911)', *Economica*, 10 (1930), 275–94.

Thomas, G. B., 'The Williams family of Dolau Aeron', *Cardiganshire Family History Society Journal*, 3 (2002–3), 105–8.

Thomas, P., *Strangers from a Secret Land* (Llandysul, 1986).

Thomas, S., 'The enumerators' returns as a source for a period picture of the parish of Llansantffraid, 1841–1851', *Ceredigion*, 4 (1963), 408–21.

——, 'The agricultural labour force in some south-west Carmarthenshire parishes in the mid-nineteenth century', *Welsh History Review*, 3 (1966–7), 63–73.

Tiller, K., *English Local History: An Introduction* (2nd edn, Stroud, 2002).

Toulson, S. and F. Godwin, *The Drovers' Roads of Wales* (London, 1977).

Trott, A. L., 'The implementation of the 1870 Elementary Education Act in Cardiganshire during the period 1870–1880', *Ceredigion*, 3 (1956–9), 207–30.

Vugt, W. van, 'Welsh emigration to the U.S.A. during the mid-nineteenth century', *Welsh History Review*, 15 (1990–1), 545–61.

Welsh Mines Society Newsletter, 48 (April 2003).

West, E., *Woollen Mills of Wales* (n.p., 1974).

Whetham, E. H., 'The London milk trade, 1860–1900', *Economic History Review*, new series, 17 (1964), 369–80.

Wiliam, E., *The Historical Farm Buildings of Wales* (Edinburgh, 1986).

Williams, A. M., 'Migration and residential patterns in mid-nineteenth-century Cardiff', *Cambria*, 6, part 2 (1979), 1–27.

Williams, D., 'Some figures relating to emigration from Wales', *Bulletin of the Board of Celtic Studies*, 7 (1935), 396–415.

Williams, D. J., *The Welsh Community of Waukesha County* (Columbus, OH, 1926).

Williams, G. A., *The Search for Beulah Land: The Welsh and the Atlantic Revolution* (London, 1980).

Williams, G. W., 'The disenchantment of the world: innovation, crisis and change in Cardiganshire c.1880–1910', *Ceredigion*, 9 (1982–3), 303–21.

Williams, J., *Digest of Welsh Historical Statistics*, 2 vols (Cardiff, 1985).

——, 'The move from the land', in T. Herbert and G. E. Jones (eds), *Wales, 1880–1914* (Cardiff, 1988), pp. 11–47.

Williams, M. A., 'Secret sins', *Victorian Studies*, 42 (2000), 343–5.

Williams, M. I., 'Commercial relations', in G. H. Jenkins and I. G. Jones (eds), *Cardiganshire County History*, vol. 3, *Cardiganshire in Modern Times* (Cardiff, 1998), pp. 198–211.

Woods, R., *The Population of Britain in the Nineteenth Century* (Basingstoke, 1992).

—— and N. Shelton, *An Atlas of Victorian Mortality* (Liverpool, 1997).

Wrigley, E. A. and R. S. Schofield, *The Population History of England, 1541–1871: A Reconstruction* (Cambridge, 1981).

ii. Online

http://www.dyfedarchaeology.org.uk/

http://www.james-son.co.uk/index2.html

http://www.theshipslist.com/ships/Arrivals/1842a.htm

http://www.theshipslist.com/1847/BPP-1847.html

http://www.theshipslist.com/1847/shipsjuly1847b.html

http://www.victorianweb.org/history/work/burnett3.html

http://www.visionofbritain.org.uk/place/place_page.jsp?p_id=1113

INDEX